Getting Started in

EXCHANGE TRADED FUNDS

The *Getting Started In* Series

Getting Started in

EXCHANGE TRADED FUNDS (ETFs)

Todd Lofton

John Wiley & Sons, Inc.

Published by John Wiley & Sons, Inc., Hoboken, New Jersey.
Published simultaneously in Canada.

For general information on our other products and services or for technical support, please contact our Customer Care Department within the United States at (800) 762-2974, outside the United States at (317) 572-3993 or fax (317) 572-4002.

Wiley also publishes its books in a variety of electronic formats. Some content that appears in print may not be available in electronic books. For more information about Wiley products, visit our web site at www.wiley.com.

Library of Congress Cataloging-in-Publication Data:

Lofton, Todd.
 Getting started in exchange traded funds (EFTs) / Todd Lofton.
    p. cm.
 Includes bibliographical references and indexes.
 ISBN-13: 978-0-470-04358-5 (pbk.)
 ISBN-10: 0-470-04358-X (pbk.)
 1. Exchange traded funds. 2. Stock index futures. I. Title.
 HG6043.L64 2007
 332.632'7—dc22
                                    2006023049
Printed in the United States of America.

10 9 8 7 6 5 4 3 2 1

In memory of our loving son, David

Contents

Preface

Welcome to a unique new way to invest.

To answer your first question, an exchange-traded fund is a basket of stocks that duplicate a stock index, such as the S&P 500 or Dow Jones. The basket trades on the exchange as a single stock.

This arrangement gives an exchange-traded fund (ETF) special qualities. For one thing, because an ETF represents the stocks of several different companies, it carries less risk than a share of stock in just one company.

ETFs can be bought and sold throughout the trading day. They can be shorted, bought on margin, and traded with stop and limit orders. They are passively managed, so they have much lower turnover and smaller expenses than actively managed funds.

ETFs also have few taxable capital gains and good transparency. (You can see what you're buying.) There is no minimum investment, and there are no fees or sales charges; the only transaction costs are normal brokerage commissions.

Should you consider having one or two ETFs in your stock account? Yes, especially if you are a relatively farsighted investor. But to decide that, you will have to know more about them, and that is where this book comes in. Here you will learn how ETFs are created, what part they can play in your investments, what ETFs are out there, and how to find one that meets your personal financial goals.

The First Pool Man   The idea of enabling a small investor to own a large portfolio is not new. The first investment trust dates from the mid-18th Century in Europe, when a Dutch financier named Adriaan Van Ketwich pooled the money of 37 individual investors and bought a large group of European government bonds.

Adriaan's fund was successful, and other funds followed, in the Netherlands and later in England. Investment trusts began to appear in the United States in the late 1800s; a landmark fund, the Massachusetts Investment Trust, was founded at Harvard University on March 21, 1924.

The first *index* mutual fund was introduced on August 31, 1976. It was unique in that its returns did not depend on the fortunes of a money manager. The mutual fund's stock portfolio duplicated the S&P 500 Stock Index, and its returns equaled the returns of the index.

Seventeen years later, in 1993, the first exchange-traded fund began trading on the American Stock Exchange. Named the S&P Depositary Receipt (SPDR) Trust Series 1, it too tracked the S&P 500 Index.

As interest in ETFs has grown, so has their number. As of late 2006, there are 293 ETFs traded on U.S. exchanges, representing some $320 billion in total assets. They are benchmarked to many different indexes, including stock indexes, fixed-income indexes, real estate indexes, a commodity index, the price of gold bullion, the price of silver, the price of crude oil, and the exchange rate of foreign currencies.

Putting ETFs to Work for You   There are several possible uses for ETFs:

- A broad-based ETF can be employed as the core of a portfolio; a foundation for other, shorter term, more risky pursuits undertaken in an attempt to increase returns. The ETF helps ensure that the portfolio's overall performance does not differ markedly from the investor's long-term goals.

- An ETF can be used as a temporary parking spot for cash. It is freely bought and sold for nominal transaction costs.

- If you want to set a certain investment benchmark—e.g., a diverse portfolio of midcap value stocks—it is much more convenient and less costly to buy, say, the iShares Russell Midcap Value Index Fund than to sort through and buy a large number of individual stocks.

- A broad-based ETF can be used for short-term trading. It is liquid, and its diversity virtually eliminates any unpleasant surprises resulting from single-stock risk.

- ETFs enable you to participate in markets that might not otherwise be available to you, such as foreign stocks or commodities.

What to Expect This book tells you what you need to know. It shows you how ETFs are created. It dissects risk. It points out what to look for when you are considering buying an ETF.

It explains the different styles of ETFs and how the different styles have fared over the years. It gives you a quick guide to futures contracts on ETFs. Same for put and call options on ETFs.

We show you several ways to forecast ETF prices. We demonstrate how to use ETFs for hedging.

We also provide you with help for day-to-day buying and selling; such as, what kind of order to use in a given market situation, how to deal with an unrealized loss, the safest way to add to a winning position.

Online access and single-digit trading commissions have made very-short-term trading feasible. If you are interested in traveling in the fast lane, we'll show you how to start your engine.

Easy Reader You'll find this book very easy to read. There's little theory, no jargon, and only a sprinkling of math. Sentences are short and sweet, and there are plenty of everyday examples to make sure that you understand. When you've finished reading, you'll be able to approach the subject of exchange-traded funds with confidence.

This book is written from the point of view of a trader, by one who was a member and floor broker on the Chicago Board Options Exchange for a number of years.

When it comes time for you to find a suitable ETF, the trail begins in Chapter 15, which lists the ETFs and the indexes that they track. The next stop is Chapter 16, where you'll find a description of the index behind the ETF. If you still like what you see, Appendix A contains a mini-prospectus for almost every ETF traded today, arranged alphabetically by trading symbol.

Acknowledgments

I would like to thank Bob Nunweiler and Mike Ritchie for allowing me to use several of their price charts in the chapter on technical analysis. Their website, *tradingcharts.com*, is an excellent online source for more than 30,000 free stock and commodity price charts and quotes.

The comprehensive information for the individual ETFs in Appendix A is drawn from *etfconnect.com*, a website sponsored by Nuveen Investments with data provided by Thomson Financial. I greatly appreciate their generosity.

I am indebted to Jim Wiandt, publisher of *Journal of Indexes*, who gave us the okay to use excerpts from the index performance tables in his March–April 2006 issue.

The pen-and-ink illustrations for the vignettes of three fictitious ETF investors were created by Anne Buchal. Her studio is in the Torpedo Factory Art Center, Alexandria, VA.

Valuable counsel was provided by Cliff Weber, senior vice president in charge of the ETF marketplace for the American Stock Exchange. Finally, I would like to thank Perry Kaufman, whose financial perception extends over the horizon, for being a friendly sounding board along the way.

Note: Although the masculine singular pronoun predominates throughout the book, it is not my intention to slight the many women in finance who are brokers, market analysts, broadcast commentators, exchange members, corporate executives, and owners.

Todd Lofton
McLean, Virginia
January 2007

A Seagull's View of an Exchange-Traded Fund

Mediterranean Charters owns one boat, a 70-foot motor yacht named *Caroline* that is moored in Naples, Italy. Summer cruises on the *Caroline* cost $10,000 a week, and the schedule is full.

To raise new capital, the owner of the *Caroline* decides to sell shares in his boat. He has no trouble selling 100,000 shares at $10 per share. Each share represents a 1/100,000 interest in the *Caroline*.

The yachting world is small and soon a *secondary market* develops in *Caroline* shares as new investors buy shares from old investors.

The value of shares in the *Caroline* depends on two factors: (1) the value of the boat and (2) what buyers are willing to pay for the shares. Those two are not always the same. Investor interest is greater in the spring and the price of *Caroline* stock rises. Prices tend to ease in the fall when cold weather arrives.

secondary market

the traditional exchanges, over-the-counter markets, and electronic exchanges where securities previously issued are bought and sold by investors.

One day, the owner decides to sell the *Caroline*, so he buys back all of the outstanding shares. He pays $11 for each share as the boat has increased in market value in the interim.

The sponsor of an exchange-traded fund (ETF) does somewhat the same. He (or she) accepts shares of the actual index stocks and secures them in a trust fund. He creates ETF share certificates, each of which represents a sliver of ownership of the stocks in the trust; and, he wire transfers the ETF shares to the person who gave him the stocks. That person sells the ETF shares to investors, who are then free to trade them on the stock exchange.

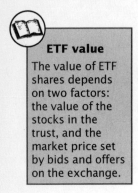

ETF value

The value of ETF shares depends on two factors: the value of the stocks in the trust, and the market price set by bids and offers on the exchange.

The *value of ETF shares* likewise depends on two factors: (1) the value of the stocks in the trust and (2) the market price set by bids and offers on the exchange trading floor.

The process that created the ETF can also be reversed. The sponsor can accept ETF shares and give back the actual shares of the index stocks that he has been holding in trust.

Chapter

The Genealogy of the Exchange-Traded Fund

The family tree of the exchange-traded fund (ETF) has a mutual fund at its head.

Adriaan van Ketwich's success in the 1770s in Amsterdam spawned more than 30 other Dutch investment trusts. The Netherlands had been instrumental in financing the American Revolution, and the objective of many of the new trusts was to speculate on the future credit of the former English colony.

By the end of the 1800s, investment trusts had crossed the North Sea. The first of these, established in London in 1868, was the Foreign and Colonial Government Trust. By 1875, there were 18 investment trusts in London. Their structures and investments varied, but the goals were the same: to provide the small investor with an opportunity own a diversified portfolio for a nominal cost.

During the 1890s, investment trusts also began to appear in the United States. One of the first was the Boston Personal Property Trust, organized in 1893.

In 1907, the Alexander Fund, which had begun as a small investment club for a few friends, was established in Philadelphia. The fund was sold in units of $100 and offered an annual return of 6 percent. By mid-1925, the Alexander Fund had 460 shareholders and assets of

$1.5 million. It is credited with originating many of the features of modern mutual funds, including allowing shareholders to sell shares back to the fund on demand.

The first true U.S. mutual fund is generally considered to be the Massachusetts Investment Trust. It was formed in Boston on March 21, 1924 by the faculty and staff of Harvard University, who pooled $50,000 of their money and retained a fund manager. Among other requirements, the fund's prospectus explicitly stated that there would be no speculation with the fund's money; that only prudent, long-term investments would be made. The arrangement was a success. Between 1926 and 1928, the Massachusetts Investment Trust earned a cumulative return of 88 percent for its shareholders, who by then numbered 200. In 1928, the fund was opened to the public.

The fortunes of mutual funds waxed and waned over the years. The 1929 stock market crash wiped out many mutual funds. In the early 1930s, investment capital was relatively scarce. The Investment Act of 1940, which regulates the mutual fund industry, ostensibly set the stage for mutual fund growth by addressing abuses in the industry. During the next 35 years, the number of mutual funds increased dramatically.

index fund

a fund designed to emulate the market performance of securities that comprise a specific stock index, like the S&P 500 or the Dow Jones Industrial Average.

expense ratio

the recurring charges against fund assets for investment management, custody, and administration, expressed as a percentage of the fund's net assets. Expense ratios do not includes nonroutine costs such as brokerage commissions or legal fees paid in a lawsuit against the fund.

The Advent of Index Funds

Up to this point, mutual funds had been *actively managed*, and the results had not been good. Beleaguered by high *expense ratios*, rapid stock *turnover*, and the difficulty inherent in forecasting prices, few fund managers did as well as the market averages, and those who had success in one year rarely repeated their winning performances.*

*In his book, *Index Funds: The 12-step Program for Active Investors* (Irvine, CA: IFA, 2005) Mark Hebner presents tables showing the top 10 performing mutual funds in each year from 1992 to 2004, a period of 13 years. The tables also show how those top 10 mutual funds fared in subsequent years. The average ranking of the top 10 mutual funds in the following year was 421; in the year after that, their average ranking was 2,576.

Economists and financial writers began calling for the establishment of a new kind of mutual fund; a mutual fund whose returns would not depend on the luck or skill of a money manager, but would equal those of a stock index; a *passively managed* fund that would have very low expenses.

John Bogle, founder of Vanguard, was of the same mind. Working with Dr. Burton Malkiel, professor of economics at Princeton University, Bogle blueprinted the first stock index mutual fund in the spring of 1976. On August 31 of that same year, the Vanguard 500 Index Fund was introduced to the world. It was designed to track the S&P 500 Stock Index.

Enter the Exchange-Traded Fund

The two principal forebears of ETFs were Cash Index Participations, which began trading on the Philadelphia Stock Exchange in 1989, and Index Participation Shares, launched on the American Stock Exchange (AMEX) the following year. Both tracked indexes and traded like stocks. However, because of their structure—a long position for every short position—they were considered a threat to futures trading and a lawsuit brought by the Chicago Board of Trade ultimately forced them to close down.

Also launched in 1989 were Toronto Stock Exchange Index Participation Shares (TIPS), designed to track the Torono-35 Index. TIPS were much like today's ETFs. Shares of the 35 underlying stocks were held in a trust in proper proportion; TIPS trust receipts, representing fractional ownership of the stocks, were bought and sold on the trading floor of the Toronto Stock Exchange.

Four years after, in 1993, the AMEX launched the first bonafide ETF, a tradable depositary receipt for a portfolio of index stocks held in a

active management
an investing style predicated on the use of good judgment and market knowledge to select securities with the potential for the greatest risk-adjusted returns.

turnover
the number of purchases and sales of stocks for the portfolio. More precisely, (Purchases + Sales) divided by (Beginning value + Ending value). If a portfolio has an average annual turnover of 30 percent using this formula, it would mean that 30 percent of the stocks in the portfolio were replaced with new stocks during the year.

unit investment trust. It was called the S&P Depositary Receipt, and it also tracked the S&P 500 Stock Index.

Today, ETFs are traded on the New York Stock Exchange, the *NASDAQ*, the Chicago Board Options Exchange, and the American Stock Exchange, which is the home exchange for the majority of ETFs.

passive management

a money management strategy that seeks to match the return and *risk* characteristics of a market index by mirroring its composition. Passive managers do not actively buy and sell securities in a search for those with the greatest returns. They make as few portfolio decisions as possible, in order to minimize transaction costs and the accrual of capital gains.

risk

The quantifiable likelihood of loss or less-than-expected returns.

unit investment trust

an investment company that holds a fixed group of securities in trust until the trust is dissolved.

NASDAQ

the acronym for National Association of Securities Dealers Automated Quotations, an electronic automated quote system. The system was established by NASD in 1968 and today reports price quotes, trading volume, and other market information for more than 5,000 *over-the-counter* stocks. NASDAQ later grew into the NASDAQ Stock Market, an electronic stock exchange where computer networks match orders from buyers and sellers.

over-the-counter

an NASD-regulated market for stocks that are not traded on traditional brick-and-mortar stock exchanges. Also included are some listed securities that are traded off the exchange, and government and corporate bonds.

NASD

the abbreviation of the National Association of Securities Dealers. NASD is a private, nonprofit organization created by the Securities Exchange Act of 1934. NASD is responsible for standardizing investment practices and setting ethical criteria for the finance industry. Nearly every brokerage firm doing business in the United States is required by law to be a member of NASD.

Chicago Board Options Exchange (CBOE)

opened in 1973, the CBOE established, for the first time, fair and orderly markets in standard listed stock options. The exchange currently trades put and call options on stocks, stock indexes, interest rates, sector indexes; and, as of this writing, options on more than 80 exchange-traded funds.

Mustering a Retirement Fund

Tim Johnson, Navy pilot, husband, father, had just retired from active duty after 22 years.

His personal balance sheet was not complicated. On one side, he had two young kids bound for college one day. On the other, he had a money-market IRA with about $18,000 and $110,000 in cash that his mother had left him when she died last year.

Tim was no student of economics. But he knew that his nest egg had to be put to work, and he was aware that historical annual returns from stock investing averaged about 10 percent.

So . . . he opened a stock account with an Internet online broker and began. He bought carefully, selecting stocks of companies with good

earnings and consistent dividends—companies that "made sense" in the light of exploding Internet commerce, the wholesale retirement of the baby-boomer generation, and the growing amount of leisure time available to workers in this country.

But this strategy did not seem to work. He was often surprised by events, some of them totally illogical, which triggered dramatic stock price movements. He also discovered that he was not immune

to the psychological effects of having his money at risk. As he looked back, he saw more than one stock that he had bought near its high and sold near its low.

At the end of the first year, he toted up the score. For all his hours of poring over research reports and exploring the Internet, his net profit was a little over $700, a return of less than a half percent on the money that he had invested. He also figured that that worked out to be about $1.20 an hour for his time.

He wondered if he were the problem, so he did a little Internet exploring. He found a study of individual investors that was done by the *Philadelphia Inquirer* in 2005. It showed that during the 20 years from 1984 to 2004, the individual investor earned an average return of 3.9 percent per year on his money. During that same period, the S&P 500 gained 13.2 percent a year.

He also read Brad M. Barber and Terrance Odean's research report (*The Journal of Finance*, April 2000). Their article analyzed the results of individual investors in 60,000 households from 1991 to 1996. It was entitled "Trading is Hazardous to Your Wealth."

Convinced, Tim looked into the possibility of someone else's managing his money. His investigation eventually narrowed down to two choices: index mutual funds and exchange-traded funds.

The biggest difference he saw between them was costs. ETFs had lower expenses, no fees, and fewer taxable capital gains. Plus, he liked the ETF's openness. It was easy to know which stocks an ETF held. And, to be honest with himself, he liked to check prices during the day occasionally, just to see how he was doing.

Not long after that, Tim went online to his broker's website and placed buy orders for three ETFs. One tracks a foreign stock index, one a U.S. small-cap *value stock* index, and one a long-term U.S. Treasury bond index.

4

How Exchange-Traded Funds Are Created

There are three players involved in creating an ETF. The first is the ETF sponsor, who is typically a bank or other large fiduciary. The names of some major ETF sponsors include Vanguard, State Street Global Advisors, and Barclays Global Investors. Second is the *Authorized Participant* (AP), a large institutional investor, specialist, or *market-maker* who is empowered to create and redeem ETF shares. Finally, there is the trust company, which holds in trust the stocks that underlie the ETF.

Authorized Participant (AP)
a large institutional investor, specialist, or *market-maker* who has signed a participant agreement with a particular ETF sponsor.

The process begins when a prospective ETF sponsor files a plan with the U.S. Securities and Exchange Commission (SEC) to create a new ETF. The plan specifies the ETF's investment objective, which securities will be included in the "basket," and how many retail ETF shares will be created. Once the plan is approved, the sponsor concludes an agreement with an AP to create the ETF shares. (In some cases, the AP and the sponsor are the same.)

The AP gathers up shares of stock in the index and delivers them in proper number and proportion to the sponsor. The sponsor forwards the shares of stock to the *Depositary Trust Company (DTC)*, which is part of

market-maker

an exchange member who enhances market liquidity by providing continuous public bids and offers for its designated ETFs. There may be more than one market-maker in a heavily traded ETF. Market-makers are required by law to give a public customer the best available bid or asked price.

specialist

responsible for maintaining fair and orderly markets in the stocks to which he (or she) is assigned. He does so by posting his best bid and asked prices, maintaining a record of orders that are away from the market, and by buying for or selling from his own inventory when there are not sufficient public buyers or sellers to maintain price equilibrium.

the U. S. Depositary Trust and Clearing Corporation. The DTC holds securities for shareholders and clients (including index shares in trust for ETFs) and arranges for the shares' electronic delivery, transfer, and settlement.

In return, the AP receives by wire transfer from the sponsor an appropriate number of new ETF shares. They arrive in large bundles called *creation units*. The AP may hold the creation units, or he can split them up and sell individual ETF shares to investors. After that, the ETF shares trade freely on the open market like any other stock, The sponsor also provides for a manager to administer the portfolio of underlying stocks.

The swap of stock shares and ETF shares is an in-kind transaction. No shares are bought or sold for cash, so no tax liabilities are created.

ETF creation can be a capital-intensive endeavor. For example, an ETF priced in the $80 range with a creation unit of 50,000 shares would require the input of some $4 million worth of underlying stock. There is also a *creation fee*, but it is nominal, typically a fraction of 1 percent. Creation fees are paid in cash and are charged per transaction, regardless of the number of creation units involved.

An AP may also redeem ETFs. To do so, the AP surrenders ETF shares to the sponsor in the specified *redemption* units, usually the same size as the creation units. The AP receives in return the actual underlying index shares that the ETF represents. There is also a nominal *redemption fee*.

The ETFs

ETFs have several different sponsors and track several different indexes. Some of their names have already been mentioned. You will be hearing the names again in the coming pages, so let us take this opportunity to introduce the whole group:

- *SPDRs* track Standard & Poor's several broad and sector stock indexes. They are sponsored by State Street Bank.

- *OPALS* (Optimized Portfolio as Listed Securities) are used mainly by large institutions.

- *Qubes* (QQQQ) track the NASDAQ 100 Stock Index. This ETF is sponsored by the Bank of New York.

- *DIAMONDs* track the Dow Jones Industrial Index. The sponsor is State Street Bank.

- *iShares* are the most numerous ETFs. They are sponsored by Barclays Global Investors and track several domestic and foreign security indexes.

- *streetTracks,* sponsored by State Street Global Advisors, track nine domestic and three foreign stock indexes.

- *PowerShares* track 36 indexes, some of them proprietary and semiactively managed. PowerShare ETFs are sponsored by PowerShares Capital Management.

- *BLDRs* (Baskets of Listed Depositary Receipts) track four Bank of New York *ADR* indexes.

- *VIPERs* (Vanguard Index Participation Receipts) are Vanguard products that track several different nonproprietary indexes, mostly MSCI indexes.

- *HOLDRs* (Holding Company Depositary Receipts) are *grantor trusts* that hold relatively small groups of stocks in a single sector or industry. Merrill Lynch sponsors most HOLDRs.

institutional investor

banks, insurance companies, hedge funds, and other large fiduciaries that buy and sell securities for their own accounts.

Depositary Trust Company (DTC)

a corporation owned collectively by broker-dealers and banks. The trust holds securities for shareholders and clients (including index shares in trust for ETFs) and arranges for the shares' electronic delivery, transfer, and settlement. DTC is part of the U.S. Depositary Trust and Clearing Corporation.

creation unit

The minimum number of ETF shares that can be created by the fund sponsor and AP in one transaction. The transaction is "in kind" and not for cash. Each ETF has its own creation unit size, ranging from 25,000 to as many as 600,000 ETF shares, with 50,000 shares being the most common size. Creation of large numbers of ETF shares are made in multiples of the creation unit.

creation fee

the fee paid by the authorized participant for delivering shares of the underlying stocks and accepting one or more creation units of ETFs. The fee is expressed in dollars and is nominal, usually less than 1 percent.

redemption

exchanging ETF shares for the shares of their underlying stocks held in trust. Redemption is made in specified redemption units.

redemption fee

the fee paid by the Authorized Participant for redeeming one or more redemption units of ETFs and receiving shares of the underlying stocks. The fee is expressed in dollars and is nominal—usually less than 1 percent—and it is paid per transaction regardless of the number redemption units involved.

HOLDR

an unmanaged portfolio of 20 or more sector or industry stocks that are bought and sold as a unit, like an ETF.

grantor trust

a trust certificate that represents literal ownership of a basket of stocks, including voting rights and the receipt of dividends. The certificate trades like a stock but is not issued by a company nor registered with the SEC. Merrill Lynch HOLDRs and Ryder Euro Currency Trust are grantor trusts.

DIAMONDS

shares in Diamond Trust Series 1, an ETF that tracks the Dow Jones Industrial Average. Organized as a unit investment trust.

ADRs

the acronym for American Depositary Receipts, which are certificates representing ownership of shares of stock in a foreign company. Most ADRs are issued by U.S. banks. They are freely traded on U. S. stock exchanges.

Qubes (QQQQ)

A heavily traded ETF that tracks the NASDAQ 100 Index, it is structured as a unit investment trust.

5

Shopping for an Exchange-Traded Fund

For the following discussion, we'll assume that your investment time horizon is months, not days. (There is a chapter on the wiles of short-term trading later in this book.)

In dissecting an individual ETF, there are several different places to make incisions. Let's consider them one at a time.

Asset Class

ETFs within the same asset class tend to demonstrate similar market performance, but there are significant differences in risk and return between asset classes.

In a study entitled "Determinants of Portfolio Performance," the results of which were published in the July/August 1986 issue of *Financial Analysts Journal,* author Gary Brinson concludes that more than 90 percent of a money manager's successful performance can be attributed to his selection of asset class.

Major ETF asset classes are:

Large-cap value   Mid–cap value

Large-cap growth   Mid–cap growth

Small-cap value

Small-cap growth

Sector/consumer

Sector/energy

Sector/financial

Sector/health

Sector/industrial

Sector/materials

Sector/real estate

Sector/technology

Sector/telecommunications

Sector/natural resources, gold

Sector/transportation

Sector/utilities

Foreign/global

Foreign/regional

Foreign/country

Specialty

Foreign/sector

Fixed income

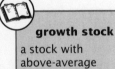

asset class

a description of the kind of stocks in an ETF, based on their location, nature, and size (e.g., large-cap U.S. value stocks). There are some 24 ETF asset classes.

If the name of the ETF does not identify its asset class, it may be found online. The easiest way is to enter *morningtar.com*, click ETFs, then click Name. You will see a list of all U.S. ETFs and the asset classes that Morningstar has assigned to them. Also shown for each ETF are its performance data for one month, three months, one year, and three years.)

The website *indexuniverse.com* has a screen for ETF asset classes, and the information is also available in the summary sheets for individual ETFs at *amex.com* and *etfconnect.com*.

Growth vs. Value

growth stock

a stock with above-average prospects for capital gains. Growth stocks typically have high price/earnings and price-to-book ratios and pay no dividends.

The distinction between *growth stocks* and value stocks is not always clear. There are some stocks that fit comfortably in each category; but there are many stocks that have attributes of both growth and value. The word "blend" is often used to refer to stocks with indeterminate pedigree.

Generally speaking, the earmarks of a value stock are a high-dividend yield, a low *price-to-earnings ratio*, a low *price-to-book ratio*, and a modest outlook. Of these, the price-to-book ratio may be the most informative as it captures one of the fundamental differences between value and growth stocks.

Value investors believe that markets are not always efficient; that it is possible to find stocks that are new or that have fallen out of favor and therefore trading for less than they are worth. Because it may take time for a value stock to be "discovered" and its price to rise, value investors have relatively distant time horizons. Value stocks typically do well early in economic recoveries.

Growth stocks have high price-to-earnings and price-to-book ratios. Some have no earnings at all. Others have earnings but pay no dividends; cash is instead funneled back into the company to finance expansion or new products. Growth stocks are bought for their potential price appreciation, and they tend to lead established bull markets. The most visible growth stocks in recent years have been in the technology and Internet sectors.

Two Ratios

A stock's price-to-earnings (P/E) ratio and price-to-book (P/B) ratio are its pulse and blood pressure.

The P/E ratio is an indication of investors' expectations for the performance of the company's stock. Historically, the average P/E ratio of the overall stock market has fluctuated between 15 and 25, with 20 being considered the watershed.

P/E ratios have on occasion reached the stratosphere when investors bid a stock's price up in expectation of the company's outstanding future prospects. Some of the new Internet companies in the late 1900s had zero earnings and stock prices in the triple digits—a P/E ratio, technically speaking, of infinity.

It is difficult to determine whether a particular P/E is "high" or "low." Its value must be viewed in light of the company's earnings history, its exposure to risk, its potential for dramatic growth, and the P/E ratios of other companies in the same business.

value stock
a stock with a high-dividend yield, a low *price-to-earnings ratio*, a low *price-to-book ratio*, and that is currently priced below similar companies in the same business.

price/earnings ratio (P/E ratio)
a component of a company's fundamental analysis. To calculate the P/E ratio, you divide the company's current stock price by the company's earnings per share (EPS). An increase in the stock price or a decline in company's earnings will cause the company's P/E to increase. A P/E ratio that is calculated using EPS data from the last four quarters is known as the *trailing P/E*. A P/E ratio calculated using estimated earnings over the next four quarters is known as the *leading* or *projected P/E*.

price-to-book ratio (P/B)

book value comprises a company's assets minus its liabilities. It is what would be left over for shareholders if the company were sold and its debt retired. The price-to-book ratio equals the stock share price divided by the per-share book value.

The P/B ratio compares the market's valuation of a company to the company's worth as shown on its books. The higher the ratio, the higher the premium the market is willing to pay for the company above its hard assets. A low ratio may signal a good investment opportunity; but the ratio is less meaningful for companies that are involved in technology or medicine because they have assets—for example, patents or other intellectual property—that are not reflected in the company's book value. In general, the P/B ratio is of more interest to value investors than to growth investors.

Comparing Returns

In the growth/value contest, the historical edge has gone to value stocks. In the 29 years from 1975 through 2003, there were 12 years during which value stocks outperformed growth stocks and six years when growth stocks predominated (based on comparisons between the S&P 500 Barra Growth Index and S&P 500 Barra Value Index).

The best year for value stocks was 2000; they gained 7 percent while growth stocks lost 23 percent. The best year for growth stocks was 1998, when the score was growth stocks plus 42 percent and value stocks plus 13 percent.

There is no pattern in the results, except that three of the relatively best years for growth stocks came in a row: 1997, 1998, and 1999.

In his book, *The Little Book that Beats the Market* (New York: John Wiley & Sons, 2006), Joel Greenblatt found similar results. During the 17-year period from 1988 to 2004, buying stocks with high returns on capital and high dividend yields—i.e., value stocks—and holding them for 3 to 5 years delivered stock returns that were almost twice those of the S&P 500 during the same time period.

Small-cap vs. Large-cap

The *small-cap/large-cap* comparison in shown in Figure 5.1, which depicts the relative performance each year from 1985 to 2005 (the Russell 2000 Index was used to represent small-cap stocks, the Russell 1000 Index to represent large-cap stocks).

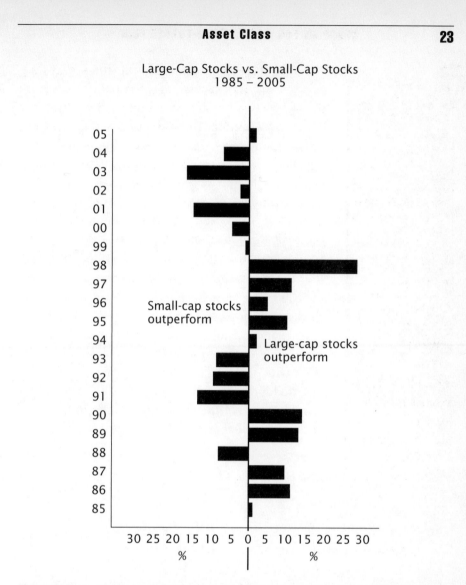

Large-Cap Stocks vs. Small-Cap Stocks
1985 – 2005

FIGURE 5.1   This graph compares the relative performance of large- and small-cap stocks. The bars show which class outperformed and by how much. For example, in 1991, the return for small-cap stocks was about 13% better than the return for large-cap stocks.

In the 20 years shown, there were 11 years when large-cap stocks outperformed small-caps, and nine years during which small-cap stocks did better. The banner year for large-cap stocks was 1998, when they outperformed small-caps by 30 percent. The best year for small-cap stocks was 2003, when they beat large-cap stocks by about 17 percent.

large-cap stock
the stock of a company with an equity market capitalization of $2 billion or more.

small-cap stock

the stock of a company whose market value is less than $250 million. Includes *microcap stocks*, which comprise companies with market values of $100 million or less.

micro-cap stock

the stock of a company with a market capitalization of "micro" proportions, generally less than $100 million.

Based on these data alone, the historical odds would seem to favor large-cap (11:9) value (12:6) stocks.

The grouping of the returns in Figure 5.1 is worth noting. As you can see, success came in bunches. A good year for growth stocks tended to be followed by more good years for growth stocks. The same was true for small caps. The longest periods of dominance: Large-cap stocks were winners each year from 1994 through 1998. For the next six years, from 1999 to 2005, small-cap stocks outperformed. It does not show in Figure 5.1, but for the first nine months of 2006, the current trend continued—small-cap stocks outperformed large caps by about 13 percent.

Craig L. Israelsen presents a broader comparison in the March/April 2006 issue of *Journal of Indexes* with tables of performance data for different indexes for the years 2001 through 2005. Each index is a composite of the five major indexes in that asset class. The annualized average performances were:

2001–2005

Large-cap Value Indexes	+3.61 percent
Large-cap Blend Indexes	+0.29 percent
Large-cap Growth Indexes	–4.19 percent
Mid–cap Value Indexes	+12.85 percent
Mid–cap Blend Indexes	+8.43 percent
Mid–cap Growth Indexes	+2.82 percent
Small-cap Value Indexes	+13.68 percent
Small-cap Blend Indexes	+9.54 percent
Small-cap Growth Indexes	+3.47 percent

From 2001 to 2005, value stocks outperformed blend and growth stocks in every capitalization category. Does this mean that growth stocks are due for a resurgence beginning in 2007? Your guess is probably better than mine.

The bottom line: Which camp you are in makes a difference.

Foreign Stocks

There are some 45 U.S. ETFs that track foreign stock indexes. As noted above, they are categorized as global, regional, country, or sector. The largest group is country ETFs. The smallest group is the five foreign global *sector ETFs*, which comprise energy, financial, healthcare, technology, and telecommunications.

sector ETF
an ETF whose underlying index contains stocks in only one market sector, such as iShares Dow Jones U. S. Telecommunications Sector Index Fund. Prices of sector ETFs are typically more volatile than the prices of broad-based ETFs.

The principal virtue of foreign securities in a portfolio is to provide diversity *among* ETFs. As we have said earlier, the prices of U.S. stocks with similar styles tend to move together; they have statistical correlations in the 90s. The correlation of the price movement between U.S. stocks and foreign stocks of similar asset class falls between 0.42 and 0.58.

The "ebbing tide that lowers all boats" in the United States does not lower foreign boats to the same extent.

Fixed-Income Securities

Six ETFs currently exist that track fixed-income indexes. They are all iShares and include short-, medium-, and long-term Lehman Treasury indexes, a corporate bond index, the Lehman TIPS (inflation protected) index, and an aggregate index that reflects the broad bond market.

Bond ETFs perform just like their stock counterparts except that, like all interest-rate securities, their prices vary inversely with the movement of interest rates. Bond ETFs pay cash dividends monthly and these dividends may be automatically reinvested.

Even though the underlying assets are bonds, there is no fixed-rate return for the investor in a bond ETF. As with a stock fund, the investor's total return comes from dividends and appreciation of the market price of the ETF. Because bonds in the index portfolio mature and must be replaced, bond ETFs are more likely to accrue capital gains than stock ETFs,

Real Estate and Gold

Gold has long been considered a store of value in times of war or economic turmoil. Historically, gold prices have moved oppositely to bond prices, as gold is used as a *hedge* against inflation. There are three ETFs

hedge

a two-position strategy whereby the loss (including opportunity loss) in one asset is largely offset by the gain in a different but economically related asset.

that track gold prices. Four ETFs track real estate prices; they are all keyed to real estate values within the United States.

Specialty

The specialty group comprises iShares Dow Jones Select Dividend Index Fund, iShares KLD Select Social Index Fund, PowerShares High Yield Equity Dividend Achievers, PowerShares WilderHill Clean Energy Fund, and the Rydex Euro Currency Trust.

Evaluating Risk

Risk is the probability that something adverse will happen. It is the likelihood that a particular undertaking will result in a loss or in less-than-expected returns.

Even though they all track indexes, ETFs vary in the risk that they present to an investor.

Certain risks are common to all ETFs. These include:

- Market risk is the risk that fluctuations in the fund's market price could cause your position to lose money.
- Asset-class risk is the risk that the types of securities in which the fund invests will under-perform other styles of securities.
- Concentration risk is the risk that a narrowly focused fund will be more susceptible to singular events that do not affect other sectors of the market.
- Management risk is the risk that, because the fund does not fully replicate the underlying index, the fund's returns will be less than the index return.

These risks can be grouped into two broad categories. One is *systemic risk*, which is defined as a risk that affects an entire financial market or system. When a broker says to you, "The tide raises all boats," he is referring to systemic risk, of the tendency of all stocks to move up or down together.

The other is stock risk, which is the risk of loss from price changes in a single stock. ETFs with a small number of stocks or in which a few stocks dominate the portfolio may also be vulnerable to stock risk.

Stock risk can be reduced or virtually eliminated by *diversification*. Systemic risk is always present; it cannot be diversified away.

Standard Deviation

The risk in owning a particular security is often expressed in terms of standard deviation.

Standard deviation describes how tightly a set of values is clustered around the average of those same values. It is a measure of dispersal, or variation, in a group of numbers. Stable investments like money market funds have standard deviations near zero. Riskier holdings may have standard deviations of 20 or more.

Calculating the standard deviation of a series of values involves complex math and is really beyond or scope here. But here is a simple example. Consider the following three series: 0, 0, 14, 14; 0, 6, 8, 14; and 6, 6, 8, 8. Each series averages 7, but because of the numbers fall at different distances from the average, their standard deviations are not the same. The actual standard deviations are, respectively, 7, 5, and 1.

In standard practice, one standard deviation comprises an area that measures 34 percent on either side of the mean value, or a total of 68 percent. If an ETF has a standard deviation of 10, it means that 68 percent of the time, the price has stayed within 10 percent of its mean (average) price.

A smaller standard deviation means less price volatility and therefore less risk.

systemic risk
risk that affects an entire system or market. Systemic risk cannot be reduced by diversification.

diversification
lowering overall portfolio risk by investing in a variety of different asset types or classes that are not all likely to move in the same direction.

standard deviation
a measure of dispersal in a group of numbers. It describes how tightly a set of values is clustered around the average of those same values. It is considered a gauge of volatility. Stable investments like money market funds have standard deviations near zero. More volatile holdings may have standard deviations of 20 or more.

volatility

a measure of the fluctuations in the market price of a security. The greater the distance between a stock's average daily high and low prices, the greater is it volatility—and the greater is the short-term price risk in owning the stock.

Sharpe Ratio

Even though two investments may have the same return, they do not necessarily have the same market risk. It is possible, for example, for a soybean futures contract and a 10-year Treasury note to have the identical return over a period, but those results would not alter the intrinsic difference in the risk between the two holdings.

The Sharpe ratio enables an investor to compare the market risks of different investment media. It provides an investor with an objective measure of the risk inherent in an investment.

The inputs for the formula for calculating the Sharpe ratio are the average monthly returns of the asset; the "risk-free" interest rate, usually represented by the return on short-term Treasury bills, the standard deviation of the monthly returns over the same period, and the average ambient short-term interest rate. The average monthly returns and standard deviation of the returns are annualized (multiplied by 12 and by the square root of 12, respectively) for the calculations.

We'll not get further into the mathematics involved, but there are some things we can tell you for the next time you meet a Sharpe ratio.

The rule of thumb is: The higher the Sharpe ratio, the higher is the ratio of reward to risk; and, from that standpoint, the more attractive is the investment. To give you a perspective, the Sharpe ratio for the cash S&P Index for the past 10 years is 0.29. For the New York Stock Exchange, the Sharpe ratio has over the years ranged from 0.30 to 0.40. So, any asset or investment strategy with a Sharpe ratio of .50 or higher would have a better-than-average ratio of reward to risk, and an asset with a Sharpe ratio approaching 1 would be extraordinary.

Measuring Volatility

The price volatility of a particular ETF can be ascertained from more than one source. An ETF's current *beta* may be found on financial websites such as *smartmoney.com* and *moneycentral.msn.com*.

A sense of an ETF's volatility can also be obtained by simply observing its daily highs and lows on a price chart.

If you are inclined to do a bit of arithmetic, you can calculate an ETF's price volatility. The procedure is as follows:

Add up the daily closing prices for the past 30 days and divide the total by 30. That is the average daily closing price. Then, take the difference between each day's high and low prices for the past 30 days. Add the daily differences up and divide that total 30. That gives you the average daily price range. Divide the average daily price range by the average daily closing price. That gives you a rough but useable volatility index.

For example, suppose that the average daily closing price for *mid–cap* SPDRs for the past 30 days was 120.00, and the average daily price range was 3.00. If we divide 3 by 120 we get 0.025. That's a rough volatility index for midcap SPDRs last month.

$$3 \div 120 = 0.025$$

Then, suppose we similarly calculate the volatilities for other ETFs, and they are:

iShares S&P 500 Index Fund	0.033
iShares MCSI Brazil	0.076
Select Sector SPDRs Energy	0.042
Select Sector SPDRs Financial	0.038

These calculations give you an indication of the normal range of volatility levels. They also provide a basis for comparing the volatility of any one ETF with the norm. For example, on the basis of

beta

an index of the volatility of a security's price, compared to the volatility of the S&P 500 Index. Securities with betas higher than 1 are more volatile than the S&P 500 Index. Securities with betas of less than 1 are less volatile than the S&P 500 Index.

mid–cap stock

the stock of a company with a market capitalization of between $500 million and $2 billion.

SPDR

the acronym for S&P Depositary Receipt, the first ETF, introduced in 1993 and designed to track the S&P 500 Stock Index. Pronounced "spider," the acronym is also part of the name of several other ETFs, including SPDR O-Strip, SPDR MidCap, and several sector SPDRs.

investment advisor

in an actively managed mutual fund, a person or company who is paid to provide specific advice for selecting securities and timing market entry and exit. Some investment advisors may also manage portfolios of securities.

index tracking

a measure of the correlation between the returns of a stock portfolio and the returns of the index to which to portfolio is benchmarked.

portfolio manager

the person or firm who is responsible to administer the portfolio of ETF's underlying index stocks held in trust.

our calculations above, the MidCap SPDRs, with a reading of 0.025, had comparatively low volatility during the period.

ETF Structure

The simplest framework for an ETF is a unit investment trust. The unit investment trust comprises a specific portfolio of securities that remain essentially unchanged throughout the life of the trust. A unit investment trust is not actively managed. It has no board of directors, corporate officers, or *investment advisor*. Expense ratios are very low. There are eight ETFs that are unit investment trusts: Diamonds Trust Series 1, SPDR Trust Series 1, Midcap SPDR Trust Series 1, NASDAQ 100 *Index Tracking* Stock, and the 4 BLDRS ADR Index Funds.

Most ETFs are organized as open-end investment trusts. An open-end investment trust is more flexible than the unit investment trust. The *portfolio manager* of an open-end investment trust has some latitude. He (or she) may be able to choose the timing of a stock purchase or sale mandated by a change in the underlying index. He may be permitted to loan stocks from the portfolio, or to invest some of the ETF's assets in derivatives. Expense and turnover ratios are higher for an open-end investment trust than for a unit investment trust.

Several ETFs are organized as HOLDRs ("holders"). A HOLDR is a receipt for ownership of a small basket of stocks. The stocks in the basket are typically in one industry or sector, but they do not comprise an index per se.

ETF Composition

An ETF that tracks a relatively small index may hold every share of stock in the index. An ETF that is benchmarked to a large index, comprising several thousand different stocks, may hold a computer-generated portfolio that mimics the performance of the index with relatively few issues.

It is not a bad idea to review the holdings of your intended, to see what you're buying. An ETF promises diversity, but it should not be taken for granted.

For example:

- The top two stocks in a Merrill Lynch Semiconductor HOLDR (SMH), Intel and Texas Instruments, comprise 38 percent of the portfolio.
- In Select Sector SPDR Fund–Energy (XLE), Exxon Mobil and Chevron together account for 28 percent.
- Genentech and Amgen dominate Merrill Lynch Biotech HOLDRs, (BBH), comprising 2/3 of the portfolio.
- In Select Sector SPDR Fund—Industrial (XLI), General Electric alone represents more than 18 percent of the portfolio. That is more than the next three stocks combined.
- In Merrill Lynch Retail HOLDR (RTH), Wal-Mart and Home Depot together comprise 35 percent of the value of the fund.
- Exxon and Chevron make up more than one-third of the iShares Dow Jones U.S. Energy Sector Index Fund (IYE).

As an ETF's holdings become concentrated, the ETF loses its diversity and begins to take on the behavior and risk of a single stock.

PowerShares Capital Management addresses this problem directly; in PowerShares ETFs, no single stock is supposed to represent more that 5 percent of the portfolio.

Other Basic Data

The following information on specific ETFs is available from several online sources. Some of the sources are listed in Appendix B.

Total Assets and Net Asset Value

net asset value (NAV)

an ETF's net asset value comprises the fund's total assets (securities and cash), minus the fund's liabilities, divided by the number of fund shares outstanding.

Total assets comprise the total market value of all the securities that the fund holds. You cannot glean much from a fund's size, but it is safe to say that moderately large size is generally best. It is possible for a fund to get so big as to be unwieldy; very small funds may suffer from a lack of diversity.

Net asset value (NAV) is derived by dividing the fund's total net assets by the number of shares the fund has outstanding.

Premiums and Discounts

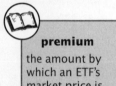

premium

the amount by which an ETF's market price is above its NAV, expressed as a percentage of the NAV.

An ETF's price is determined by the bids and offers received in the marketplace. An ETF's net asset value is determined by the value of its underlying stocks. Because the criteria are different, it is possible for an ETF to trade at a *premium* or at a *discount* to its net asset value.

A proxy calculation to ascertain the current net asset value of the securities in the ETF's portfolio is made every 15 seconds during the trading day. This is referred to as its intraday portfolio value, or intraday value, and is publicly available under its own ticker symbol.

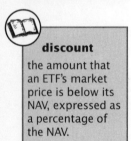

discount

the amount that an ETF's market price is below its NAV, expressed as a percentage of the NAV.

When the spread between an ETF's market price and its intraday value becomes too great, *arbitrage* is possible. Such arbitrage would require swapping units of ETFs and their underlying stocks, and so could be conducted only by Authorized Participants.

For example, if the intraday value is less than the ETF price, arbitrageurs could buy the underlying securities, swap them for creation units of ETFs, and sell the ETFs on the open market. If the intraday value is greater than the ETF price, arbitrageurs could do the reverse: buy ETF shares on the open market, form redemption units, swap them for the underlying securities, and sell the securities. The actions of the arbitrageurs force the spread between the intraday value and the ETF price to narrow, reducing or eliminating the temporary discount or premium.

Premiums and discounts for domestic ETFs are very small, typically in a range from 0.00 percent to 0.08 percent. Premiums and discounts are bigger and more persistent in U. S. ETFs that track foreign stocks, as trading volume in these markets is often comparatively low, and the ETFs may trade in the United States when the foreign stock markets are closed.

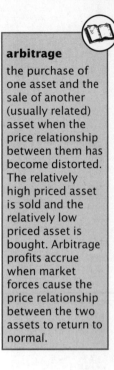

arbitrage
the purchase of one asset and the sale of another (usually related) asset when the price relationship between them has become distorted. The relatively high priced asset is sold and the relatively low priced asset is bought. Arbitrage profits accrue when market forces cause the price relationship between the two assets to return to normal.

Current Yield

There are 2 kinds of current yield. One is dividend yield, which is the return based on the ETF's market price. For example, if the ETF is selling for $20 and pays a monthly dividend of 10 cents, the ETF has an annual dividend yield of 6 percent ($20 × 06 = $1.20 per year = 10 cents per month). The other is called market yield. It is calculated the same way, but it is based on the ETF's net asset value.

Annualized Total Returns

Annual percent returns usually are shown for the most recent 1-, 3- , 5-, and 10-year periods and since inception. Annual returns may be expressed in two ways: the return on the share price or the return based on the NAV. The difference between them is typically very small.

Creation and Redemption Features

These data show the size of the creation and redemption units, expressed in number of ETF shares. Also shown are the creation and redemption fees, which are expressed in dollars per transaction.

Average Daily Trading Volume

Average daily trading volume is a count of the average number of ETF shares that change hands on the exchange each day. As of late 2006, the top-10 most-traded ETFs in descending order of trading volume are as follows:

1. NASDAQ 100 Index Tracking Stock (QQQQ)
2. SPDR Trust Series 1 (SPY)
3. iShares Russell 2000 Index Fund (IWM)
4. Merrill Lynch Semiconductor HOLDRs (SMH)
5. Select Sector SPDR Fund—Energy (XLE)
6. iShares MSCI Japan Index Fund (EWJ)
7. Merrill Lynch Market Oil Services HOLDRs (OIH)
8. streetTRACKS Gold Shares (GLD)
9. DIAMONDS Trust, Series 1 (DIA)
10. Select Sector SPDR Fund—Financial (XLF)

Fundamentals of the Underlying Stocks

Underlying stocks differ from ETF to ETF, even between those in the same sector. All else being equal, the ETF whose stocks have the better underlying fundamentals will have better market performance.

According to a University of Michigan study described in their news release of March 2005, the positive effects of company good news, such as a surprise announcement of increased earnings, can continue to affect the market performance of the company's stock for as long as two years after the event.

Returning to the Mean

There are market analysts, not the least of whom is Dr. Burton Malkiel, author of *A Random Walk Down Wall Street* (New York: Norton, 1990), who hold that stocks that have performed poorly over the past two or three years are good candidates to produce above-average returns in the next two or three years.

If you are interested in pursuing this algorithm, the periodic returns of all Wilshire Associates stock asset classes since 1987 may be gleaned with the index calculator at *wilshire.com*. Click Indexes, Index Return Calculator, Cumulative Returns, and select the desired time span.

Expense Ratio

An ETF's expense ratio represents the percentage of the ETF's assets that are deducted each year to pay for the general operation of the ETF. Included in the expense ratio are office expenses, administrative fees, and other asset-based costs. Direct costs such as brokerage commissions or legal fees for a specific lawsuit are not.

ETFs, by their very nature, have low costs. Individual ETF expense ratios (not including HOLDRS) range from 0.08 percent to 0.65 percent, with a median of about 0.28 percent. The expense ratio for HOLDRs is virtually nil.

According to Morningstar, the average annual expense ratio for all mutual funds in 2005 was 1.52 percent, but that's not a fair comparison. There are index mutual funds today with expense ratios close to the ETF average.

In addition to identifying ETFs with the lowest expenses, the expense ratio can be used an informal quality check. As a general rule, ETFs with low expense ratios outperform those with high expense ratios.

Turnover

Stock turnover within an ETF incurs commission costs and creates potential capital gains. Commission costs are paid out of ETF assets and reported as "other expenses." Capital gains are ostensibly passed through to ETF holders at yearend.

However, turnover in an ETF is characteristically low, and capital gains are few. And even then, effective portfolio managers often find a way to offset intra-year capital gains and end the reporting period flat.

Barclay's iShares, for example, have had zero capital gain distributions for the past four years. SPDR Trust Series 1 has had annual capital gains of less than 0.02 percent of invested assets over the past 11 years.

The ETF asset classes with the lowest average tax-cost ratio over the past five years were mid- and small-cap blend and growth stocks.

Fifty-Two-Week High and Low Price

It is valuable to know the dimensions of the playing field. Prices near their annual highs have, speaking technically, a greater probability to go down than up. The inverse is true for prices sitting near their 52-week lows.

Top 10 Stock Holdings

The fund's top 10 holdings will likely present few surprises; but if you are unfamiliar with the index's composition, the nature of the top 10 securities it holds will give you an insight.

Industry Diversification

Industry diversification provides a breakdown of the portfolio by sector (e.g, healthcare, information technology, mining.) The breakdown also shows the percentage that each sector represents.

Availability of Options

Availability of options indicates whether puts and calls are available on the ETF.

Getting Help

Many stock brokers are equipped to help you to determine the best investments for you to hold, given your age and personal financial situation.

Selecting and working with a financial advisor is a subject beyond our scope here, but there are professional advisors who can help you with allocating assets. They are often found in financial firms. The top tier of certified consultants includes the Chartered Financial Analyst (C.F.A.), the Certified Financial Planner C.F.P.) the Registered Financial Consultant, (R.F.C.), the Chartered Financial Consultant (Ch.F.C.), and the Certified Fund Specialist (C.F.S.).

Other sources of help in allocating assets may be found in Appendix B.

Lastly, you should consider reading *Exchange-traded Funds as an Investment Option* by A. Seddik Meziana (New York: Palgrave McMillan, 2005) and *Active Index Investing* by Steven A. Schoenfeld (Hoboken, NJ: John Wiley & Sons, 2004).

Pork Bellies Don't Fit in a Safe Deposit Box

Hugh Williams is 26 years old and single. He lives in Philadelphia where he works as a commodity broker in a major firm. Hugh is a numbers nerd. His office desk is cluttered with commodity price charts and computer printouts.

One of Hugh's favorite off-duty pastimes is playing $50 blackjack in the Atlantic City casinos, which he does two or three weekends a month. He always takes $20,000 cash with him, deposits it in the cage, and writes markers at the tables when he needs to buy chips.

Casinos do not send a limousine for Hugh. He understands that blackjack is not a game of chance; and he knows the strategies that can keep the house odds at blackjack close to zero, or even slightly in his favor. As a consequence, he usually goes home even, or with modest winnings, and on occasion he has won several hundred dollars.

Hugh has a very good annual income—and he has become aware recently that his growing money market account should probably be put to better use. He does some personal commodity trading, but only on a small scale, and that's the way he wants to keep it. What he needs, he feels, is an anchor to windward, a counterbalance, something solid at the other end of the spectrum from blackjack and pork bellies. Maybe gold or real estate? He wonders about mutual funds.

tax efficiency

the tax efficiency of an ETF is a function of the fund's capital gains that are passed through to the ETF holder. An ETF that is managed with tax efficiency as a goal will distribute few or no taxable capital gains to its holders.

He discusses the subject with one of his friends at the firm who worked previously as a stockbroker. The friend tells Hugh that broad-based, exchange-traded funds have yielded 10 percent over the years; and that there are narrower funds such as the S&P MidCap 400, for example, whose average annual gains over the past decade are closer to 15 percent.

Hugh becomes interested and looks further. In addition to favorable returns, he learns that ETFs also offer nominal costs and good *tax efficiency*. He also likes the idea that they are low maintenance; he doesn't have to watch over them constantly.

Over the next few weeks, Hugh gradually transfers funds from his money market account into ETFs, choosing from a different assert class each time.

Chapter

7

Position Management

If you are new to the stock market or have been dealing mostly with mutual funds, exchange-traded funds may cause you to work with some unfamiliar concepts. If that is the case, you'll want to become more familiar with them.

Intraday Prices

Intraday ETF price quotes are available from several sources. Broker-dealer websites typically provide their clients with real-time prices, and some display streaming prices. The ETF exchanges also provide intraday price quotes, although they are usually delayed.

> **broker-dealer**
> a securities firm that sells stocks, bond, funds, or other investments to the public.

Two good online sources for free, real-time streaming price quotes, plus a peek at electronic open bid and asked prices, are *tradingday.com* and *midnighttrader.com*.

The Orders

Orders vary in three ways: time, action, and contingency.

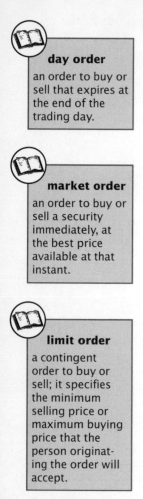

day order
an order to buy or sell that expires at the end of the trading day.

market order
an order to buy or sell a security immediately, at the best price available at that instant.

limit order
a contingent order to buy or sell; it specifies the minimum selling price or maximum buying price that the person originating the order will accept.

Time refers to how long the order stays open. A *day order*, as the name implies, is open for just that day. If it is still unfilled at the close of trading in that market, it is automatically cancelled. Most traders like to use day orders, reentering the order each morning if necessary.

Orders that remain open until they are specifically cancelled are known as "good-till-cancelled orders" (GTC). The problem, familiar to anyone who has been around markets for very long, is that GTC orders tend to be forgotten. A surprise fill on a GTC order placed a month ago may not be a pleasant surprise.

The most important orders specifying action are: the *market order*, the *limit order*, and the *stop order*.

Market Order

A market order contains no contingencies. An example of a market order is:

Buy 100 SPY at the market.

When this order reaches the exchange, it will be filled at the best bid available at that moment. You won't know the price you paid until you get the confirmation of your trade.

In an ETF like SPY, that trades 60 million shares a day, there is probably not much risk in using a market order. It is a different matter in a market where trading is slow. The bid and asked prices may be relatively far apart, and the fill you get may not be what you expected.

Limit Order

A limit order contains a price provision. It is expressed as:

Buy 100 SPY at 121.20

If you place this order when SPY is trading at 121.85, for example, it cannot be filled immediately. The current price is .65 above the maximum price that you will pay. The order will be held in abeyance. If the price later eases and SPY trades at 121.20, your limit order will be activated.

But there is no assurance that your entire order will be filled. The most that you will pay remains 121.20. If prices immediately rallied again, there could be a portion of your order left unfilled at the end of the day.

Market-if-Touched (MIT) Order

First cousin to a limit order, an MIT order solves the problem of partial fills. As the name implies, a market-if-touched order becomes a market order when its specified price is touched. Like any other market order, it will be filled completely at the best price available at the time.

Stop Order

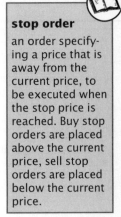

The most familiar employment of a stop order is to close out a losing short-term position when losses reach a specified level. In this context, it is sometimes referred to as a "stop-loss" order.

stop order
an order specifying a price that is away from the current price, to be executed when the stop price is reached. Buy stop orders are placed above the current price, sell stop orders are placed below the current price.

To take an example, say that you had bought SPY at 119.40, and it is now trading at 121.80. You have a nice gain, and you would like to keep most of it. You decide that if the ETF gives back 30 points, you will sell it. You would use a stop order. It would take the form of:

Sell 100 SPY at 121.50 stop

Nothing will be done on this order until SPY reaches 121.50, when it will convert to a market order and be filled immediately. If SPY never gets down to 121.50, your stop order will never be activated. Your profitable position will remain intact.

Once again, there is no assurance that you will get the stop price. If you are concerned about the price you will get when your stop is activated, you add a limit to the order. The order might now read:

Sell 100 SPY at 121.50 stop, limit 121.40

The stop part of the order is unchanged. But now, when the stop is activated, it becomes a limit order, not a market order. The order cannot be filled at a price below the limit, 121.40. Believe it or not, there's still a small risk. In a fast-moving market, prices could fall below the 121.40 limit before all of your shares have been sold, and you would be left with a partial fill. You can reduce this risk by making the stop price different from the limit price, as in example just above.

A stop order may also be used to enter a market. For example, you might want to wait to buy an ETF until it puts on a display of strength, such as breaking out to new highs. To do so, you could use a buy stop placed just above the old highs.

There are other orders that can be used in buying and selling ETFs; but they are known more for their exotic qualities than their usefulness, and you will find few occasions to use them.

Short- versus Long-Term Trading

"Short" and "long" are relative terms; the distinction between them is often a matter of interpretation.

Traders generally break position times down into three categories: a day trade, which means in and out in the same trading session; a swing trade, which spans a couple of days to a couple of weeks; and a position trade, which comprises everything else.

How long you keep a market position is a matter of your personal goals. If your investment horizon is relatively distant and you do not have a lot of time to devote to your investments, a few positions in broad ETFs might be very suitable. You won't ever "beat the market," but you are relatively certain to receive market returns on your money.

If you are a short-term trader at heart, today's information technology and low commissions make frequent buying and selling financially feasible.

The big difference, of course, is that short-term trading requires a market "view," an opinion about where prices are headed in the next few hours or days. If your view is wrong, your account balance will pay the penalty. We will elaborate in Chapter 13, where we talk about day trading.

Short Sales

A short seller borrows stock and sells it in the expectation that its price will go down. If his expectation is correct, he can buy the stock back later at a lower price and return the stock to the lender. The difference in the two prices is the short seller's profit.

If the short seller's expectation is wrong, and the price of the stock starts to go up, the short seller will begin to accrue losses on his short position.

The crux is whether the short seller owns the identical stock that he is borrowing. If the short seller owns the identical stock (in another account), his market losses on the short position are offset by the gains in his long position. His loss is only one of opportunity.

If the short seller does not own the identical stock that he is borrowing, his short stock position is "uncovered," and his market risk is theoretically unlimited.

Margins for stock short sales reflect these differences. Minimum initial margin for an uncovered stock short sale is 100 percent of the proceeds from the short sale plus 50 percent normal margin. Minimal initial margin for a covered short sale is 100 percent of the proceeds from the short sale.

In both cases, if market losses erode the value of the short seller's equity below a certain level, a margin call will go out to him asking for additional, maintenance margin.

opportunity loss
the return that the money could have earned elsewhere if it were not committed to that particular investment.

short seller
a short seller borrows stock, sells it in the expectation that its price will go down, and then buys it back later and returns it to the lender.

margin
a cash deposit made by the stock buyer to secure a margin loan.

The Process

To begin, the appropriate ETF shares are borrowed, through a broker, from another investor or from the brokerage firm itself. These borrowed shares are sold on the open market and the proceeds deposited in the short seller's margin account.

While the short position is on, the short seller will be charged interest on the margin loan to buy the shares; and, if the ETF should pay a dividend in the interim, he will have to remit the money to the lender of the shares.

To close out his short position, the short seller would buy the ETF shares on the open market and return them to the lender.

Short selling is a complicated process. There are simpler, equally effective ways for an individual investor to offset or profit from a decline in an ETF's price. One is to buy a put option on the ETF; another is to sell short a futures contract, if one is available on the ETF. Options and futures on ETFs are discussed in later chapters.

What to Do with a Losing Position

> *Even being right three or four times out of ten should yield a person a fortune if he has the sense to cut his losses quickly on the ventures where he has been wrong.* —Bernard Baruch

Preserving your investment capital is the single most important consideration in position management. The most dangerous mind-set when facing growing unrealized losses is a stubborn refusal to acknowledge your mistake and take the loss.

More than one study has shown that traders who curtail their losses have better results than those who do not. In one study of futures traders, conducted some years ago by the U.S. Department of Agriculture, closing out losing positions early was the defining factor between winners and losers.

technical analysis
the forecasting of stock prices based solely on the interpretation of price movement and trading volume. Supply, demand, and company business conditions are not components of technical analysis.

Stanley Kroll, a legendary commodity trader in the 1970s, made a fortune trading wheat futures before he was 40 years old. Kroll was also a prolific writer. In his book, *The Professional Commodity Trader* (New York: HarperCollins, 1974), he details the results of 38 individual trading accounts that he managed from 1971 through 1973. Thirty-seven of the 38 accounts had profits, most with annualized returns of more than 200 percent. One of his most important trading rules: a tight, inviolate stop-loss order protecting each position.

Technical analysis can be used effectively to identify a logical point to exit the market. Or, you can simply select the maximum loss that you are willing to accept.

All of this can be summed up in the white-haired adage:

Cut your losses short and let your profits run.

The stop order is designed to do just that. It rests quietly below current price levels, waiting to cut your losses short. If prices never come down to the level of the stop, it will sit there, unexecuted, letting your profits run.

Margin versus Paying in Full

Trading on margin magnifies your gains and losses. Trading with the minimum ETF margin of 50 percent doubles your risk and reward. This effect is known as *capital leverage*.

capital leverage constructive ownership of an asset while owning less than 100 percent of equity; for example, buying stocks on 50 percent margin. Changes in the value of the asset are multiplied in their effect on investor equity.

For example, Table 7.1 shows a comparison of two 100-share IYT trades, one made on margin, the other not.

In the margined trade, capital leverage doubled the return on equity. As you might expect, this effect cuts both ways. If prices start to retreat, capital leverage will see to it that your losses are also doubled.

Other Suggestions

1. *Stick to your guns.* Once you have decided to take a position in the market, keep your own counsel. Ignore the "experts." If new information arrives that fundamentally changes the investment

	Purchase		Price		Percent Change	Percent Change
ETF	Price	Now	Margin	Equity	in ETF Price	in Equity
IYT	72.20	73.90	100%	$7,220	+2.35%	+2.35%
IYT	72.20	73.90	50%	$3,610	+2.35%	+4.70%

TABLE 7.1 Two 100-Share IYT Trades

scenario, it may be necessary to modify your plan. But be slow to discard the original analysis that you did.

2. *Be open to divorce.* Psychologists tell us that people tend to stay with less-then-the best relationships or courses of action because the relationships and courses of action are familiar, and to change them would disrupt the status quo. Such a mind-set is a potential disaster in investing. There is not much you can do about it except to be aware of the phenomenon the next time that you are thinking about divorcing a losing position.

3. *Be skeptical of "bargains."* An ETF that was at $60 four months ago and is now trading at $32 may not necessarily be a good buy. There are reasons for the decline, and it is good practice to determine what they are before you hurry to take advantage of the markdown.

4. *Keep the market at arm's length.* It is possible to get too close to the markets. If you start reacting to every price tick, your objectivity will go out the window. Online trading is an ideal environment for acting on impulse. It puts the price action in your lap. It also enables you to change your market position by tapping a few computer keys. That's not a recipe for success.

Chapter

8

Price Forecasting Using Fundamental Analysis

There are two approaches to forecasting the price of any stock. *Fundamental analysis* involves evaluating the company itself. The fundamental analyst looks at the supply of and demand for the company's products or services and the business environment in which the company lives. Under the microscope are the company's earnings, sales, competitive position, financial health, demand for the company's products, and quality of management

fundamental analysis
the study of a company's business and financial situation in an attempt to predict the course of the company's stock price in coming weeks or months.

Technical analysis gives no weight to business and economic conditions. A technical analyst theorizes that all external market forces will eventually be reflected in the stock's price and trading volume, and he will interpret the information then.

The fundamental analyst looks down the road 6 to 12 months. The technical analyst is more concerned with what prices are going to do in the next few days. Or, to say it another way, fundamental analysis

market timing

an attempt to predict the movement of security prices, thereby enabling the purchase of shares just before their prices go up or the sale of shares just before their prices go down.

attempts to unearth secular price trends; technical analysis is used for short-term *market timing*.

This chapter provides an overview of fundamental analysis. In the next chapter, we will look at technical analysis.

Guidelines

Fundamental analysis of financial markets has been likened to solving a jigsaw puzzle where the pieces change shape when you are not looking. There are many variables to be considered, and not all of them behave predictably.

There are a couple of actions you can take to enhance the success of any fundamental inquiry. One is to exercise great care in making your initial assumptions. In some cases (complex systems), a small difference in the starting point can make a big difference in your final conclusion.

Another is to keeps things as simple as possible. The more steps in an analytical process, the more opportunities there are for inconsistencies and ambiguities to creep in.

According to a 2001 University of Chicago study, there is a point of diminishing returns in the amount of information available to a decision-maker. The study evaluated of a group of professional horserace handicappers over several months. The handicappers were given differing amounts of background and performance data on the horses, and their resulting forecasts were graded.

It was not surprising to learn that too-little information reduced the effectiveness of the handicappers' predictions. What was surprising was that too much information was just as deleterious. It overwhelmed the handicappers, actually impairing their decision-making ability.

You might also take a page out of Jack Schwager's book, *A Complete Guide to the Futures Markets* (New York: John Wiley & Sons, 1984). Schwager suggests that, wherever possible, fundamental values be expressed as ranges rather than single numbers to signify that, despite their appearance of mathematical precision, the values are approximations.

Exchange-Traded Funds

The fundamental landscape is not the same for all ETFs. Fundamental forces affecting a large, broadly-based ETF are those that affect the stock market as a whole. On the other hand, an ETF that tracks a small number of stocks in only one industry or market sector can be treated almost as a single company for the purpose of fundamental price forecasting.

These are extremes. They mark the opposite ends of a spectrum. For ETFs that fall somewhere in between, it will be up the analyst to decide, on a case-by-case basis, which fundamental factors are most important.

Narrowly Based ETFs

Much has been written about how to gauge a company's economic health. An excellent source, *Security Analysis,* by Benjamin Graham, is referenced at the end of this chapter. In the meantime, you can still perform some triage. The vital signs include:

1. *Small corporate debt.* A debt/asset ratio (total liabilities divided by total assets) of less than 1.00 is desirable, as it indicates that the majority of the company's assets are financed through equity. A detailed ratio analysis for a selected company, including comparative ratios of other companies in the same industry or sector, may be found at *finance.yahoo.com.*

2. *A 10-year history of regular dividend payments on common stock* (better still, increasing dividends).

3. *An ongoing program to repurchase the company's own stock*, thereby reducing the float and raising the book value of remaining shares.

4. *Insulation from competition* through market dominance or patent protection.

5. *Positive free cash flow.* Free cash flow (money left after all the bills are paid) does not get as much press as earnings, but there are some who consider free cash flow to be a better yardstick.

6. *The presence of new products* on the drawing boards or in the pipeline.

7. *A history of increasing earnings.* Growing earnings provide a powerful undercurrent of long-term stock price improvement.

8. *Effective management.* Quality of management is hard to gauge, but it can be inferred. The company's return on capital is a measure of how effectively the company uses money (its own or borrowed) in it operations.

9. *A flat or rising stock price* for the most recent 12 months.

You can find key ratios, company profile, and price and share information for individual companies at *marketguide.com*.

Broad-Based ETFs

Fundamentals for ETFs that track a large number of diverse stocks come mainly from the economic environment. They include the level of U.S. interest rates, the degree of investor confidence, the employment rate, the strength of the U.S. dollar, overall corporate earnings, the U.S. economy's current stage in the business cycle, foreign currency exchange rates, and governmental monetary and fiscal policies.

yield curve
a graph representing the interest rates of securities that differ only in their time to maturity. A "normal" yield curve slopes upward to the right—long-term interest rates are above short-term interest rates at each time interval—as investors are paid more to compensate them for the risk of higher inflation farther down the road.

The Strength of the Dollar   A strong U.S. dollar makes U.S. goods more expensive for foreign customers. The prospect of a weakening dollar would augur for greater exports of U.S. products and improved balance sheets for companies who sell overseas.

Interest Rates   Short-term interest rates respond to current economic conditions; long-term interest rates reflect long-term expectations for inflation. When the U.S. economy is expanding, as it was during the first half of 2006, demand for capital pushes interest rates up. During times of recession, as in 1991 and 1992, the demand for credit ebbs and interest rates drop.

Historically, short-term rates have been below long-term rates, and this relationship is considered normal. In the past 40 years since 1966, however, there have been times when long-term rates have fallen below short-term rates, as anticipation of inflation increased demand for longer term paper. The yield curve was "inverted" (long-term interest rates were below short-term interest rates) for much of the year 2000. The yield curve inverted again briefly in early 2006, but has remained normal or flat for the rest of the year. An inverted yield curve traditionally signals a slowing economy. According to an analysis made by the Federal Reserve Bank of San Francisco in 2003, each of the six recessions since 1970 was proceded by a yield curve inversion.

The principal forces affecting interest rates in the United States are the actions of the Federal Reserve Board, the status of the current U.S. budget deficit (whether the government is issuing or retiring debt), and our foreign balance of trade.

Low interest rates are generally good for U.S. business, but they contain the seeds of inflation. High rates attract investment capital from overseas. Virtually all industries in the United States are affected in some way by the level of interest rates. Those most directly affected include banking, construction, and real estate.

Expectations Expectations fuel speculative buying and selling, which are the wildfire of stock prices. Conventional wisdom holds that speculation creates 10 times more market volatility than earnings changes, and 100 times more volatility than dividend changes.

Those may be gross understatements. From mid-November 1999 to mid-March 2000, the NASDAQ 100 Index doubled, climbing from 2,400 to 4,800. That's a gain about 25 percent a week for four weeks. The S&P 500 was no slacker. In the five years from 1995 to 2000, it increased 344 percent. In the following two years, it fell 45 percent.

Those roller-coaster rides had nothing to do with earnings or dividends.

Demographics The United States is graying. Baby-boomers are now reaching retirement age, and some 70 million of them are expected to join the ranks of retirees by 2009. Their investment objectives will not be the same after they leave the work force. Income and preservation of capital will become more important than growth. These new goals will be reflected in their investment choices in coming years.

New Frontiers Bill Gates likens the advent of the Internet to the invention of the telephone. Any long-range fundamental assessments must consider the directions that electronic commerce will take in the next generation.

World Markets   Foreign exchange-rate risk has been greatly reduced by the adoption of the euro. There are twice as many nations using the euro now than in 1993, when the Economic Union was formally created, and the list is still growing. The effect of lower currency risk is to encourage international commerce, especially with the smaller euro nations, whose currency had before been prohibitively illiquid.

Alternate Energy Sources   Petroleum is exponentially the most important commodity in the world. In the near future, alternate, low-emission energy sources—solar, wind, geothermal, bio, tidal—will increasingly replace fossil fuels. The change will create massive shifts in world economic balances.

Getting Advice

If you are interested in conducting your own fundamental analysis, the books listed below will provide guidance and insights. For individual investors who want to leave the digging to someone else, several firms make a business of conducting fundamental stock market research and selling their conclusions and stock recommendations to subscribers. The price for their services can range from less than $100 to several thousand dollars per year. Advice may be given by U.S. mail, e-mail, or, in the case of some high-ticket accounts, in person.

The impartial *Hulbert Financial Digest*, published monthly, provides the names and track records of successful stock advisors and market newsletter writers going back as far as 25 years. For more information, contact the publisher at 5051-B Backlick Road, Annandale, VA 22003, or at *marketwatch.com*.

For further suggested reading, see *Security Analysis* by Benjamin Graham New York: McGraw-Hill, 2004); *Corporate Financial Analysis in a Global Environment* by Diane R. Harrington (New York: Thomson Learning, 2003); and *Strategic Management and Business Analysis* by David Williamson et al. (London: Elsevier Buttersworth-Heinnemann, 2004).

Technical Analysis

Forms of technical analysis range from exotic computer trading programs to the simple perusal of a price chart. However, virtually all methods incorporate five basic technical tools: moving averages, trading volume, price trend, market momentum, and the companion concepts of price support and price resistance. This chapter shows you to use these tools to forecast ETF prices and identify optimum price points for entering or leaving the market.

Trends

A trend is the tendency for a series of results to keep moving in the same general direction.

Gasoline prices have been trending upward in the past several years. As winter approaches, daily outside air temperatures trend lower. There has been an increasing trend in the number of working mothers in the United States.

If you have ever sat on an ocean beach and watched the tide go out, you have seen a lowering trend. Each wave laps up a bit less on the sand and recedes a bit more.

Financial prices also trend, and the trends can be persistent. The weekly price chart in Figure 9.1, for example, shows a downward price trend that lasted for 22 months.

Recognizing a Trend

When prices have been moving sideways for an extended period and then begin to set new highs or lows, it is possible that a fresh price trend has been set in motion. But you won't be able to tell right away. It takes three price points to establish a trend.

In the case of a downtrend, they would be a new low, a lower high, and a lower low. A downward price trend is not confirmed until the second low is registered.

This sequence can be readily visualized on a price chart. In Figure 9.1, the downtrend was established when prices closed below the lows that were set nine weeks earlier. The signal proved to be a reliable forecast. The ensuing decline carried prices all the way down to 1.

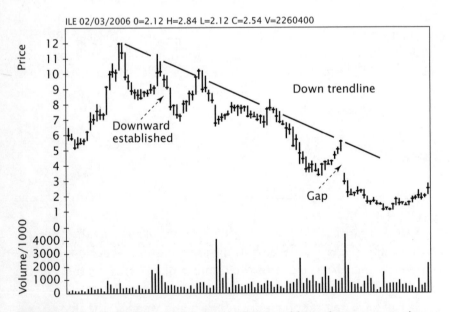

FIGURE 9.1 A persistent downtrend. The trend line, drawn across the peaks, provides technical entry points for new short positions. Chart courtesy of tradingcharts.com.

Traders sometimes draw a straight line across the peaks in a down-trend. This is referred to as a *trend line*. It takes a minimum of two peaks to define a trend line, after which the line can be extended. It is possible that a trend line may have to be adjusted later in the light of new price action.

Each time that prices return to the trend line, touch it, and then reverse course, the trend line's legitimacy is verified. The downtrend line in Figure 9.1 is an unusually powerful example; it turned away rallies on five separate occasions.

A chart uptrend is a mirror image of the downtrend. In an uptrend, the "stair steps" are rising: a new high, a higher low, and a higher high. The uptrend is confirmed by the second high, and an uptrend line is drawn across the price valleys.

Figure 9.2 shows an example of a chart uptrend and its trend line. This trend is also very well delineated. After more than two years, the trend is still intact.

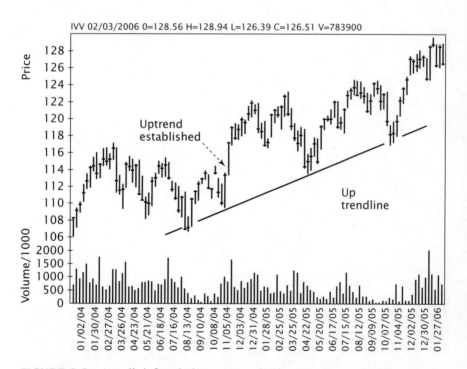

FIGURE 9.2 A well-defined chart uptrend. The trend was established in early November 2004, when prices closed above the high set 2 months earlier. Chart courtesy of tradingcharts.com.

Using Trend Lines

A clearly defined trend line can serve two purposes. It can provide a market entry point with minimal technical price risk; and, its penetration by daily price action provides a technical warning that the current price trend is losing its momentum.

Take another look at Figure 9.1. The downtrend line could be drawn when the second peak was made. If you believed that prices were indeed heading lower, you had an opportunity to establish a short position about four months later, when price revisited the trend line for three days. There would have been a similar shorting opportunity about six months after that. There was even some downside left on the day before the volume spike downward, when prices returned to the trend line for the fourth time.

Figure 9.3 provides an example of a yellow caution light. The downtrend line is well demarcated and has been unbroken for seven months. When prices punch up through the trend-line in August 2004, a technical analyst would sit up and take notice. He would check his other technical indicators to see if there are other signs that the lower

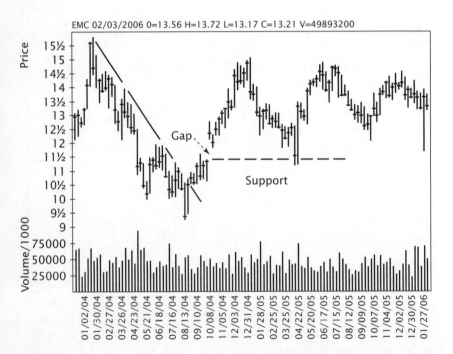

FIGURE 9.3   The breaking of the downtrend line in the week of August 13, 2004 signaled the end of the bear's seven-month domination. Chart courtesy of tradingcharts.com.

price trend has run its course. If he is short the market, he would start giving thought to closing out his position.

In retrospect, it is clear that the breaking of this particular downward trend line was valid technical signal. The ensuing rally carried prices back up to near their recent highs.

Trend Reversals

Established trends change very deliberately. The end of an uptrend does not signal the beginning of a downtrend, and vice versa. Trend changes are usually marked by periods of trend-less, sideways price action. The previous market momentum has dissipated and new market forces have yet to muster.

The sideways price action can last for an extended period. Figure 9.4 provides an example; prices were trapped in a narrow trading range for 1–½ years.

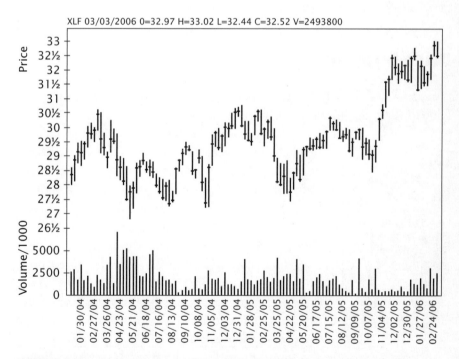

FIGURE 9.4   A trend-less chart, where the market action was trapped between $27 and $30.50 for 18 months, It doesn't show on this chart, but the rally after prices broke out of the long trading range continued to new highs in the following weeks. Chart courtesy of tradingcharts.com.

Some technical analysts refer to an extended rectangular pattern like the one in Figure 9.4 as a "coil," in the sense that prices are gathering the strength necessary to break out of the range—like a snake coiling to strike.

Technicians also assert that the longer that prices remain trapped within such a trading range, the farther they will travel when they finally exit. There is some logic to the premise. The average daily trading volume for XLF during those 100 trading days was about 5 million. So the total trading volume for the entire period was about 500 million.

That means that literally millions of traders had a vested interest in that narrow price range—they had bought or sold at prices between 27.50 and 30.75—and when prices broke out through the top that range, they reacted. Longs smiled and added to their winning positions. New buyers were attracted by the show of strength. Holders of short positions began to accrue losses and started to close out their positions. Those three market forces all point the same direction.

Price Support

A *support level* is defined as a price level where downward momentum falters; where declines tend to stop.

support level
a price level where declines tend to pause or stop. A strong support level can turn prices around and form the foundation for a subsequent rally.

If a stock's price falls from, say, $40 to $23, goes nowhere for a week or so, and then turns upward and begins to rally, the turning point of $23 is considered by chart technicians to be a potential price support level. Prices found a temporary floor there. When prices come back down to that level again, the decline should again tend to run out of gas.

The chart in Figure 9.5 provides an example of chart price support at a previous low. The strong downward momentum of the previous four weeks dissipated when prices returned to the level of the lows set in the week of August 22, 2005.

Price support is also found in other neighborhoods. One location is a previous price peak. Prices tend to find support when they come back

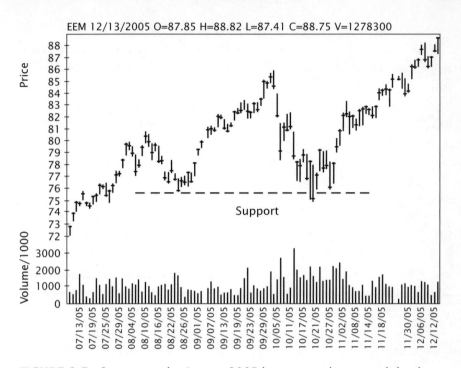

EEM 12/13/2005 O=87.85 H=88.82 L=87.41 C=88.75 V=1278300

FIGURE 9.5 Support at the August 2005 lows not only stopped the decline, it provided the foundation for a subsequent rally to new highs. Chart courtesy of tradingcharts.com.

down to that level. Figure 9.6 shows an example. Support at the highs made in the spring of 2004 sponsored a rally a year later.

Figure 9.6 provides an example of another technical phenomenon: the ability of price support and resistance to swap roles. The $112 price level provided resistance throughout 2004 and support for the following six months.

Support is also found around price *gaps*, which are small blank spaces in a chart where no trading took place; and, near price congestion areas, where prices backed and filled in a small trading range for several days or weeks. You will see chart examples of both a little later in this chapter.

gap
on a bar chart, the white space left when the trading ranges of two consecutive trading days do not overlap.

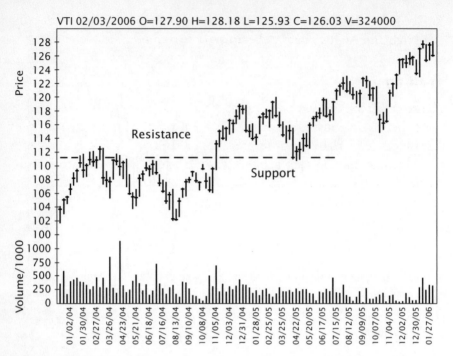

VTI 02/03/2006 O=127.90 H=128.18 L=125.93 C=126.03 V=324000

FIGURE 9.6 Price support and resistance often demonstrate chameleon-like qualities. As shown in this example, the same price level acted as both a ceiling and a floor within a short time span. Chart courtesy of tradingcharts.com.

Price Resistance

Price resistance is the opposite side of the coin. Resistance lies overhead, waiting to act as a roadblock to further gains.

Price resistance is found at the same landmarks as price support: at previous highs and lows, at gaps in the price action, and at price congestion areas. The difference is that prices approach the resistance area from below.

Figure 9.7 provides an example. After an extended price rise from 51 to 69, prices began to move sideways. Price resistance near the highs set in December 2004 turned back two further attempts to resume the rally, in March and August, before the bulls took over again in November.

Trading

Figure 9.8 is Figure 9.4 with support and resistance lines labeled. It is presented to demonstrate that the price action, although trendless, does offer short-term trading opportunities. A technician would trade within the rectangle, buying near support at the bottom and selling near resistance at the top, always keeping stop-loss orders resting just outside the rectangle's boundaries.

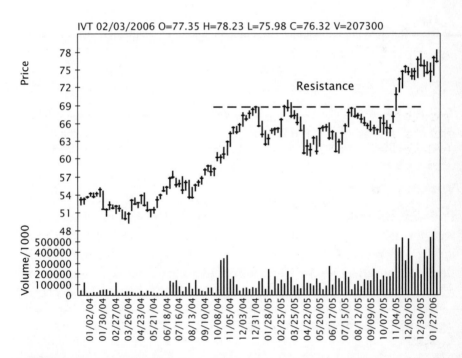

FIGURE 9.7 An example of price resistance at a previous high. Chart courtesy of tradingcharts.com.

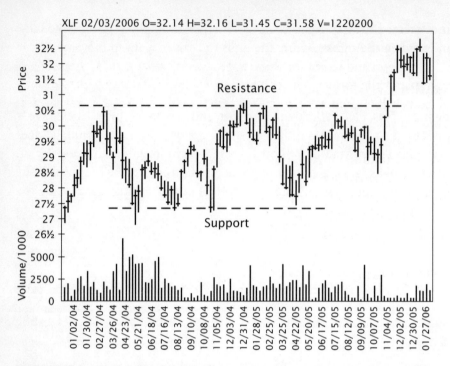

FIGURE 9.8 Well defined lines of support and resistance like these offer good technical opportunities for short-term trading within the rectangle, buying near the bottom and selling near the top. Chart courtesy of tradingcharts.com

Without Charts

Price support and resistance levels may also be identified mathematically, without the use of price charts. Computers are used to track daily price action and measure a market's relative strength or momentum. Some firms use proprietary algorithms to calculate mathematical support and resistance levels and provide the information to their subscribers.

Gaps

In most high-low-close price charts, the days overlap. Each day's price action falls at least partially within the previous day's trading range. When it does not, a price gap is created on the chart.

Price gaps are created on the opening of trading, when powerful market forces cause the opening price to be outside of the previous day's range. Most such price gaps are "closed" during the same day, as prices sooner or later trade within the previous day's high and low. If the forces that created the gap remain strong throughout the day, the gap will still open when the market closes.

Support and resistance are often found near price gaps. Figure 9.9 is an example of the former. The gap formed in the first week of October provided a shelf of support six months later. If you flip back to Figure 9.3 (page 58), you will see another example of support at the edge of a price gap.

Gaps serve other technical purposes. When prices break out of an extended trading range, the new momentum will sometimes cause a gap to form. Chartists refer to this as a "breakaway" gap; it is considered an augury of further price movement in the direction of the breakout.

Similarly, a relatively wide, high-volume price gap may be seen at the end of an extended price move. Chartists refer to this as an "exhaustion" or "blow-off" gap, the last lunge before the current market momentum disappears. Figure 9.1 (page 56) shows an example.

Gaps may also be found at the midway point in an extended price move. They are called "measuring" gaps. Figure 9.9 provides an example. The gap formed at a price of 32 was just halfway between 27 and 37.

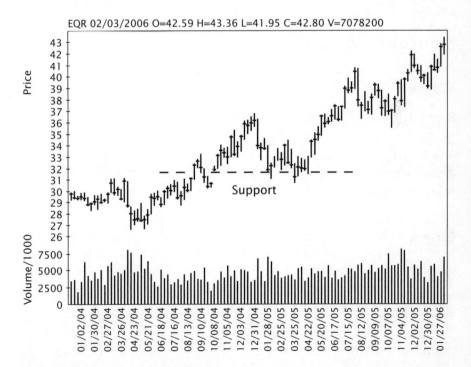

FIGURE 9.9 An example of support found at the edge of price gap. Chart courtesy of tradingcharts.com.

Congestion Areas

Often an ongoing rally or decline will pause, prices will move within a narrow trading range for several days or weeks, and the previous rally or decline will then resume. This period of close-knit price action is called a *price congestion area*. It will tend to provide support the next time prices approach it from above, or resistance if it is approached from below. Figure 9.10 provides and example of the latter. When prices declined in Juen 2005 and then later climbed back to that area, they dug into the resistance a bit, but finally capitulated.

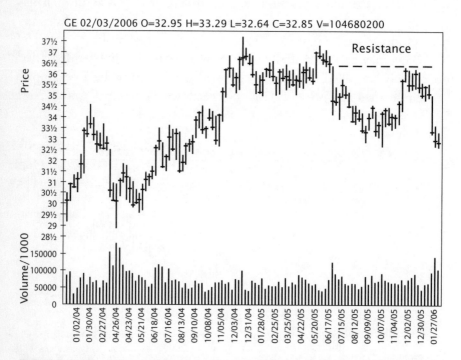

FIGURE 9.10 Price resistance in the neighborhood of a price congestion area. The longer the price congestion lasts, the bigger the roadblock it presents. This congestion area is 6 months long, making it a formidable obstacle. Chart courtesy of tradingcharts.com.

Trading Volume

Daily trading volume is defined as the number of shares that changed hands that day. There are two considerations: The day's total trading volume and, more importantly, the variation in the amount of daily trading volume over time.

High trading volume means that the market is liquid. There are many buyers and sellers; trades can be executed without delay and with a minimum of impact on the price level.

Volume versus Price

If trading volume increases when prices start to climb, it is a sign of increasing interest in the rally. That has bullish overtones. By the same token, if volume picks up when prices fall, it means that the decline is attracting an increasing number of followers.

The opposite situation—a rally or a decline on unchanged or diminishing trading volume—is, technically speaking, more likely to be a head fake.

Figure 9.7 provides a chart example. When prices finally broke through the overhead resistance at 69, they did so on extremely high trading volume. It is not shown on this chart, but the ensuing rally continued to new all-time highs.

Moving Averages

A moving average is simply an ordinary average that is updated every time new information arrives.

The most well known moving average may be a baseball player's batting average. It is updated with every at-bat. Moving averages of daily stock and commodity prices are updated at the market's close each day.

Moving averages are an integral part of almost all trading algorithms. Richard Donchian (1905–1993), considered by many to be the father of trend-following, pioneered the use of 5- and 20-day moving averages to generate price points at which to enter or leave commodity markets. Ten- and 20-day moving averages are also widely used in the commodity markets.

In the stock markets, 50- and the 200-day moving averages are more familiar benchmarks. Major price support is often encountered at the level of a security's 200-day moving average, and the breaking of that support level is considered by technical analysts to be a harbinger of lower prices.

Moving Average Defined

Before we talk about price forecasting, let's review how moving averages are constructed. If this is old news to you, you can skip down to the section on trading.

A moving average begins with a single number, typically the simple average of the last several days closing prices. Any number of days can be used in the moving average. To keep the numbers simple, we're going to build a five-day moving average.

For our example, suppose that the closing prices for XLE for the last five days are as shown in Table 9.1. The average closing price of XLE over the five days is calculated by totaling the prices (227.61) and dividing by 5. The answer is 45.52. That's the static five-day average.

On day 6, we add the new closing price and re-calculate. Let's say that the day 6 closing price is 45.85, as shown in Table 9.2. The new five-day average (the average of days 2 through 6) is 45.77. Our average is now longer static; it is moving forward in time.

TABLE 9.1   Closing Prices for XLE for Days 1 through 5

Day	Price	5-day Average
1	44.57	
2	45.03	
3	45.80	
4	46.16	
5	46.05	45.52

TABLE 9.2 Closing Prices for XLE for Days 1 through 6		
Day	Price	5-day Average
1	44.57	
2	45.03	
3	45.80	
4	46.16	
5	46.05	45.52
6	45.85	45.77

Over the next several days, we repeat the process, adding each day's closing price and calculating the average of the five most recent days. The results are shown in Table 9.3.

We now have a picture of a simple five-day moving average of XLE prices over 10 trading days. The price action on days 5 through 7 demonstrates an important quality of moving averages. The daily price went down each day, but the moving average continued to increase. It was not until day 8 that the moving average finally reflected the falling daily prices and turned downward.

TABLE 9.3 Closing Prices for XLE for Days 1 through 10		
Day	Price	5-day Average
1	44.57	
2	45.03	
3	45.80	
4	46.16	
5	46.05	45.52
6	45.85	45.77
7	45.48	45.87
8	45.20	45.75
9	44.83	45.48
10	44.96	45.30

The moving average "tuned out" the minor downward price swing on days 5 through 7. It delayed changing its course until more information was available. This delay is one of the benefits of moving averages. It helps a trader to avoid overreacting to short-term price changes. It is also one of the moving average's "costs." In some cases, the delay can cause a trader to miss a significant part of a developing price move.

We used five days for our moving average, but that number has no special significance. The optimum number of days to use depends on the market. The fewer the number of days in the moving average, the more sensitive it will be to new information.

The analogy to the baseball player is again appropriate. On the second day of the season, a single hit could raise his batting average 25 points; in September, one hit might add only a fraction of a point.

It follows, then, that in very volatile markets, longer moving averages would tend to work better. They would generate fewer false trading signals, because they are slower to react to spurious short-term price changes. By the same token, a shorter moving average would tend to produce better results in a quiet market, as it would respond sooner to the slow changes in trend.

Prices and their moving averages are easier to interpret when their numbers are plotted on a price chart. Figure 9.11 is a chart of XLE prices and their five-day moving average that uses the data from Table 9.3. The chart demonstrates moving average lag and also displays a "sell" signal.

Weighted Moving Averages

The previous example is a simple moving average—the calculations give equal weight to each day's price. But the daily prices are not all of equal importance. No matter what you are talking about, the most recent information is almost always the most indicative. A weather forecast made today is more accurate then one made a week ago. Last night's stock price is a better indication of the market than the price 10 days ago.

Weighted moving averages put this effect to work. Weighted moving averages give the recent prices more importance than the more distant prices.

XLE

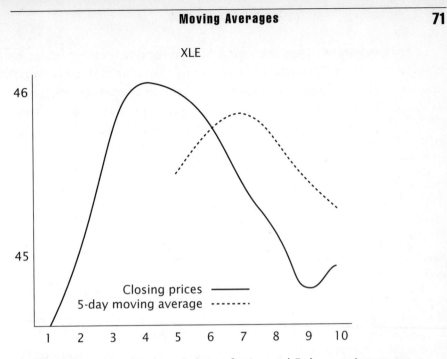

FIGURE 9.11 This combined chart of price and 5-day moving average demonstrates moving average "lag"; prices turned downward 3 days before the moving average did. The chart also shows the moving-average sell signal generated on Day 6, when prices fell below their moving average.

A typical weighting scheme for a five-day moving average would be:

$$1 \ldots 2 \ldots 3 \ldots 4 \ldots 5$$

That is, the most recent closing price would be multiplied by 5, the next most recent price would be multiplied by 4, and so on back to five days ago. The days' values are then totaled and divided by 15, the total number of the weights.

To see the effect of weighting, let's take a hypothetical example. Let us say that the closing prices for stock of the fictitious Neverlast Corporation over the past five days have been 77.78, 78.12, 78.90, 79.25, and 79.74.

The simple average of those prices is their total (390.79) divided by 5 (the number of days) = 78.76.

Now let's weight those same 5 prices according to the scheme above:

Neverlast Corporation, Five-day Weighted Average

$$77.78 \times 1 = 77.78$$

$$78.12 \times 2 = 156.24$$

$$78.90 \times 3 = 236.70$$

$$79.25 \times 4 = 317.00$$

$$79.74 \times 5 = \underline{399.00}$$

$$\text{Total} = 1,186.75 \div 15 = 79.12$$

The five-day weighted average is 79.12. That is 0.36 higher than the simple average. Why? Because the prices were trending higher over the five-day period. The weighted average recognized the upward price trend, providing a more accurate picture of the behavior of Neverlast stock.

This is just an example. Weights may assigned to any number of days in any amount. But the weights should become decreasingly less as you move back in time, so that more recent prices will have a greater effect on the outcome than older prices.

Exponential Moving Averages

The ultimate in weighting is the exponential moving average. Recent days still get the most emphasis, but every day gets some weight all the way back to start of the calculations.

The theory was developed during World War 2, when exponential moving averages were used in antiaircraft fire control to forecast the position of a moving target.

To begin an exponential moving average, we need a starting point. A convenient (and workable) one is a simple moving average of the last 10 days' prices.

This number is plugged into the following formula as *MO*:

$$MN = MO + \frac{CP}{(P - MO)}$$

where

> *MN* = The new moving average
>
> *MO* = Yesterday's moving average
>
> *P* = Today's closing price
>
> *C* = A smoothing constant

In succeeding days, the original starting point is abandoned. *MO* is always the previous day's moving average.

The key to the calculation is *C*, the smoothing constant, which controls the number of days that will be included in the calculations. *C* is always a value between 0 and 1.

The smaller is *C*, the more days will be included in the moving average. For example, if *C* = 0.05, the past 44 days will have about 90 percent of the total weight. With a smoothing constant of 0.20, the past 10 days get 90 percent of the total weight. If *C* = 0.40, the past four days will have 90 percent of the total weight.

The value of *C* for current calculations is chosen by the trader to reflect the market that is under scrutiny. In keeping with what we discussed above, it would follow that more volatile markets would be assigned smaller values for *C*.

Trading with Moving Averages

Figure 9.11 also demonstrates a basic way to use a moving average to create trading signals. The algorithm is as follows:

Be long when the daily price is above the moving average, and be short when the daily price is below the moving average; reverse your position when the two lines cross.

In Figure 9.11, the price closed below the moving average on day 7, generating, in keeping with our trading system, a signal to close out our long position and establish a new a short position in XLE at the opening of trading on day 8. A variation of this algorithm that avoids short selling is to be long when the price is above the moving average and on the sidelines when the price is below the moving average.

Moving averages may also be used in combination. The 50- and 200-day moving averages are a popular combination for stock markets. Figure 9.12 shows an example of a chart depicting daily closing prices (the gray line), their 50-day moving average, and their 200-day moving average. Also presented in Figure 9.12 is a possible combined trading strategy that provides for being on the sidelines when the present price trend is indeterminate.

The following rule would allow for being on the sidelines while the trend is changing:

Be long when the price is above both the 50-day and the 200-day moving averages; be short when the price is below both moving averages; and be out of the market at other times.

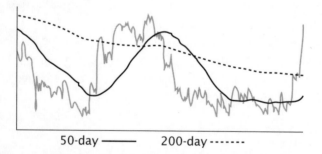

50-day ———   200-day -------

FIGURE 9.12 A trading algorithm: closing out an existing short position (shifting to neutral) when the price crosses above the 50-day moving average, and waiting until the price crosses above the 200-day moving average to take a new long position. A similar strategy could be followed with descending prices and moving averages.

Consensus

As with other technical tools, moving averages should be considered as only one input to a trading decision. The signals produced by the analysis of moving averages should be blended with evaluation of other technical criteria—price support and resistance, trading volume, chart patterns, historical price ranges—to arrive at a consensus technical forecast of the probable movement of prices in coming days or weeks,

Market Momentum

Momentum is a measure of the rate at which prices are changing. The gauge used to take the measure is called a *momentum oscillator.*

The simplest and most widely know momentum oscillator is the Relative Strength Index (RSI), developed by J. Welles Wilder and first published in 1978 in his book, *New Concepts in Technical Trading Systems.*

The RSI does not attempt to compare the relative strength of two different securities, but rather the strength of a single security in relation to its past performance. The principal goal of the RSI is to identify markets that are, technically speaking, oversold or overbought.

The index is calculated by comparing the number of the stock's up days and down days over a given time period. The final result of the calculations is a relative strength index number that falls on a scale from 0 to 100.

To be more specific, the formula for the Relative Strength Index is:

$$\text{Relative strength} = 100 \times \left(\frac{RS}{1+RS}\right)$$

where

$$RS = \frac{AU}{AD}$$

AD = The number of days in the last 14 trading days with lowerr closes

AU = The number of days in the last 14 trading days with higher closes.

We assume that, in the market that we are evaluating, there were nine up days and five down days in the past 14 trading days. If we plug those values into our formula, we get:

$$RS = \frac{AU}{AD} = \frac{9}{5} = 3.6$$

We go back to the first formula and plug in the value of 3.6 for RS:

$$\text{Relative strength} = 100 \times \left(\frac{3.6}{1+RS}\right) = \left(\frac{3.6}{4.6}\right)$$

or

$$\left(\frac{3.6}{4.6}\right) = .782$$

$$\text{Relative strength} = 100 \times .782 = 78.2$$

The current relative strength in this market is 78.2. To keep the process moving forward, you drop off the oldest price, add the newest price, and recalculate.

Putting the RSI to Work

The RSI can be used in several ways. Generally, the RSI value of 50 is considered to be a watershed; from 50 up to 70 is bullish territory, from 50 down to 30 is bearish country.

RSI values higher than 70 signify a market that is overextended, or "overbought," and vulnerable to a setback. RSI values below 30 signal the opposite; the market is considered to be "oversold," the decline to have run its course, at least for now. Some analysts adjust these benchmarks to allow for bias in trending markets; for example, using an upper threshold of 80 instead of 70 in a strong bull market.

A divergence between the direction of prices and the direction of the RSI acts as a kind of early warning radar. A rally accompanied by a falling RSI would be considered suspect. A price decline on rising RSI would be equally suspicious.

Welles Wilder used 14 trading days as the basis for his calculations when he first introduced the Relative Strength Index. He felt that 14 days represented the "normal" distance between price peaks or price valleys, or half of the natural price cycle of 28 days.

But that number is not sacred. It is possible that 14 days do not represent a half-cycle in the market you're studying; and that, as with moving averages, using a larger or smaller number of days in your calculations would produce more accurate values.

If the actual half-cycle in a particular market is greater than the number of days you're using, the resulting daily RSI values will be too high; and, vice versa.

Finally, some of the technical phenomena found in bar charts—for example, support and resistance levels—may also be applied in charts of daily RSI values.

Point-and-Figure Charts

We have been using high-low-close charts for our examples. There is another kind of price chart that technicians use. It is called a point-and-figure chart, and it is more than a record of prices. It comprises a defined trading method.

The point-and-figure chart is the typically hand drawn and posted daily by the chartist. Figure 9.13 shows an example. Prices are on the left-hand scale, in the spaces between the lines. There is no calendar across the bottom; point-and-figure charts are kept without regard to time. The "X" symbol is used to record rallies and the "O" to record declines. Each time the chartist shifts from one symbol to another, he begins a new column to the right.

The size of each "box" is chosen by the chartist. It is generally some conveniently divisible number. For example, if you were constructing a point-and-figure chart for Select Sector SPDR Fund – Financial (XLF), you might assign each box the value of 0.50 points. If a rally were underway and Xs were being plotted, a new X would be added to the top of the column with every 0.50-point gain. If prices were falling and Os were being plotted, a new O would be added to the bottom of the column each time the price fell by another 0.50 points.

Shifting from Xs to Os (or vice versa) is called reversal, and the chartist has to decide for himself how far prices must move against the prevailing trend before he shifts to the next column to the right and starts plotting the other symbol. A "three-box" reversal criterion is common;

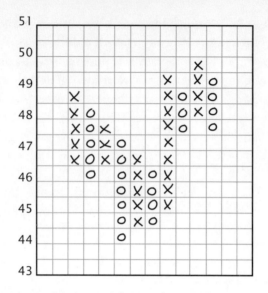

FIGURE 9.13 A typical point-and-figure chart. Rallies are marked by ascending columns of "X"s, declines are marked by descending column of "O"s.

that is, if prices would fill three or more boxes in the direction opposite to the direction you are presently plotting, you move one column to the right and shift symbols.

Adjusting Values

Because you select the box size and reversal criterion yourself, it is possible for you to "fine tune" the point-and-figure chart. The smaller the box size, the more sensitive the chart is to price changes. The smaller the reversal criterion, the greater the number of trend changes that will be signaled. For volatile markets you would use relatively large box sizes and reversal criteria, so the chart would ignore jittery short-term price fluctuations. In a quieter market you would use smaller values, to pick up the more subtle price movements.

The key is to strike a happy medium. What you want your point-and-figure chart to do is to send you a signal when the underlying price trend has changed, but ignore as much as possible meaningless minor price fluctuations. Selecting the values to be used in a point-and-figure chart is as much art as science, and is accomplished mainly by trial and error.

Trading Signals

Point-and-figure charts have another attribute not found in bar charts: point-and-figure charts can give unequivocal "buy" and "sell" signals. A simple point-and-figure sell signal occurs when the column of Os presently being plotted falls below the immediately preceding column of Os. A buy signal is given when an ongoing column of Xs tops by at least one box the immediately preceding column of Xs. Both signals are shown in Figure 9.14.

It is also possible to use trend lines in point-and-figure charts. The downtrend line in Figure 9.14 is well established before the rising column of Xs breaks through.

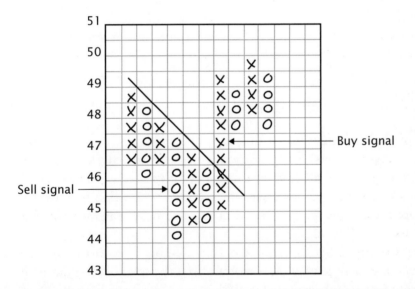

FIGURE 9.14 A sell signal is created when a column of "O"s falls below the immediately preceding column of "O"s. A buy signal is created when a column of "X"s rises above the immediately preceding column of "X"s. As shown, trend-lines may also be used on point-and-figure charts.

Point-and-figure chartists recognize and use several other price patterns in making their trading decisions, but most patterns are variations on these simple buy and sell signals.

Optimizing

Technical analysts use computers to reconstruct past market activity and test trading theories. The underlying assumption is that a trading algorithm which worked well in the past will work well in the future. Some analysts sell their findings in the form of proprietary trading methods, providing specific point-and-figure box sizes and reversal criteria that have worked well in a certain markets over recent months.

The process is called "optimizing" because it seeks the optimum balance between the values that produce the greatest profit and the values that produce the smallest loss.

The problem is, of course, that today's price behavior may not resemble yesterday's price behavior at all. Factors that affect prices change constantly. The conditions that caused a .50-point box and five-box reversal to work well for midcap SPDRs last month, for example, may not be repeated this month or ever again.

The Stock Market Itself

Prices of all ETFs are affected to some degree by changes in the major market averages. Those most affected, of course, are the large, diverse ETFs, some of which are literally surrogates for the overall market.

We have restricted our discussion so far to forecasting the prices of individual ETFs. Many of the same technical criteria can also be applied to price charts of the market averages.

In addition, there is an important technical benchmark that is unique to the stock market. Market breadth is the ratio of the number of advancing issues to the number of declining issues. It is a measure of authenticity, and its interpretation is straightforward. A price movement accompanied by an extreme advance/decline ratio—for example, a rally during which 2,200 issues were up and 477 issues were down (a ratio of 4.61), or a decline in which losers outnumbered gainers 2.5 to 1 (a ratio of 0.40)—would be on a much more sound technical footing than a price movement in which advances and declines were about even (a ratio near 1).

Market breadth readings can also stand in for prices. A moving average of daily breadth values would reveal trends in broad market strength or weakness. Daily breadth values plugged into the above formula for relative strength (instead of prices) would provide a measure of broad market momentum.

Other Avenues

There are many other aspect of technical analysis. Some technicians interpret chart price patterns, and there are some patterns that do seem to have predictive powers. Elliott Wave analysis is applicable to long-range price forecasting. Named after a man who lived in the early 1900s, the Elliott Wave theory proposes that major price movements are complete after five legs in the direction of the trend, and that major price retracements along the way comprise three legs.

There are other kinds of price charts. Equivolume charts combine price and volume data into a single indicator. Candlestick charts, named for their candle-like appearance, make it possible to spot the current price trend at a glance by the color (black or white) of the candlestick. Candlestick charts also have their own unique forecasting tools.

Some technicians use no charts or visual media at all, but base their conclusions on purely mathematical thresholds.

A good source for daily ETF price charts is *tradingcharts.com*, which is mentioned in the preface and whose price charts are shown in this chapter. The web site *archeranalysis.com* has software for creating and evaluating point-and-figure charts.

For further reading, the following books have detailed information on technical analysis. These include *Technical Analysis* by Jack D. Schwager (New York: John Wiley & Sons, 1996); *Technical Analysis of the Financial Markets* by John J. Murphy. (New York: New York Institute of Finance, 1999; *Stock Trading with Moving Averages* by Clif Droke (New York: Publishing Concepts, Inc., 2002); and, *Point and Figure Charting* by Thomas J. Dorsey (Hoboken, NJ: John Wiley & Sons, 2007).

The Tuesday Investors

etty Call had always been interested in the stock market. Her major in college was business, and she wrote her senior thesis on the New York Stock Exchange.

For years, Betty could only observe the stock market. Now that her two children were grown and out on their own, she decided to start a small stock investment club.

She recruited five other women. Each of them put up $6,000, and Betty opened a club cash stock account at a local brokerage firm. The club, which they named the "Tuesday Investors," began meeting in one of the member's homes every Tuesday morning for coffee and discussion.

The drill was simple. At each meeting, one of the women was assigned a single stock to research as a possible club investment. At the next meeting, that woman made a presentation on the company. Presentations covered the company's fundamentals in detail, including earnings and dividend history, new products on the way, possible competition, exposure to foreign currency risk, stock price history, and the quality of the company's management.

After the presentation, the members voted. If a majority favored buying the stock, Betty put the order in that afternoon.

On occasion, the club had guest speakers. One man, a friend of Betty's husband, talked about trends and patterns on price charts. Another spoke of options. The women nodded agreeably and stayed their course.

Everything did go swimmingly for a while as the broad market averages climbed over the next several months. On the first anniversary of the club's formation, their account stood at $77,000, more than twice their beginning stake. They had a dinner party and invited the spouses.

Then dark clouds appeared on the horizon. A major telecommunications company announced that it was revising its earnings downward, and the company's stock collapsed in one day. The club heaved a collective sigh of relief. They had talked about buying the stock just last month ago, but had decided to pass.

A few weeks later, a pharmaceutical company came under scrutiny for continuing to promote a major proprietary drug that the company suspected had adverse side effects. The stock fell 35 percent in three days and there was even talk of the company's failing. The club owned that stock.

Soon thereafter, a college economics professor whom Betty had met at a neighborhood cookout came to speak to the club. He talked about randomness and about the difficulty of forecasting stock prices. He said that he understood that the club members liked the challenge and excitement of speculating in the stock market, but that there was a way to reduce the possibility of sudden sharp losses in a single stock. That way, he said, was exchange-traded funds, which offered low individual stock risk, low costs, and market flexibility. As he put it, "You don't have to look for a needle in a haystack because you have the whole haystack."

The women had several questions, and the coffee and pastries were gone by the time the professor left.

At the next meeting, the women agreed unanimously that exchange-traded funds should be a part of their portfolio. To start, they decided to allocate one-third of their trading capital to broad-based ETFs. On that they would build a superstructure of carefully chosen individual stocks and sector ETFs, both of which would still allow the group to exercise their market judgment.

Chapter

11

Futures Contracts on Exchange-Traded Funds

The first futures contract that had to do with stocks appeared at the Kansas City Board of Trade in February 1982. It was a futures contract on the venerable Value Line Stock Index. Soon after that, a futures contract on the S&P 500 Index began trading at the Chicago Mercantile Exchange. In succeeding years, other stock index futures appeared, eventually representing virtually all of the major stock indexes.

The first single-stock futures contract did not appear until January 2001, and it wasn't here. It was on the London Financial Futures and Options Exchange (LIFFE) in London, England. The most recent single-stock futures contracts are those on ETFs, which were launched in the summer of 1994.

There are presently four ETF futures contracts. Three are traded on the Chicago Mercantile Exchange, and one is traded on OneChicago.

Overview

Futures markets differ from stock markets in many ways. To begin with, there is no ready-made supply of futures contracts standing around waiting to be bought. A new futures contract is created only when a new buyer and a new seller step up and agree to make the transaction. The buyer is long, the seller is short. If they both later reverse their actions, the futures contract disappears.

Margin

The minimum margin on a single-stock futures position, including ETFs, is 20 percent. That amount is set by law. Both the buyer and seller must post margin, but it is not a down payment; it is considered a "good faith" deposit or a performance bond. No money is borrowed.

The margin deposited to open a trade is called original margin. If price changes reduce the equity of either the buyer or seller beyond a certain point, he or she may be asked to put up additional money, to restore what was lost. That is called maintenance margin. The point at which maintenance margin is required varies from exchange to exchange, but a common trigger point is an unrealized loss of 20 percent.

If price changes increase the equity of either the buyer or the seller, he may withdraw the funds, but he cannot draw the account below the level of original margin.

The Futures Contract

A futures contract is a forward contract with most of the terms standardized. The underlying asset, the quantity, and the delivery months are all predetermined, set by the exchange when the futures contact is first listed for trading. All that is left to be set is the price.

Futures contracts are bought and sold only by exchange members and only on the trading floors of futures exchanges. When you buy a futures contract, you are agreeing to accept delivery of the underlying asset, during the delivery period, at the agreed price. When you sell a futures contract short, you agree to make the delivery under the same conditions.

If you change your mind in the interim, you can close out your futures position simply by making an offsetting futures trade.

Futures contracts that are still open when the delivery month is reached are settled by either transfer of cash or by the delivery of the actual underlying physical asset from seller to buyer. All ETF futures are settled by physical delivery of ETF shares on the day after the futures contract expires. After that, the futures contract is removed from the board and no longer exists.

Open Interest

Open interest is a concept unique to the futures and options markets. It is defined as the number of contracts that are open, that have not yet been closed out by delivery of the underlying asset or an offsetting market transaction. It takes two positions to make one unit of open interest: one long and one short.

Open interest changes from minute to minute during the trading day, as buyers and sellers create and uncreate futures contracts. But not every transaction causes open interest to change. It depends on who is buying from whom:

- *Open interest increases*—when a new long buys from a new short, as there are now two new players in the market.
- *Open interest decreases*—when an old long sells to an old short. Two previous players, an old long and an old short, are now gone.
- *Open interest does not change*—when a new long buys from an old long or a new short sells to an old short, as the new player simply replaces the old player in the standings.

Changes in open interest provide technical analysts with an insight into why prices are moving. There are four scenarios:

1. *Prices and open interest are both going up.* A rally that is accompanied by rising open interest is on a sound footing. Buying pressure is coming from new players who are bullish on the market's prospects. Something positive has coaxed them off the sidelines. They are forcing the issue, creating new futures contracts, forcing prices higher.

2. *Prices and open interest are both going down.* Prices are losing ground, but falling open interest suggests a temporary condition. Selling pressure is coming mainly from exiting longs, not new shorts, and it will subside when all the old longs have closed out their positions.

3. *Prices are going up, but open interest is flat or going down.* A price rise accompanied by flat or falling open interest is suspect. The rally is being sponsored by shorts who are buying to leave the market, and will last only as long as they last. If no new factor enters the picture in the meantime, the rally will run out of steam when the last short has bought.

4. *Prices are going down, open interest is going up.* If prices are falling while open interest is increasing, the presumption is of a legitimate bear market. A lot of selling is going on. The rise in open interest tells us that the selling pressure is coming from aggressive new shorts that have suddenly been drawn into the market. The lower price trend is therefore on a relatively good technical footing.

The four scenarios can be summarized in one statement:

When price and open interest go up or down together, the current price trend is given a vote of confidence; when prices and open interest diverge, the market may be about to change course.

We hasten to add that these scenarios are not etched in granite. They are guidelines, to be applied along with other technical indicators to develop a rounded picture of the status of a particular market.

The ETF Futures Contract

OneChicago, the home of single-stock futures in the United States, trades a futures contract on Diamonds Trust Series 1. The Chicago Mercantile Exchange trades futures contracts on the SPDR Trust Series 1, iShares Russell 2000 Index Fund, and the NASDAQ 100 Index Tracking Stock.

The delivery unit for DIA and SPDR Trust Series 1 is 100 ETF shares. The minimum price fluctuation is $0.01, which translates to a $1.00 change in the value of the contract ($.01 × 100).

The delivery unit for IWM and QQQQ is 200 ETF shares. The minimum price fluctuation for those futures contract is also $0.01, but it translates to a $2.00 change in the value of the contract ($.01 × 200).

Maturity months for all ETF futures contracts fall in the typical quarterly cycle for financial futures: March, June, September, and December. The two nearest months are listed for trading. Expiration day is the third Friday of the contract month. Settlement is by physical delivery of ETF shares.

There are no daily limits on futures price movement of any ETF futures contract.

ETFs versus Futures

If you are bullish on small-caps, you could buy IWM outright, or you could take a long position in IWM futures.

There are several differences between owning an ETF and owning a long futures position in the ETF.

The first difference is the stock dividend. The owner of the ETF gets any dividends that the underlying stocks pay; the owner of a futures position in the ETF does not. ETF short sellers must borrow the actual shares to sell; sellers of ETF futures do not. A stock position can be held indefinitely; all futures contracts eventually expire.

Finally, you get more bang for your buck in futures. The reason is capital leverage, which we have talked about before. The minimum margin for an ETF purchase is 50 percent; the minimum margin for an ETF futures purchase is 20 percent. If you trade ETF futures with minimum margin, the effect of a change in the futures price is magnified.

An example is shown in Table 11.1. The lower margin for the futures contract makes the percent change in equity in futures more than twice that in the cash ETF. Of course, if prices go down, losses would be equally magnified.

leverage
the effective ownership of an asset while possessing less than 100 percent of its equity. Leverage creates both opportunity and risk. In 50 percent margin trades, for example, a $1.00 price change in the asset will cause a $2.00 change in the investor's equity. In single-stock futures, where the minimum margin is 20 percent, a $1.00 change in asset value can result in a $5.00 change in investor equity.

The Speculator

The simplest use of an ETF futures contract is for speculation; that is, to place a *leveraged* bet that the ETF price will make a meaningful price move, up or down.

TABLE 11.1   An Example of ETFs versus Futures

	Margin	Purchase Price	Later Price	Change in Price	Change in Equity
Cash ETF	50%	53.00	57.00	3.7%	7.4%
ETF futures	20%	53.00	57.00	3.7%	18.5%

Spread positions are also practicable. A spread comprises two positions—one long and one short—in the same asset or two closely related assets. The idea is that the prices of the two tend to go up and down together. The spreader profits by changes in the *difference* between the two prices.

For example, IWM tracks small-cap stocks; DIA tracks 30 large-cap stocks. If you believed that small-cap stocks were going to outperform large-cap stocks in the near term, you could set up a spread to take advantage of the situation.

The spread would comprise a long position in IWM futures and an equal short position in DIA futures. Regardless of the absolute change in the two ETF futures prices, you will earn a trading profit in your spread position as long as the price of IWM futures goes up more or down less than the price of DIA futures

In the example shown in Table 11.2, both futures prices advanced. But IWM futures prices were stronger; they gained ground on DIA futures. That generated a net gain in the spread.

If both futures prices declined, the spread would still have profited as long as the futures contract you bought (December IWM) went down less than the futures contract you sold (December DIA) This effect is shown in Table 11.3.

TABLE 11.2   Long IWM/Short DIA Futures: Example 1

December IWM			December DIA	
Bought	65.50	July 6	Sold	125.50
Sold	68.00	August 3	Bought	128.00
Gain	3.50		Loss	2.50
		Net gain = 1.00		

TABLE 11.3   Long IWM/Short DIA Futures: Example 2

December IWM			December DIA	
Bought	65.50	July 6	Sold	125.50
Sold	63.00	August 3	Bought	122.00
Loss	2.50		Gain	3.50
		Net gain = 1.00		

Hedging with ETF Futures

A short position in ETF futures can be used to protect a long position in the ETF itself. Because the futures price follows the ETF price, losses in the ETF are largely offset by gains in the short futures position.

The short hedge is placed when a downturn is expected in the ETF price, and the hedge is lifted when the ETF price has stabilized or is expected to increase.

Let's take an example. You own 1000 shares of IWM, and you have reason to believe that IWM is in for a near-term setback. You do not want to sell the ETF. That would create roundtrip transaction costs and disturb your portfolio. You believe that IWM is a good long-term holding, but you would just as soon avoid any possible losses in the next several weeks. You decide to sell IWM futures as a hedge.

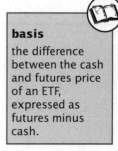

basis
the difference between the cash and futures price of an ETF, expressed as futures minus cash.

It is July. IWM is selling for $65.50, and the nearby IWM December futures on the Chicago Mercantile Exchange (CME) are trading at $65.70 (that .20 difference between the cash price and the futures price of IWM is called the *basis*. It represents the cost of carrying the cash ETF from July to December, and is a factor in advanced hedging and arbitrage. To keep our example simple, we'll ignore it here).

You figure that any shakeout will be over in a couple of months, so you sell five September IWM futures contracts as a hedge. The numbers are shown in Table 11.4.

IWM went down as you anticipated. But the short hedge did its job. Although IWM lost $2.00, your futures position gained $2.00. Your unrealized loss on the combined position is zero.

What would have happened if your assessment had been wrong, and IWM had rallied after you put on your short hedge? This is shown in Table 11.5.

TABLE 11.4 Short Hedge in IWM Futures: Example 1				
Cash			*Futures*	
IWM	65.50	July 6	Sell 5 Sept. IWM futures	65.50
IWM	63.50	September 3	Buy 5 Sept. IWM futures	63.50
Loss	(2.00)		Gain	2.00
		Net gain/loss = 0		

TABLE 11.5 Short Hedge in IWM Futures: Example 2

	Cash		Futures	
IWM	65.50	July 6	Sell 5 Sept. IWM futures	65.70
IWM	66.80	July 27	Buy 5 Sept. IWM futures	67.00
Gain	1.30		Loss	(1.30)
		Net gain/loss = 0		

In this case, the short hedge worked against you. It would have protected you from losses if IWM had gone down, but it also offset any windfall gains when IWM unexpectedly went up.

At this point, you would want to revaluate your outlook for IWM. If you believe a near-term loss is still in the cards, you could keep your hedge in place. If you now think that IWM's prospects have improved, you could lift your hedge by buying five September IWM futures.

Your cost for the protection of the hedge? Your commissions and the opportunity cost of the margin you put up. The $1.30 gain in the stock that you missed out on is not part of the cost of the hedge. That is the cost of misjudging IWM's near-term outlook.

Long Hedge

A long hedge in an ETF future allows you set the purchase price of an ETF now, even though you won't actually buy the ETF for several days or weeks.

Let us say that you will not have the funds until a CD matures next month, but you believe that the market will rally while you're waiting, and you want to effectively buy the ETF now. The transactions are shown Table 11.6.

TABLE 11.6 Long Hedge in IWM Futures: Example 1

	Cash		Futures	
IWM	65.50	July 6	Buy 5 Sept. IWM futures	65.70
IWM	67.80	August 25	Sell 5 Sept. IWM futures	68.00
Opportunity loss	(2.30)		Gain	2.30
		Net gain/loss = 0		

IWM went up while you were waiting, as you expected, but the gains in the long futures position offset your opportunity loss in the ETF. You can buy IWM now at an effective price of 65.50, the price when you initiated the long hedge.

What would happen if IWM went down while your long hedge was in place? Look at Table 11.7.

On August 25, you would still buy IWM at an effective price of 65.50, which is the price you originally sought to lock in with your long hedge. The windfall gain from the unexpected decline in IWM while you were waiting is cancelled out by the loss in your long futures position.

These two examples demonstrate a rule that applies to all hedges:

A futures position taken to hedge against an adverse movement in the cash price will generally negate any favorable movement in the cash price.

Arbitrage

Merriam-Webster defines arbitrage as "the simultaneous purchase and sale of the same or equivalent security in order to profit from the price discrepancies." Here is a real-world example. Suppose that you are a secondary dealer in U.S. Treasury bonds. You buy and sell outstanding issues. Your customers are banks, insurance companies, pension funds.

U.S. Treasury securities are the international benchmark for interest rates. T-bond prices are quoted in markets all over the world, and you keep a close eye on them. One morning you see that the November 2018 T-bond is bid in London at 141-12, and you know that you can buy the identical bond in New York 141-08. (In standard bond prices, the number after

TABLE 11.7 Long Hedge in IWM Futures: Example 2				
	Cash		*Futures*	
IWM	65.50	July 6	Buy 5 Sept. IWM futures	65.70
IWM	62.80	August 25	Sell 5 Sept. IWM futures	62.80
Opportunity gain	2.70		Loss	2.70
		Net gain/loss = 0		

the dash is 32nds, and each 32nd = $31.25), The London/New York price difference is 4/32, or $125 per $1,000 bond.

That is a big discrepancy, and it won't last long. You immediately sell 100 of the November 2018 in London for 141-12 and buy 100 November 2018 in New York for 141-08. It is all done in seconds, at the touch of a few computer keys. No gilt-edged certificates change hands. Your profit on the transaction is $12,500 ($31.25 × 4 × 100), less commissions.

Note that arbitrage is, in effect, self-destructive. The very act of selling London and buying New York drives the two prices back together, reducing and soon eliminating altogether the profit opportunity that the difference presented.

Futures

In the futures markets, arbitrage is done between the cash price and the futures price of the same asset. As mentioned earlier, the difference (futures price minus cash price) is known as the basis. If the basis gets big enough to cover transaction costs and provide a few pennies of profit, arbitrageurs (arbs) will step in take the profit.

For example, if the ETF futures price has drifted too far above the ETF cash price, an arb would sell the futures and buy the cash ETF. When the futures mature, he would deliver the cash ETF against his short futures position, closing it out.

A typical potential arbitrage situation is shown in Table 11.8.

An arb's ears would prick up when he (or she) sees a situation like this. An instant gross profit of 12 cents per ETF is potentially available. From this he would have to deduct his transaction costs. These would include commissions on both the cash and futures trades, and the opportunity cost (what his money could have earned elsewhere) of carrying the two positions. If that all figures out to, say, 7 cents per ETF, the arb would have a certain 5-cent profit.

TABLE 11.8   iShares Russell 2000 Index Fund (IWM)

Date	Cash	December Futures	Basis
October	77.20	77.32	+0.12

Conversely, if an ETF's cash price is above its futures price—less likely, but possible in unusual circumstances—the arb would short the ETF and buy the futures. When the futures mature, he would accept delivery of the underlying ETF shares. He would then pass ETF shares along to his broker to close out his short ETF position. As in the foregoing bond example, the arbitrage creates market forces that cause the price difference—and the arbitrage opportunity—to diminish.

Of course, saying and doing are not the same. First of all, you must use two limit orders, and one or both could fail to be filled. In the numerical example above, separate orders must be placed in two different markets. If one side remains unfilled, you would be left with a net position in the other, and that is not what you want. Or, the favorable price discrepancy could vanish before you can even have a chance to get your orders placed.

The actions of arbs ensure that cash and futures prices gradually converge as the futures contract approaches the delivery period, And that, in turn, ensures that hedging, the futures markets' reason for being, can be done effectively.

The prerequisites for successful arbitrage: an electronic link to the markets, up-to-the-second price data for both ETFs and futures, low commissions, and, ideally, some sort of computer software designed to recognize and act quickly in fleeting arbitrage opportunities.

Online Classes

Lind-Waldock—*single-stock-futures.com*—offers a free, 13-chapter online course devoted to single-stock futures. The course defines single-stock futures, outlines their relative benefits, explains their pricing, and describes how they may be used in several different strategies for speculation or hedging.

Also available online at the same web site is an informative, 10-page, color brochure on single-stock futures published by OneChicago. For additional reading on futures trading, check out *Getting Started in Futures,* 5th ed, by Todd Lofton (Hoboken, NJ: John Wiley & Sons, 2005) and *Single Stock Futures: An Investors Guide* by Kennedy E. Mitchell (Hoboken, NJ: John Wiley & Sons, 2003).

Chapter 12

Options on Exchange-Traded Funds

Your wife's 40th birthday is next month, and for some time she has wanted a painting to hang over the stone fireplace in the family room. She favors scenes of nature and already owns several small watercolors that were painted by a local woman artist.

One day you spot a painting in a downtown gallery window. You go inside the gallery and inquire. The painting is by the same artist, but it is done in oils, and it is large. It shows a winter forest scene, with two cardinals, one male and one female, perched in vivid contrast on a snow-covered tree branch. The price is $2,000.

While you are looking at it, the gallery owner says that the painting is unusual because the artist rarely works in oils (true), that $2,000 is a good price (probably true), and that there is another potential buyer who is very interested in the painting and who is coming in this very afternoon (possibly true).

Nevertheless, to be sure that you do not lose the painting, you offer the dealer a nonrefundable $100 to hold it off the market until tomorrow, when your wife can see it. If she approves, you will buy the painting then. The dealer agrees.

You have bought an option on the painting. During the next 24 hours, you can exercise the option and buy the painting for the agreed price of $2,000. If you do not exercise the option, it will expire at the close of business tomorrow, and the gallery owner will keep your $100.

Background

For many years there was an over-the-counter market in options on common stock in the United States. The owner of the stock arranged with a private dealer to sell an option on it. The dealer advertised in the newspapers for option buyers and earned a commission on each option he sold.

Those old over-the-counter stock options were not transferable. Unless a special arrangement could be made with a dealer to take it back and resell it, there were only two courses of action open to the option buyer. If the stock price changed enough to make the option worth exercising, he could do so and acquire the stock. If not, he simply abandoned the option when it expired.

Since 1973, stock options have been traded on stock exchanges, where their financial integrity is warranted by the exchange and an option clearing corporation. The assets underlying these options are common stocks of major U.S. companies. Exercise of the option is settled by the transfer of stock.

Exchange options, in addition to enhancing investor confidence, added an important third possible course of action for the option buyer. No longer were his choices limited to exercising the option or letting it expire. Like a futures contract, an exchange option position can be offset with an opposing market transaction, and the option holder is then out of the market. The same holds true for short positions in options. This innovation opened the door to a dramatic increase in option activity.

ETF Options

Options on ETFs are traded on the American Stock Exchange (AMEX), Chicago Board Options Exchange (CBOE), and NASDAQ. The AMEX and CBOE also trade options on HOLDRs.

A total of about 250 ETF options is traded on the three exchanges. All are American style: that is, they may be exercised on any business day before they expire, and they are settled by delivery of shares of the underlying ETF.

Options market activity varies greatly. Some ETF options have little or no open interest, while others are very actively traded. The most active ETF options, as you might expect, are those on the most actively traded ETFs.

Trading

ETF options offer several different trading strategies, including spreads, hedges, and limited-risk speculation. But before we get into that, let us review some option basics.

Options come in two types: calls and puts. A call confers the right to buy an asset within a certain period time at an agreed price. (It gives you the privilege of calling the asset to you.) The husband in the chapter-opening example bought a call option on the painting. The premium was $100, the exercise price was $2,000, and the expiration date was tomorrow.

A put entitles you to sell something to someone else. (It gives you the right to put it to the other person.)

The exercise price of an option is the price at which the underlying stock changes hands if the option is exercised. The expiration date is the day the option dies. The premium is the amount of money that the option buyer pays the option seller in the *opening transaction*; it is equal to the market price of the option at that instant.

opening transaction
the purchase or sale of an option that establishes a new position.

Open Interest

As in futures, open interest in options comprises the number of out-standing option contracts, those that have not yet been closed out by exercise or an offsetting market transaction. Puts and calls are treated separately; each has its own open interest tally.

Changes in open interest are interpreted in the same way as in futures. When option prices and open interest are moving in the same direction, the ongoing price movement is considered to be on a sound technical footing. If prices and open interest are both going up, the buying is coming from new longs rather than exiting shorts. If prices and open interest are both going down, the selling pressure is coming from shorts leaving the market, not aggressive new sellers.

For the same reason, when the movement of prices and open interest diverge, the current price trend is deemed suspect, or vulnerable to change.

Specs

An option's exercise price is set by the principal exchange when it first lists the option for trading. Exercise prices are always even dollars (no pennies) and do not change during the life of the option. They are set at $1 intervals above and below the prevailing price of the underlying ETF.

The option contract comprises 100 shares of the underlying ETF. If you buy a call on SPY and exercise it, for example, you will receive 100 shares of SPY. The price you pay each share of the SPY would be the option's exercise price.

Option market prices (premiums) are established by open bids and offers on the exchange trading floor and are quoted in dollars and cents. Incremental price changes depend on the option's price. For an option trading under $3, the minimum tick is $0.05; for options trading at $3 and above, the minimum tick is $0.10.

Naming Options

A stock option takes its name from the stock underlying it. For example, a call option on Midcap SPDR Trust Series 1 (MDY) with a striking price of $130 and December expiration would be referred to as:

MDY December 130 call

The ETF's trading symbol is first. This is followed by the expiration month and the exercise (striking) price; and, lastly, the kind of option (put or call).

If you buy this option and exercise it you would receive 100 shares of ETF at an effective price of $130.00.

A March put option on Merrill Lynch Semiconductor HOLDRs (SMH) with a striking price of 65 would be referred to as:

SMH March 65 put

If you bought this option and exercised it, you would receive a short position comprising 100 shares of SMH at an effective price of $65.00

More Nuts and Bolts

You met some of the special terms for options above. There are a few others you should know.

In the Money

Because it confers the right to obtain a long position, the value of a call option increases when the price of the underlying stock increases. When the call becomes profitable to exercise—that is, when it is more advantageous to exercise the call option to obtain the ETF than it is to buy the ETF outright—the option is said to be *in the money*. A call is in the money, therefore, whenever its striking price is below the ETF's market price.

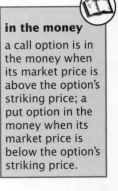

in the money
a call option is in the money when its market price is above the option's striking price; a put option in the money when its market price is below the option's striking price.

If a call option's striking price is above the ETF's market price, the call is said to be *out of the money*. If you want the ETF, it would be cheaper to buy it outright than by exercising the option.

On the rare occasions when the option's striking price and the price of the underlying ETF are the same, the option is said to be *at the money*.

The mechanics of a put are just the opposite. The owner of a put has the right to sell the underlying ETF at the striking price. Short positions gain in value when prices decline; so, therefore, does a put. A put is in the money when its striking price is above underlying ETF's market price, because it is more advantageous to acquire the short ETF position via exercise than through an open market short sale.

at the money
a call or put option is at the money when its market price and striking price are the same.

For example, suppose the exercise price of a put is 55 and the underlying ETF is trading at 58. The put is out of the money. If you want to be short the ETF, you can sell it on the open market for 58. If you exercise the put to obtain a short position, you will be short at 55. That is a $3 disadvantage.

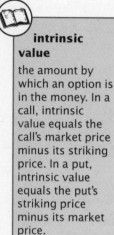

intrinsic value

the amount by which an option is in the money. In a call, intrinsic value equals the call's market price minus its striking price. In a put, intrinsic value equals the put's striking price minus its market price.

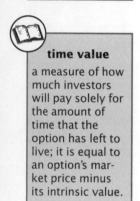

time value

a measure of how much investors will pay solely for the amount of time that the option has left to live; it is equal to an option's market price minus its intrinsic value.

An option price example from the daily newspaper is shown in Table 12.1. Let's translate it: The iShares Russell 2000 April 72 call closed at 1.10 yesterday, up .30 or 37.5%. The underlying ETF closed at 73.00, so the call is in the money. The day's trading volume was 19,800 options.

A line of call option information on a typical broker-dealer's online trading screen would resemble Table 12.2 (SFBEA is the option's trading symbol).

Option Value

If you were to dissect the price of an option, you would find that it is not homogeneous. It comprises two kinds of value added together. One is called the option's *intrinsic value*. The other is called its *time value*.

Intrinsic value is the difference between the option's striking price and the underlying ETF price. An option that is in the money has intrinsic value. An option that is out of the money has no intrinsic value. Intrinsic value changes when the price of the underlying ETF changes.

For example, suppose the conditions shown in Table 12.3 pertained for a PowerShares Dynamic Large-Cap Growth Index Fund (PWB) 70 call.

TABLE 12.1		Option Price Example					
Option Name	Exp. Date	Strike	Vol.	Option Price	Net Chg.	Pct. Chg.	Stock Close
iShRs 2000	Apr 07	72.00 c	19.8	1.10	+ .30	+ 37.5	73.00

TABLE 12.2	Broker-Dealer Screen's Call Option Information Example					
SPY	Last	Chg.	Bid	Ask	Vol.	Open Int.
MAY 131 SFBEA	2.05	+ 0.25	1.95	2.10	4,880	25,870

This table demonstrates a couple of options features: (1) The intrinsic value of a deep in-the-money options changes penny for penny with the market price of the underlying stock; when the option market price went up $1.10 (column A to column B), the intrinsic value also went up $1.10; and (2) an option's intrinsic value (column C) can never be a negative number; the lowest it can go is zero..

Time value is more ephemeral. It represents what market participants are willing to pay simply for the time the option has left to run. Time value is a residual; it is found by removing the intrinsic value from the premium.

For example, suppose iShares Russell 2000 Index Fund (IWM) is trading at 66.20, and the premium for the IWM December 65 call is 2.30.

When an option has no intrinsic value, it is premium comprises entirely time value. This means that if nothing else changes, the premium will drop to virtually nothing when the time runs out and the option expires. That is why you sometimes hear an option referred to as a "wasting asset."

Time value does not change when the option's market price changes. Time value reacts to the ticking of the clock. The more days an option has until it expires, the greater will be its time value. As an option ages, its time value does not diminish at a steady rate. The closer the option gets to expiration, the faster its time value disappears. On the day the option expires, its time value is zero.

TABLE 12.3 PBW 70 Call			
	A	**B**	**C**
Striking price	70.00	70.00	70.00
PBW price	75.20	76.30	69.80
Intrinsic value	5.20	6.30	0

TABLE 12.4 IWM December 65 Call Time Value	
IWM price	66.20
Call price	2.30
Call intrinsic value	1.20 (66.20 minus 65.00)
Call time value	1.10 (2.30 minus 1.20)

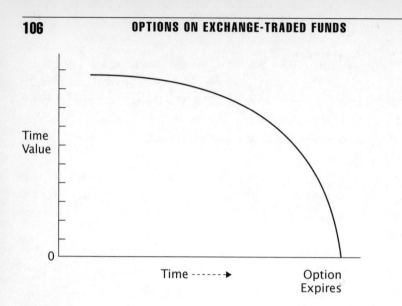

FIGURE 12.1   As shown, an option's time value dissipates at an increasing rate as the option approaches expiration and the hopes of option holders fade. Time value will always be zero on the day that the option expires.

A graph of the behavior of time value as an option approaches expiration is shown in Figure 12.1. As you can see, the closer an option gets to expiring, the faster its time value falls.

Other Influences

There are two other major influences on the prices that option buyers and sellers are willing to accept: they are (1) the option's striking price, and (2) the volatility of the underlying ETF price.

The first is self-evident. If an in-the-money 50 call has a premium of $3, the same call with a striking price of $45 is going to be worth $8, as it has an additional $5 of intrinsic value.

The effect of volatility is not as concrete—but it is very important. Buyers of ETF options do so in the hope that the underlying ETF price will move favorably, and the option will increase in value. If the price of the underlying ETF does not move, but instead trades quietly in a narrow range, there is no possibility of gains. Buyers are therefore willing to pay more for options on high flying ETFs, and option sellers likewise insist on receiving more for them.

Option Strategies

1. Buying calls or puts outright to speculate that the ETF's price will rise or fall, respectively.
2. Buying a put to hedge a long ETF position.
3. Buying a call to hedge a short ETF position.
4. Selling a call or a put outright.
5. Spread positions using calls or puts.

Buying Options

The simplest, most direct use for an option is as a straight bet on the direction of prices over the next several days or weeks. If you believe conditions are right for streetTracks Gold Shares (GLD) to stage a rally, you could buy a call option it. If the price of GLD does go up, so will the value of your option, and you can then sell the option at a profit.

Conversely, a put could be bought in anticipation of a decline in the price of the underlying ETF.

Why would a speculator choose an option over the ETF itself in these situations? One important reason is limited risk. The option buyer's risk is limited to the price he paid for the option. No matter how far prices go against him, the option buyer will never receive a margin call. The worst that can happen is that the option will expire worthless and the entire premium be lost.

Another reason that a speculator might choose an option over the actual ETF is leverage. An out-of-money option can register large percentage gains if the price of the underlying ETF makes a big move.

For example, suppose it is March, iShares Russell 2000 (IWM) is trading at 80, and the following call options are available:

Call Option	*Option Price*
IWM May 80	3.25
IWM May 81	3.00
IWM May 82	2.60
IWM May 83	1.10
IWM May 84	.90

If you bought the at-the-money May 80 call for 3.25, and the price of IWM advanced to 84, your call would now be worth about 7.00 (4.00 intrinsic value + 3.00 time value). A 5 percent increase in the price of IWM caused a 115 percent increase in the value of the May 80 call.

Let's compare that to buying the May 84 call. It is out of the money, so it has no intrinsic value. Its price reflects only time value.

If the price of IWM were to advance to 84, the May 84 call would now be at the money and would be worth about 3.00. The 5 percent increase in the price of the IMW caused a more than 300 percent increase in the value of the IMW May 84 call, from 0.90 to 3.00.

That is the rosy side. The dark side: All IWM has to do for you to lose your entire premium is nothing. If the price of IWM stays flat, the time value of the out-of-the-money May 84 call will slowly run out, and option will eventually expire worthless.

Selling Options

Selling options short is an entirely different matter than buying them. If you sell an option short and do not own the underlying ETF, the sale is considered to be "uncovered." You must post option margin. You are subject to margin calls if prices move against you, and your market risk is virtually unlimited. The amount of margin required may differ among brokerage firms, but the minimum original margin for a short position in an ETF option is 100 percent of the market value of the option plus 10 percent of the value of the underlying security.

To take a bad-case example, suppose IWM is trading at 63.25 and you sell 10 uncovered IWM December 65 calls for a premium of 2.20. You would receive $2,200 ($2.20 × 100 shares × 10 options).

A month later, IWM is trading at 69.80, the premium for the December 65 call is 5.20, and the call that you sold is exercised. But you do not own the IWM calls, so you have to buy them now. You pay the current price of 5.20 for 10 IWM December 65 calls, a total of $5,200, and immediately deliver them to the call buyer to satisfy the exercise.

You received $2,200 when you sold the uncovered calls in the opening transaction. You later paid $5,200 to buy the calls to meet the options' exercise. The result: a loss of $3,000 plus commissions. (To be picky, you are also out the opportunity cost of financing the short position for the month.)

Covered Sale

If you already own the underlying ETF and sell a call on it, the sale is considered to be "covered." You do not need to post margin on the short call because you already have the asset (the ETF) to deliver to the call buyer if the call is exercised. This is considered a more conservative option strategy, amenable to use by nonprofessional traders.

The acquisition of an ETF and the simultaneous sale of a call option on it can treated as a single trading strategy in itself. The goal is to keep the ETF but earn most or all of the call option premium.

Note that the sale of a covered call is not a neutral strategy. Gains are greatest when the price of the underlying ETF stays flat or advances a bit. A decline in the ETF's price begins to eat into potential profits.

The sale of a covered put against a short ETF position would likewise fare better in a mildly bearish environment.

Environment

If buyers want options on high flying stocks, sellers of ETF options want the underlying ETFs to go to sleep. Most sellers of options do so for only one reason: to earn the premium. Risk is least if the option is out of the money when it expires. (For a full description of the profits and pitfalls in the sale of covered and uncovered options, Lawrence McMillan's *Options as a Strategic Investment*, referenced at the end of this chapter, is complete and very readable.)

Option Spreads

So far we have discussed only net positions in options—that is, the buying or selling of calls and puts. It is also possible to establish spread positions with options. A call spread comprises a long position in one call option and an offsetting short position in a different call option. A put spread comprises a long position in one put option and an offsetting short position in a different put option.

In a simple spread, the two options differ only in their exercise prices. They have the same underlying ETF and the same expiration month. For example, a simple call option spread on DIA might comprise:

Buy DIA December 110 at 11

Sell DIA December 120 at 6

The two most popular spreads—and, not coincidentally, the two that are perhaps easiest to understand—are: (1) a bullish spread constructed of two calls and (2) a bearish spread constructed of two puts. These are the only spreads discussed here.

Bullish Call Spread

As you might surmise, a bullish call spread is established when the price of the underlying ETF price is expected to advance. The call with the lower striking price (higher premium) is bought; and the call with the higher striking price (lower premium) is sold. (The DIA spread example in the previous section is a bullish call spread.) The two opening transactions therefore create a debit. That debit is the spreader's maximum market risk.

The two striking prices define the playing field. The bullish call spread gains the maximum if the underlying stock price is at or above the higher striking price at option expiration; it loses the maximum if the underlying stock price is at or below the lower striking price at option expiration.

This effect is easier to see with an example. We continue with the DIA opening spread positions as previously described—and we assume that, when the options are near expiration, the DIA price is 130. That means the time value is gone and the options are trading at their intrinsic value.

As shown in Table 12.5, the spreader earned a trading profit of 5.00, minus commissions.

TABLE 12.5 DIA Bullish Call Spread

DIA Dec. 110 call			DIA Dec. 120 call	
Bought at	11	now	Sold at	6
Sold at	20	later	Bought at	10
Result	+9		Result	−4
		Net result = +5		

There are two other possible outcomes: (1) The DIA price falls and both options expire out of the money. In that event, you would lose the amount of the opening debit plus commissions. Or (2) the call you sold goes into the money is exercised. Exercise puts an end to the spread and generates some unwanted commissions, but it does not force you buy the ETF on the open market. You could obtain the ETF you need by exercising the call you bought.

Bearish Put Spread

You put on a bearish put spread by buying the put with the higher strike price (higher premium) and selling the put with the lower strike price (lower premium). The two transactions create an opening debit and, as with the call spread, that is the most you can lose. The bearish put spread delivers its maximum gain, as you might expect, when the underlying ETF price is weak.

To take an example, suppose that it is October 30 and iShares Dow Jones Transportation Average Index Fund (IYT) is trading at 77. You buy the December 80 put and sell the December 75 put. The 80 has 3 points of intrinsic value (80 − 77) and 3 points of time value, so it costs you 6. The 75 is out of the money, so the 3 you receive when you sell it is all time value. Your opening debit is 3.

Two weeks later, IYT has declined to 72, both puts are now in the money, and the bearish spread has generated a small gain. The numbers are in Table 12.6.

Caveats

Making speculative profits in option spreads is not as facile as these examples may imply. Many ETF option markets are still very thinly traded; occasionally, limit orders that look like they should have been filled, are

TABLE 12.6 IYT Bearish Put Spread				
IYT Dec. 80 put			*IYT Dec. 75 put*	
Buy at	6	October 30	Sell at	3
Sell at	11	2 weeks later	Buy at	6
Result	+5		Result	−3
		Net result = +2		

not. Trading commissions, although low by historical standards, represent a relatively large percentage of the potential spread gains.

The difference between the bid and asked prices, especially for low-priced options, is wide. It is not unusual, for example, to see a bid of 0.25 and an asked of 0.35. That 0.10 difference is 40 percent.

Hedging with Options

Delta

Greek letters are used to identify various aspects of option behavior. There are several, but we will mention only one—delta—because it is the most important one.

Delta is a decimal stands for an option's reaction to a change in the underlying stock price. If the option premium goes up 1 when the underlying stock price goes up 1, the delta is 1.00. If the option goes up 0.47 when the stock price goes up 1, the option's delta is .47.

It follows, then, that in-the-money options have high deltas; out-of-the-money options have low deltas.

Previously, in the discussion about out-of-the-money options, we learned that one of the problems with buying them is that the underlying stock has to move a long way before the option's premium reacts very much. Another way of saying that is: Out-of-the-money options have low deltas.

By the same token, an option that is deep into the money will have a delta approaching 1, and the option premium will change virtually dollar for dollar with changes in the underlying stock. An option that is at the money will normally have a delta of about .50.

Option Hedge Example

You have probably realized that a put option would make a good short hedge. There would never be a margin call. The hedger's risk is limited to the premium paid and is fully known at the outset.

If it is to serve as a hedge, the option's premium must change when the price of the underlying stock changes. In other words, the option must have a high delta (be in the money). If the option price does not change when the price of the underlying asset changes, the hedge offers no protection.

Let us take a numerical example. You own 1,000 shares of IWM. It is mid-July, IMW is trading at 65, and you believe that a market correction is coming. You decide to hedge your IWM position by buying 10 IWM September 63 puts, for which you pay 1.75 each. Your opening transaction would look something like the example shown in Table 12.7.

By the middle of August, the market has eased, as you expected; IWM is trading at 61.50, and the put premium has risen to 3.10. As shown in Table 12.8, the unrealized loss of $1.50 in the ETF is largely offset by the gain in the value of the put.

The reasons that the put did not fully offset the loss are: The delta is less than 1, so the option price and the ETF price did not move exactly in unison; and, over the intervening few weeks, the put option characteristically lost a few ticks in time value.

Although we have only just scratched the surface, this is all we are going to say about options. The books referenced below are good sources for further information on speculating, spreading, hedging, and other strategies for trading put and call options. In addition, *yahoo.finance.com* contains a great deal of educational information on the subject of options.

The books are: *Options as a Strategic Investment* by Lawrence G. McMillan (New York: New York Institute of Finance, 2005); *Getting Started in Options,* 6th ed. by Michael C. Thomsett (Hoboken, NJ: John Wiley & Sons, 2003); and *Trade Options Online* by George A Fontanills (New York: John Wiley & Sons, 1999).

TABLE 12.7 Short Hedge Opening Transaction			
IWM		IWM Sept 65 Put	
63.00	mid-July	Bought	1.75

TABLE 12.8 IWM Short Hedge as of mid-August			
IWM		IWM Sept 65 Put	
63.00	mid-July	Bought	1.75
61.50	mid-August	Sold	3.10
−1.50			+1.35

Chapter 13

Day Trading

Buying a broad-based ETF and holding it for five years may be prudent. But then, so is eating broccoli.

There are investors who like the excitement of the game, who enjoy pitting their skill and acumen against the market. Whether they keep a position for a few hours or a few days, their objective is the same—to earn a quick trading profit.

Short-term trading may be more a mind-set than a measure of time. Long-term investors expect their portfolios to increase in value, of course. That is why they are in the stock market. But they do not look for sudden gains. The closest they get to monitoring prices may be a glance at the newspaper financial section on Sunday morning. Day trading is the quintessential short-term trading.

From what we know about the difficulty in forecasting prices, you might suspect that day traders do not fare well. There is not much recent evidence, but there is some. In his book, *All About Exchange Traded Funds* (New York: McGraw-Hill, 2003), Archie Richards Jr. reports on a study of the accounts of 124 stock day traders for the years 1998 and 1999, a period of rising stock prices. According to the author, some 77 percent lost money.

A Look Back

Time was, day trading was out of reach of most private individual investors. Access to real-time prices required special equipment and cost a monthly fee. Order execution was slow and cumbersome. And triple-digit commissions put the trader in a deep hole before he hung up the telephone.

The personal computer has changed all that. Today, streaming quotes are free, trades are executed electronically, and competition has driven trading commissions down to bedrock.

This streamlined trading has spawned new players. Online brokerage firms offer sophisticated trading platforms and low commissions. Day-trading salons provided their clients, for a fee, with office space, sophisticated technical trading tools, and direct access to markets.

Electronic Communications Networks

ECN

an acronym for "electronics communications network." ECNs are electronic trading systems for matching buy and sell orders received from the ECNs' subscribers, typically institutional investors, broker-dealers, and market-makers. ECNs connect buyers and sellers directly, bypassing third parties. An individual investor who wishes to trade via an ECN must have an account with a subscriber. Only limit orders are accepted.

Another new player is the electronic communications network or *ECN*.

An ECN is an electronic stock market where buyers and sellers meet directly, without intermediaries, for order execution and direct market access. An ECN executes trades by computer-matching the highest bid with the lowest offer, providing an alternative to traditional people-based order fulfillment by exchanges or market-makers. Virtually all NASDAQ orders are handled by ECN.

ECNs typically offer low execution costs, full access to their electronic order books, and order execution outside of normal exchange hours (pre-market and after-hours trading). To place orders with an ECN, you must be a subscriber. Subscribers comprise market makers, individual investors, institutional investors, program traders, and other broker-dealers. An order is displayed only on the ECN where it is entered, and only limit orders are accepted.

ECNs sprung up in the 1990s. By the year 2000, there were a dozen or so ECNs in operation, accounting for a rapidly growing percentage of total stock transactions. Familiar ECN names included Archipelago, Bloomberg, Tradebook, Instinet, Island, NexTrade, REDIBook, and BRUT.

The number of independent ECNs has been shrinking in recent years, as they have merged with each other and with major exchanges and broker-dealers. Archipelago, for example, merged with the New York Stock Exchange on March 7, 2006. Instinet and Island ECNs were acquired by NASDAQ in April 2006.

A Good Vehicle

An ETF is amply suited to day trading. It has all of the tradability of a stock, plus an added feature: Short sales are exempt from the downtick rule. Typical short interest in U.S. common stocks runs 1 percent to 2 percent; it is not uncommon for short interest in an ETF to be 15 percent or more.

More importantly, an ETF is a single stock without single-stock risk.

On Good Behavior

ETFs are what technical analysts describe as "well behaved." To explain what that means, we give you an example of "not well behaved" because that is easier to define.

Years ago, the Chicago Mercantile Exchange had a futures market in plywood. The demand for plywood is seasonal, of course; most houses are built in warm weather. Plywood supply is also erratic, as rain and snow in the timbering areas can slow or stop tree-cutting for weeks at a time.

To compound the problem, there was little public interest in plywood. Trading volume in plywood futures was very low and, at times, the plywood pit (actually, a small section of one pit) on the Chicago Mercantile Exchange trading floor resembled a ghost town.

As a result, plywood futures prices often went ballistic. They would suddenly go up the allowable limit for five or six days in a row, pause for a day or two, and then plunge the limit for the next four days.

Even if a single stock in an ETF were to show such volatility, the other stocks in the index would act as shock absorbers, and any price change of the ETF itself would be muted.

What It Takes

Day trading requires the right physical setup. You need a fast personal computer and a high-speed connection to the Internet such as DSL or cable modem or fiber-optic cable or satellite.

Your trading account must be online. In addition to accepting orders and reporting fills, your online broker should provide you with price charts, streaming quotes, your current account balance, a list of your present positions, a summary of gains or losses for the day, settled cash available for trading, your account's trading history; and, a phone number to call to ask a question or place a trade when you are not online. Some online brokers also provide their clients with direct access to ECNs. The brokers include Tradescape, TradeCast, and CyBerCorp.

You also may want to have some outside help. An excellent web site for day traders is *tradingday.com*. It offers streaming real-time quotes, a view of INET's order book, technical buy and sell signals, a tally of the most active ETFs, and the biggest percent gainers and losers for the day. And everything is free.

There are several other firms who provide technical tools, online training courses, and specific stock recommendations for their clients or subscribers. A Google search of "day trading" will hit the mother lode.

Trading

A day trader should be aware of underlying market fundamentals, but they will not play a major role in his trading. It is of no help for a day trader to know that the stocks in his ETF are expected to be 50 percent higher four months from now.

The day trader's game is played on a much smaller field. He is concerned with very short-term movement in prices and the precise timing of his market entry and exit.

If that sounds to you like a prescription for technical analysis, you are right. Day trading is based almost entirely on the evaluation of trends, market momentum, price support and resistance levels, and other technical criteria (discussed in Chapter 9).

Selecting the ETF

The ETF you choose to day trade should be a mover and shaker. There is no point in buying a ticket on an airplane that never leaves the ground.

One way to identify potential day-trading candidates would be to set an arbitrary benchmark; for example, you could select only ETFs whose prices have fluctuated by at least 10 percent in recent sessions.

A more accurate way would be to compare betas. Beta is an index of volatility. It is derived by comparing an individual stock's average volatility over time, typically five years, with the volatility of a major market index, like the Wilshire 5000 or the New York Stock Exchange Composite Index during the same period. The results are expressed as a ratio. A stock with a beta of 1, therefore, has the same average volatility as the market as a whole. A stock with a beta of 1.25 is 25 percent more volatile than the overall market.

Table 13.1 shows ETFs and their betas as of mid-2006, so they may have changed by the time you read this. Because of their relatively high volatility, any one of these ETFs would be a good potential candidate for day trading.

Mechanics

A market that is trending has strong undercurrents. Identifying and trading with the present price trend is especially important in day trading, as there is little time to recover from a setback. A day trade in consonance with the ongoing trend may not always succeed, but at least you will have the technical odds on your side.

TABLE 13.1 ETFs and Their Betas as of mid-2006	
ETF	*Beta*
Merrill Lynch Internet Infrastructure HOLDRs	1.72
iShares MSCI Taiwan	1.22
Merrill Lynch Oil Service HOLDRs	1.23
iShares Goldman Sachs Semiconductor Index Fund	1.36
Merrill Lynch B2B Internet HOLDRs	1.65
iShares MSCI Brazil	1.40

A day trade should not be taken without a protective stop order to cut your losses at a predetermined point. As we have talked about before, the point can be generated by technical analysis, or it can be simply the maximum dollar loss you are willing to accept in the trade.

It is also not a bad idea to place a standing limit order at your profit objective. If it happens to be reached when you are not looking, the limit order will act for you.

Losses

Losses take on a special significance in day trading. You are trying to harvest quick, small profits; a large loss could undo several successful trades. And there is something else—losses are not as straightforward as they seem. Recovering from a loss requires a bigger percentage gain than the percentage lost. If you lose 10 percent, for example, you have to gain 11.1 percent to get back to even.

Take a numerical example. Suppose that you have $1,500 equity in a position and you lose $225. Your equity drops to $1,275. That is a loss of 15 percent (275 divided by 1,500). To get back to your original level of $1,500, you have to earn that $225 back. But that would be a gain of 17.6 percent of your present equity.

It is like walking along the edge of a grassy slope. It is easier to slip down than to get back up. Table 13.2 shows the effect.

TABLE 13.2 Recovering From a Loss	
Percentage Lost	Percentage Gain Needed to Recover the Loss
5	5.3
10	11.1
15	17.6
20	25.0
25	33.3
30	43.9

Commissions

Trading commissions are also more important in day trading because they represent a larger percentage of your potential profits than they would in a longer term trade. There are several online brokers who advertise trading commissions of $10 or less. There is no reason for you to pay more.

Bid-Asked Price Spread

One of the unseen "costs" of trading ETFs is the spread (difference) between an ETF's bid and asked prices. Few individual investors are able to avoid buying at the offering price or selling at the bid price. They, in effect, pay the spread. This cost is negligible for a long-term trader, as it is amortized over weeks or months. It is more significant for a day trader.

ETF bid-asked price spreads tend to widen during periods of market volatility and tighten when prices are relatively stable. The spread may also be slightly wider in ETF shares that do not trade actively.

The typical spread for a broad-based, large-cap domestic ETF is in the neighborhood of 0.20 percent, but there are better neighborhoods. A recent study done by State Street Global Advisers over 160 trading days found that the average bid-asked spread in SPDR 500 Trust Series 1 (SPY), which is based on the S&P 500 Stock Index, was 0.09 percent.

Trading on Margin

The SEC defines a "pattern day trader" as one who is in and out of the same security in the same trading day at least four times in a five-day period and for whom the same-day trades make up at least 6 percent of the trader's activity during that period.

Under the rules of NYSE and NASD, an investor who is deemed to be a pattern day trader must have at least $25,000 on deposit, and his day trades must be made in a margin account.

Number of Open Positions

There are jugglers who can keep four balls in the air. There are few day traders who can. You will find your own capacity as you gain experience, but it is a good idea to start slow. For a lone investor, having more than three day trades open at the same time could be self-defeating.

Accept an Unexpected Gift from the Market

If you buy an ETF, and the next time you look its price has suddenly gone up several percentage points, sell it immediately and accept the windfall. There is no scientific rationale for the policy, but it is something that many experienced traders do. After you are out and counting your gains, you can investigate the possible causes for the sudden price change.

Beware of Success

Success can be dangerous. It is human nature to let your guard down after a big win. You may feel that you are on a roll or that you are playing with house money. But that is the time to slow down and proceed with extra caution.

Double Check

Electronic trading removes the live broker from your line of communication. There is no other human intelligence to evaluate your intentions, no one to say to you, "Are you sure that is what you want to do?"

Errors can get through, as was demonstrated recently at Mizuho Securities in Japan. A trader there intended to sell one share of stock in a company called J-com for 610,000 yen (about $5,000). Instead, he keyed in an order to sell 610,000 shares for 1 yen each and clicked the "submit" button. Despite the fact that the order was out of range, the Tokyo Stock Exchange reportedly processed it. According to the newspaper report, the mistake cost Mizuho Securities more than $200 million.

In *The Almanac of Online Trading* (New York: McGraw-Hill, 2000), Terry Wooten tells of a London trader who, after making an electronic trade in bonds, inadvertently leaned his elbow on the keyboard and sent out a wave of 145 separate sell orders for bonds.

Morphing into a Swing Trade

Buying a stock the day before its price *jumps* $15 is satisfying, but it does not begin to compare with the satisfaction of *selling* a stock the day before it *falls* $15. These emotions demonstrate what psychologists tell us about risk takers: They are more concerned about not losing than with winning.

One of the ostensible advantages of a day trade is its immunity to events that occur overnight or when the market is closed for the weekend. There are only two reasons why a day trader would decide to carry a position overnight: (1) He has a loss that he doesn't want to take; or (2) he has a profit in the position and believes that the stock still has good upward price momentum.

The first reason is, of course, taboo. It is tantamount to lowering an established stop-loss order; it demonstrates the hazardous mindset described just above.

Never Add to a Losing Position

A losing position should be closed out, not increased. So-called "averaging down" has no place in day trading. It is O.K. to add to a winning position—but do it very circumspectly so as not to create a top-heavy structure that will topple over at the first market tremor.

For example, suppose you believed that energy stocks were going to have a good day, and you bought 300 Sector Energy SPDRs (XLE) in the premarket for 50.10.

You were correct; by 11:30, XLE is trading at 51.00, and you have a $270 gain. You believe that there is more upside to come, and you now have a profit "cushion"; so, instead of selling the position, you increase it. How much more should you buy? A good rule is:

> When adding to a winning position, make any new increment equal to or smaller in size than the original position.

Table 13.3 shows what happens if you were now to buy, say, 700 shares at 51.00, increasing your total number of XLE shares from 300 to 1,000.

The new 700 shares bought at 51.00 raised your average price per share from 51.10 to 50.73. Your average price is now only 27 ticks below the current price. You have removed any wiggle room. Any setback of more than 1/2 percent will put your entire position into a loss.

How would that compare to adding, say, only 200 shares, raising your holdings to 500 shares (Table 13.4)? Your position has been increased to take advantage of any further gains, but in this scenario you are not living on the edge. Your average price per share is 50.46, which is 54 ticks away from the current market price. There is room for the market price to make small random swings without pushing your entire holdings into a loss.

TABLE 13.3	Adding to a Winning Position: Example 1		
	300 shares	*1,000 shares*	*Current price*
Average price	50.10	50.73	51.00

TABLE 13.4	Adding to a Winning Position: Example 2		
	300 shares	*500 shares*	*Current price*
Average price	50.10	50.46	51.00

The Final Factor: You

Day traders typically suffer financial losses in their first months of trading, and many never make the leap to profit-making status. Given these outcomes, it is clear that you should risk only money you can afford to lose. A good rule: If the loss of all your trading capital would make a significant change in your standard of living, you are overextending.

Day trading creates a lot of expenses: for your computer setup, high-speed online connection, training, seminars, trading commissions. You should know up front how much you will need to make to cover expenses and break even.

Successful day trading requires a certain personality. Day traders have to takes losses philosophically. A several-hundred-dollar debit cannot be viewed as a forgone fishing trip or a lost vacation in Las Vegas. The debit has to be viewed as a cost of doing business, as simply a bump in the road to a successful trading week.

The day trader also has to be able to devote sufficient time to the activity of trading. You do not have to be handcuffed to your desk. It will often be possible to put on a trade, place your stop and limit orders, and divert your attention to other matters for a while. But by and large if you are going to be a day trader, you should plan to be wedded to your computer for much of the day.

You may not be suited for day trading. The only way to find out is to do it. If the risk gives you a stomachache, if the memories of losses tend to haunt you, day trading may not your cup of java.

Day-Trading Firms

There are (were) small commercial enterprises set up for strictly day trading. Clients supplied initial working capital of $50,000 and paid a monthly rent and a per-trade fee. In return, they were given a desk and access to the equipment and technical support necessary to conduct hyperactive online buying and selling.

Six years ago, there were an estimated 100 of these stock daytrading "salons" in the United States. The largest, All-Tech Investment Group, had 23 offices in 15 states. Momentum Securities was headquartered in Houston and had branches in New York, Chicago, and Atlanta. Datek was another day-trading firm, at the time the nation's fifth-largest online broker.

Day trading became the subject of adverse publicity at the end of the 1990s. The industry was accused of mishandling customer funds, false advertising, and making illegal loans to its customers. The bad publicity peaked on July 29, 1999, when Mark O. Barton, who had lost over $100,000 in day trading in previous weeks, returned to Atlanta and shot and killed nine people in two different day-trading offices before turning the gun on himself.

In the year 2000, Momentum Securities merged with MarketXT. In the period from 1999 to 2001, All-Tech was fined on 3 occasions for a total of $1.28 million by the state of Massachusetts and NASD. It is no longer in business. Datek dropped off the radar screen in the summer of 2002 when it was acquired by Ameritrade.

You don't hear much about exclusively day-trading firms any more, but there are brokers who cater especially to day traders. A list of some

20 of them may be found at *daytrading.about.com*. There are also some full-service brokers who enable day trading.

Among the services offered by day-trading firms are online order entry, customizable technical support, online tutorials, level II NASDAQ quotes, direct access to ECNs, and commissions as low as 1 cent per share or $4.95 per trade. A few even offer commission-free day trading, covering their costs with the bid/asked price spread.

The Anatomy of a Successful Day Trade

You begin with beta, to identify those ETFs whose prices have above-average volatility. Once you have this group assembled, you check their average daily trading volumes. The ETFs you want need not be wildly popular, but you weed out those who trade, say, less then 200,000 shares a day.

From this group of moderately active, volatile ETFs you cull those whose prices are going up, those that are setting new highs. (You want to trade from the long side).

From this smaller group you look for ETFs who are near a chart price support level, like the bottom edge of a rectangular trading pattern, a previous price peak, the edge of a price gap, a price congestion area, or a previous low.

Let us assume that your analysis has narrowed down to one ETF: Goldman Sachs Semiconductor Index Fund (IGW). Its beta is 1.35, well above the average of 1.00; and, it trades 300,000 shares a day, which is adequate.

If you have a source, you might also check the current trend of IGW by other technical criteria or get a verbal assessment from a market advisory service on the current momentum in semiconductor stocks.

You go online and click the NASDAQ web site to view pre-market indications, and you see that the broad index futures prices are almost unchanged; markets are expected to open flat.

You next enter your online brokerage account and open the IGW page. IGW closed yesterday at 67.20. It is 8:30 EST, one hour before the exchanges start trading, so you have plenty of time.

You take another look at the price chart for IGW. It is essentially featureless, but you note that IGW has closed lower each day for the past three days.

You retrieve a small book from the shelf in your office. First published in 1975 and long out of print, it is called *Success in Commodities: the Congestion Phase System* by Eugene Nofri and Jeanette Nofri Steinberg. These authors advance a simple thesis: If prices are in a trading range, three consecutive down days—or two down days separated by a small retracement—have a 75 percent probability of being followed by an up day. The inverse holds for three consecutive up days. The four basic patterns from the book are shown in Figure 13.1.

The Nofris have added a small favorable portent to your intended trade. At 9:20, using your margin account, you place a limit order to buy 1,000 IGW at 67.20, yesterday's close and go for coffee.

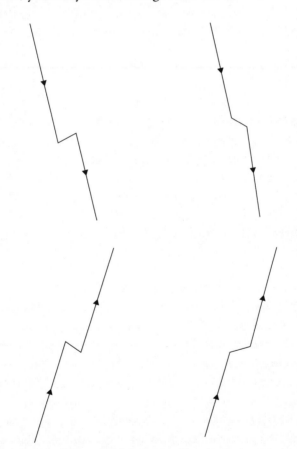

FIGURE 13.1 Day-trading patterns. When prices are within a trading range. three days of price action that follows one these patterns has, according to the authors of *The Congestion Phase System*, a 75% probability of being followed on the fourth day by a close in the opposite direction

Later, 10 minutes after the opening, you check your order screen and see that you bought 1,000 IGW at 67.00 at the time of 9:31. IGW is now trading at 67.09, nine ticks above where you bought it. This is a good sign.

Your policy is never to risk more than $200 (plus commissions) on any single short-term trade, so you immediately place a sell-stop order for 1,000 IGW at 66.80.

You go about other business, but you keep one eye on IGW. Your assessment proves to be correct. At 11:00 o'clock, your sell stop is still sitting there, unexecuted, and IGW is trading at 67.28. That is a $280 gain, and you consider taking it.

Instead, you decide to let your profits run. You move your sell stop up to 67.03, to get you out of the position with no loss if the market turns down. One of the unwritten day-trading commandments:

Thou shalt not allow an unrealized gain to turn into an unrealized loss.

At noon, all of the market indexes are higher and IGW is going across the CNBC ticker at 67.41. Your gross profit is now $410. That is more than twice the loss you were willing to accept, a 2:1 reward-to-loss ratio. So you put in a limit order and sell your 1000 shares of IGW at 67.41.

You made about $400 after commissions. And, once prices got above your entry level, your raised sell stop ensured that the trade would not be a loss.

For further reading about day trading, see *Electronic Day Traders' Secrets* (New York: McGraw-Hill, 1999, a compendium of knowledge on this subject; *How to Get Started in Electronic Day Trading* by David Nassar (New York: McGraw-Hill, 1999); *Winning the Day Trading Game: Lessons and Techniques from a Lifetime of Trading* by Thomas L. Busby and Patsy Busby (Hoboken, NJ: John Wiley & Sons, 2005); and *Success in Commodities: the Congestion Phase System*, by Eugene Nofri and Jeanette Nofri Steinberg (New York: Poseidon Press, 1975. Though this last title is out of print, you can find second-hand copies at such online used book dealers as *alibris.com* and *amazon.com*.

Chapter

A Very Short Word about Taxes

As with any investment, tax considerations for your ETF transactions should be discussed with your accountant.

When you do, there is a subject about which you should inquire. The Securities Exchange Act of 1934 sets forth a "wash-sale" rule, written to preclude investors from taking artificial losses for federal income tax purposes. The rule says that if you sell a stock for a loss, it won't count if you buy a substantially similar stock within 30 days before or after the loss sale.

They key words are "substantially similar." An ETF, even one that tracks stocks in the same industry or sector as the stock you sold, may not be deemed to be a substantially similar investment.

15

An ETF Menu

The following is a list of U.S. exchange-traded funds and their trading symbols. The list is complete as of this writing. Appendix A contains a miniprospectus of each individual ETF.

Foreign ETFs are traded in many markets around the world, including Amsterdam, Australia, Canada, Frankfurt, Hong Kong, Israel, Japan, London, Mexico, Paris, Stockholm, Singapore, South Africa, Taiwan, Toronto, Turkey, and New Zealand. A discussion of these foreign ETFs is beyond the scope. of this book.

The following ETFs are grouped by asset class. In most cases, the ETF's underlying index is identified in its name. If not, the name of the underlying index is shown in parentheses after the fund name.

Exchange-traded Funds Based on Stocks	Trading Symbol
Broad-based Large Cap ETFs	
DIAMONDS Trust Series 1 (Dow Jones Industrial Average)	DIA
Fidelity NASDAQ Composite Index Tracking Stock	ONEQ
iShares DJ U.S. Total Market index Fund	IYY
iShares Morningstar Large Core Index Fund	JKD
iShares Morningstar Large Growth Index Fund	JKE
iSahres Morningstar Large Value Index Fund	JKF
iShares NYSE 100 Index Fund	NY
iShares NYSE Composite Index Fund	NYC
iShares Russell 1000 Growth Index Fund	IWF
iShares Russell 1000 Index Fund	IWB
iShares Russell 1000 Value Index Fund	IWD
iShares Russell 3000 Growth Index Fund	IWZ
iShares Russell 3000 Index Fund	IWV
iShares Russell 3000 Value Index Fund	IWW
iShares S&P 100 Index Fund	OEF
iShares S&P 500 Index Fund	IVV
iShares S&P 500/BARRA Growth Index Fund	IVW
IShares S&P 500/BARRA Value index Fund	IVE
iShares S&P 1500 Index Fund	ISI
NASDAQ 100 Index Tracking Stock	QQQQ
PowerShares Dynamic Market Portfolio	PWC
PowerShares Dynamic OTC Portfolio	PWO
PowerShares Dynamic Large-Cap Growth	PWB
PowerShares Dynamic Large-Cap Value	PWV
Rydex Russell Top 50 Trust	XLG
Rydex S&P Equal-Weight Trust	RSP
SPDR O-Strip	OOO
SPDR Trust Series 1 (S&P 500 Stock Index)	SPY
streetTracks DJ U.S. Large-Cap Growth Index Fund	ELG
streetTracks DJ U.S. Large-Cap Value Index Fund	ELV
streetTracks Total Market (DJ Wilshire 5000 Composite Index)	TMW
Vanguard Growth VIPERS (MSCI US Prime Mkt Growth Index)	VUG

Exchange-traded Funds Based on Stocks	*Trading Symbol*
Vanguard Large-Cap VIPERS (MSCI US Prime Mkt 750 Index)	VV
Vanguard Total Market VIPERS (MSCI US Broad Market Index)	VTI
Vanguard Value VIPERS (MSCI US Prime Mkt Value Index)	VTV

Broad-based Mid–cap ETFs

iShares Morningstar Midcap Core Index Fund	JKG
IShares Morningstar Midcap Growth Index Fund	JKH
iShares Morningstar Midcap Value Index Fund	JKI
iShares Russell Midcap Growth Index Fund	IWP
iShares Russell Midcap Index Fund	IWR
iShares Russell Midcap Value Index Fund	IWS
iShares S&P Midcap 400 Index Fund	IJH
IShares S&P Midcap 400 BARRA Growth Index Fund	IJK
iShares S&P Midcap 400 BARRA Value Index Fund	IJI
Midcap SPDR Trust Series 1	MDY
PowerShares Dynamic Midcap Growth Fund	PWJ
PowerShares Dynamic Midcap Value Fund	PWP
Vanguard Extended Market VIPERs (Wilshire 4500 Index)	VXF
Vanguard Midcap Vipers (MSCI US Midcap 450 Index)	VO

Broad-based Small-Cap ETFs

iShares Morningstar Small Core Index Fund	JKJ
iShares Morningstar Small Growth Index Fund	JKK
iShares Morningstar Small Value Index Fund	JKL
iShares Russell 2000 Growth Index Fund	IWO
iShares Russell 2000 Index Fund	IWM
iShares Russell 2000 Value Index Fund	IWN
iShares S&P Small Cap 600 Index Fund	IJR
iShares Small Cap 600 BARRA Growth Index Fund	IJT
iShares Small Cap 600/BARRA Value Index Fund	IJS
PowerShares Dynamic Small Cap Growth Fund	PWT
PowerShares Dynamic Small Cap Value Fund	PWY
streetTracks DJ U.S. Small Cap Growth Index Fund	DSG
streetTracks DJ U.S. Small Cap Value Index Fund	DSV
Vanguard Small Cap Growth VIPERs (MSCI US Small-cap Growth Index)	VBK

Exchange-traded Funds Based on Stocks	Trading Symbol
Vanguard Small Cap Value VIPERs (MSCI US Small-cap Value Index)	VBR
Vanguard Small Cap VIPERs (MSCI US Small-cap 1750 Index)	VB

Broad-based Micro–cap ETFs

iShares Russell Microcap Index Fund	IWC
PowerShares Zacks Micro Cap Portfolio	PZI

Speciality ETFs

iShares DJ Select Dividend Index Fund	DVY
iShares KLD Select Social Index Fund	KLD
PowerShares High Yield Equity Dividend Achievers Fund (Mergent Dividend Achievers 50 Index)	PEY
PowerShares Wilderhill Clean Energy Fund	PBW
Rydex Euro Currency Trust	FXE

Sector/Consumer ETFs

iShares DJ U.S. Consumer Goods Sector Index Fund (Dow Jones US Consumer Non-cyclical Sector Index)	IYK
iShares DJ U.S. Consumer Services Sector Index Fund (Dow Jones US Consumer Cyclical Index)	IYC
Merrill Lynch Retail HOLDRs	RTH
PowerShares Dynamic Food & Beverage Index Fund	PBJ
PowerSharse Dynamic Leisure and Entertainment Index Fund	PEJ
PowerShares Dynamic Media Index Fund	PBS
Select Sector SPDR Fund—Consumer Discretionary	XLY
Select Sector SPDR Fund—Consumer Staples	XLP
Vanguard Consumer Discretionary VIPERs (MSCI US Investable Mkt Consumer Discretionary Index)	VCR
Vanguard Consumer Staples VIPERs (MSCI US Investable Mkt Consumer Staples Index)	VDC

Sector/Energy ETFs

iShares DJ U.S. Energy Sector Index Fund	IYE
Merrill Lynch Market Oil Service HOLDRs	OIH
Select Sector SPDR Fund—Energy	XLE
Vanguard Energy VIPERs (MSCI US Investable Mkt Energy Index)	VDE
The U.S. Oil Fund	USO

Exchange-traded Funds Based on Stocks	Trading Symbol
Sector/Financial ETFs	
iShares DJ U.S. Financial Sector Index Fund	IYF
iShares DJ U.S. Financial Services Sector Index Fund	IYG
Merrill Lynch Regional Bank HOLDRs	RKH
Select Sector SPDR Fund—Financial	XLF
Vanguard Financial VIPERs (MSCI US Investable Mkt Financials Index)	VFH
Sector/Health ETFs	
iShares DJ Healthcare Sector Index Fund	IYH
Merrill Pharmaceutical HOLDRs	PPH
PowerShares Dynamic Pharmaceuticals	PJP
Select Sector SPDR Fund—Healthcare	XLV
Vanguard Healthcare VIPERs (MSCI US Invest Mkt Health Care Index)	VHT
Sector/Industrial ETFs	
iShares DJ Industrial Sector Index Fund	IYJ
Select Sector SPDR Fund—Industrial	XLI
Vanguard Industrials VIPERs (MSCI US Invest Mkt Industrials Index)	VIS
Sector/Materials ETFs	
iShares DJ Basic Materials Sector Index Fund	IYM
Select Sector SPDR Fund—Materials	XLB
Vanguard Materials VIPERs (MSCI US Invest Mkt Materials Index)	VAW
Sector/Natural Resources ETFs	
iShares Goldman Sachs Natural Resources Index Fund	IGE
iShares COMEX Gold Trust	IAU
streetTracks Gold Shares	GLD
Deutsche Bank Commodity Index Tracking Fund	DBC
Sector/Real Estate ETFs	
iShares Cohen & Steers Realty Majors Index Fund	ICF
IShares DJ U.S. Real Estate Index FundIYR	
streetTracks Wilshire REIT Index Fund	RWR
Vanguard REIT VIPERs (MSCI US REIT Index)	VNQ

Exchange-traded Funds Based on Stocks	*Trading Symbol*
Sector/Technology ETFs	
iShares DJ U.S. Technology Sector Index Fund	IYW
iShares Goldman Sachs Networking Index Fund	IGN
iShares Goldman Sachs Semiconductor Index Fund	IGW
iShares Goldman Sachs Software Index Fund	IGV
iShares Goldman Sachs Technology Index Fund	IGM
iShares Goldman Sachs Biotechnology Index Fund	IBB
Merrill Lynch B2B Internet HOLDERs	BHH
Merrill Lynch Biotech HOLDRs	BBH
Merrill Lynch Broadband HOLDRs	BDH
Merrill Lynch Internet Architecture HOLDRs	IAH
Merrill Lynch Internet HOLDRs	HHH
Merrill Lynch Internet Infrastructure HOLDRs	IIH
Merrill Lynch Semiconductor HOLDRs	SMH
Merrill Lynch Software HOLDRs	SWH
PowerShares Dynamic Biotech and Genome Portfolio	PBE
PowerShares Dynamic Software Portfolio	PSJ
PowerShares Dynamic Networking Portfolio	PXQ
Select Sector SPDR Fund—Technology	XLK
streetTracks Morgan Stanley Technology Index Fund	MTK
Vanguard Information Technology VIPERs (MSCI US Investable Market Information Technology Index)	VGT
Sector/Telecommunications ETFs	
iShares DJ U.S. Telecom Sector Index Fund	IYZ
Merrill Lynch Telecom HOLDERs	TTH
Merrill Lynch Wireless HOLDRs	WMH
Vanguard Telecommunications VIPERs (MSCI US Investable Market Telecom Services Index)	VOX
Sector/Transportation ETF	
iShares DJ Transportation Average Index Fund	IYT
Sector/Utilities ETFs	
iShares DJ U.S. Utilities Sector Index Fund	IDU
Merrill Lynch Utilities HOLDRs	UTH

Exchange-traded Funds Based on Stocks	Trading Symbol
Select Sector SPDR Fund—Utilities	XLU
Vanguard Utilities VIPERs(MSCI US Invest Mkt Utilities Index)	VPU

Foreign/Global ETFs

BLDRS Developed Markets 100 ADR Index Fund (Bank of New York Developed Mkts 100 ADR Index)	ADRD
iShares MCSI–EAFE	EFA
iShares MSCI–EAFE Growth	EFG
iShares MSCI–EAFE Value	EFV
iShares S&P Global 100 Index Fund	IOO
Merrill Lynch Market 2000+ HOLDRs	MKH
streetTracks DJ Global Titan Index Fund	DGT

Foreign/Regional ETFs

BLDRS Asia 50 ADR Index Fund (Bank of New York Asia 50 ADR Index)	ADRA
BLDRS Emerging Markets 50 ADR Index Fund (Bank of New York Emerging Mkts 50 ADR Index)	ADRE
BLDRS Europe 100 ADR Index Fund (Bank of New York Europe 100 ADR Index)	ADRU
iShares MSCI–EMU Index Fund (EMU = European Monetary Union)	EZU
iShares MSCI–Pacific Ex-Japan Index Fund	EPP
iShares S&P Europe 350 Index Fund	IEV
iShares S&P Latin America 40 Index Fund	ILF
iShares MSCI–Emerging Index Fund	EEM
Merrill Lynch Europe 2001 HOLDRs	EKH
streetTracks DJ Euro STOXX 50	FEZ
streetTracks DJ STOXX 50	FEU
Vanguard Emerging Market VIPERS (Select Emerging Mkts Index)	VWO
Vanguard European VIPERS (MSCI Europe Index)	VGK
Vanguard Pacific VIPERS (MSCI Pacific Index)	VPL

Foreign/Country ETFs

iShares FTSE/Xinhua China 25 Index Fund	FXI
iShares MSCI–Australia	EWA
iShares MSCI–Austria	EWO
iShares MSCI–Belgium	EWK

Exchange-traded Funds Based on Stocks	Trading Symbol
iShares MSCI–Brazil	EWZ
iShares MSCI–Canada	EWC
iShares MSCI–France	EWQ
iShares MSCI–Germany	EWG
iShares MSCI–Hong Kong	EWH
iShares MSCI–Italy	EWI
iShares MSCI–Japan	EWJ
iShares MSCI–Malaysia (Free)	EWM
iShares MSCI–Mexico (Free)	EWW
iShares MSCI–Netherlands	EWN
iShares MSCI–Singapore (Free)	EWS
iShares MSCI–South Africa	EZA
iShares MSCI–South Korea	EWY
iShares MSCI–Spain	EWP
iShares MSCI–Sweden	EWD
iShares MSCI–Switzerland	EWL
iShares MSCI–Taiwan	EWT
iShares MSCI–United Kingdom	EWU
iShares S&P TOPIX 150 Index Fund (S&P/Tokyo Stock Price 150 Index)	ITF
PowerShares Golden Dragon Halter USX China Fund (Halter USX China Index)	PGJ

Foreign/Sector ETFs

iShares S&P Global Energy Index Fund	IXC
iShares Global Financial Index Fund	IXG
iShares Global Healthcare Index Fund	IXJ
iShares Global Information Technology Index Fund	IXN
iShares Global Telecommunications Index Fund	IXP

Exchange-traded Funds Based on Fixed-Income Securities

iShares Lehman 1–3 Year Treasury Bond Fund	SHY
iShares Lehman 7–10 Year Treasury Bond Fund	IEF
iShares Lehman 20+ Year Treasury Bond Fund	TLT
iShares GS $Investop Corporate Bond Fund	LQD
ISharers Lehman TIPS Bond Fund	TIP
iShares Lehman Aggregate Bond Fund	AGG

16

The Underlying Indexes

The first stock indexes were created to measure the performance of the broad market. These indexes date from the beginning of the 20th century and include the Dow Jones Industrial Average, the New York Stock Exchange Composite, and the NASDAQ Composite.

Stock indexes to measure the performance of more narrow areas of the markets came later, starting in the 1950s. Among them were the S&P 500, the Morgan Stanley Consumer Index, the Wilshire 5000, The Russell 1000 and Russell 2000, and Dow Jones U.S. stock sectors indexes. Narrower still are the S&P Select Sector indexes and the NASDAQ 100, introduced in 1998.

Today there are hundreds of securities indexes. Not every one is suitable for use as the benchmark for an ETF. Ideal ETF indexes are well diversified (not dominated by a few large companies), have low index turnover, comprise *capitalization-weighted* stocks, and abide by strict rules for changing the composition of the index. And, it does not hurt if the index has a recognizable name, like S&P 500 or Dow Jones Industrial Average.

capitalization-weighted

in a capitalization-weighted index, each stock's contribution is equal to its share price multiplied by its total number of shares outstanding. Large-cap stocks therefore play a much greater role than small- or midcaps in determining index performance.

Weighting

There are four methods for determining an individual stock's weight in an index: capitalization weighting, price weighting, *equal weighting*, and *equal-dollar weighting*.

In a capitalization-weighted index, each stock's contribution is equal to its share price multiplied by its total shares outstanding. Large-cap stocks therefore play a much greater role than small- or mid–caps in determining index performance. Most indexes are capitalization-weighted.

In a *price-weighted* index, a stock's weight is determined by share price only, without regard for the number of shares outstanding. A company with expensive shares and a small market cap will have a greater influence on the index than a huge company with low-price shares.

In an equal-weighted index, all stocks receive the same weighting regardless of the share price or the company's capitalization.

An equal-dollar-weighted index is constructed assuming that an equal amount of money is invested in each stock in the index.

The Indexes

Following are descriptions of the stock indexes that underlie current ETFs. Unless otherwise noted, the indexes are capitalization-weighted. The list is in alphabetical order by index name or, where appropriate, by index family.

Bank of New York Indexes

American Depositary Receipts (ADRs) are dollar-denominated certificates that represent ownership of shares of stock in a non-U.S. company. The foreign stocks are owned by U.S. banks or other

equal weighting

in an equal-weighted stock index, all stocks receive the same weighting regardless of the number of shares outstanding.

equal-dollar weighting

an equal-dollar-weighted index is constructed assuming that an equal amount of money is invested in each stock.

price weighted

in price-weighted indexes, like the Dow Jones Industrial Average (DJIA), a stock's weight is determined by share price only, without regard for the number of shares outstanding. A company with expensive shares and a small market cap will have a greater influence on the index than a huge company with low-price shares.

fiduciaries that issue the ADRs. ADRs trade freely on U.S. stock exchanges.

The Bank of New York has established four ADR indexes. The ETFs that track the indexes are called BLDRs, which stands for Baskets of Listed Depositary Receipts. BLDRs were introduced in November 2002 and were the first ETFs to be benchmarked to indexes comprising ADRs. They are also the first ETFs to be listed on NASDAQ.

The four ADR indexes include:

Bank of New York Developed Markets 100 ADR Index comprises a broad array of American Depositary Receipts (ADRs) for 100 major companies in developed nations. Virtually all major industries are represented, but the three largest sectors—banks, oil and gas producers, and companies involved in pharmaceuticals and biotechnology—account for 47 percent of the index.

Bank of New York Asia 50 ADR Index comprises ADRs for the securities of 50 companies in Asia. Banks, automotive companies, and technology hardware are the dominant sectors. The top three companies represented are Toyota (13 percent) and Mitsubishi Financial Group (11 percent), and BHP Billiton (5 percent).

Bank of New York Emerging Markets 50 ADR Index consists of ADRs for the securities of 50 companies in the emerging markets in Asia and Latin America. Oil and gas producers, banks, and mobile telecommunications companies constitute about 40 percent of the portfolio. The top three companies are Taiwan Semicondcutor, Amercian Movil SA de CV, and Teva Pharmaceutical.

Bank of New York Europe 100 ADR Index is made up of ADRs for the securities 100 major European companies. The largest market sectors are banks, oil and gas producers, and pharmaceutical and biotechnology companies. These three sectors account for about half of the portfolio.

Cohen & Steers Realty Majors Index

The Cohen & Steers Realty Majors Index comprises the stocks of large real estate investment trusts (REITs) in the United States. Both residential and commercial properties are represented. The top five stock holdings in the index are Simon Property Group, Equity Office Properties, Equity Residential, Vornado Realty, and General Growth Properties.

Deutsche Bank Commodity Index

The Deutsche Bank Commodity Index, introduced in 2006, tracks six of the most liquid futures markets in the world. The commodities and their proportional representation in the index are: 35 percent light sweet crude oil, 20 percent heating oil, 12.5 percent aluminum, 11.25 percent corn, 11.25 percent wheat, and 10 percent gold. The light sweet crude oil and heating oil futures contracts are rolled monthly, while the gold, aluminum, corn and wheat futures contracts are rolled annually. Rolling comprises closing out contracts that are nearing expiration and entering into new contracts with expirations either one month or one year distant, respectively.

Dow Jones Industrial Average

The Dow Jones Industrial Average (DJIA) was born on July 3, 1884, when Charles Dow introduced his Customers Afternoon Letter. At the time, railroads were among the biggest and sturdiest companies in America, and the few industrial companies that were publicly traded were considered highly speculative. Of the 11 stocks reported on in the Customers Afternoon Letter, nine were railroads. The constituency of the Index continued to change over the years as stocks were added and replaced. By May 23, 1896, the Dow average comprised only industrial stocks.

The present Dow Jones Industrial Average of 30 stocks was introduced on October 1, 1928. Today, the Dow's 30 stocks have a total market value of $3 trillion and represent one-fifth of the market value of all U.S. stocks.

The DJIA is calculated on a price-weighted basis. That is, stocks with higher prices are given a greater weighting in the index than lower-priced stocks (regardless of each company's actual size). Whether the DJIA is a true barometer of the marketplace is moot. But it is the oldest and certainly the most well known of the stock market averages.

The following 30 stocks are members of the DJIA as of August 2006:

United Technologies	MMM
IBM	Caterpillar
Johnson & Johnson	Procter & Gamble

Wal-Mart Stores	Coca-Cola
Boeing	American Express
Altria Group	Merck & Co.
Citigroup	Exxon Mobil
General Motors	E. I. DuPont de Nemours
JPMorgan Chase	Honeywell International
Verizon Communications	Home Depot
Pfizer	General Electric
Alcoa	Microsoft
McDonald's	Intel
Walt Disney	SBC Communications
Hewlett-Packard	American International Group

Dow Jones U.S. Total Market Index

Dow Jones U.S. Total Market Index is designed to embrace a constant 95 percent of the U.S. stock market's capitalization. The top market sector is financial, which represents 20 percent of the Index. The next four biggest sectors are technology, consumer, industrial, and health care; together, they account for about 54 percent of the Index's holdings.

The Index's Top 10 holdings include:

General Electric	Exxon Mobil,
Microsoft	Citigroup
Pfizer	Bank of America
Johnson & Johnson	IBM
American International Group	Intel

Dow Jones Sector Indexes

Dow Jones maintains indexes on 13 market sectors. Each is a subset of the Dow Jones U.S. Total Market Index.

Sectors include consumer goods, consumer services, energy, financial, financial services, healthcare, industrial, basic materials, real estate, technology, telecommunications, transportation, and utilities. There is also a Dow Jones select dividend index.

Dow Jones U.S. Consumer Goods Sector Index includes companies that produce automobiles and automotive parts, beverages, food producers, household goods, leisure goods, personal goods, tobacco, food and beverages, and cosmetics. Household goods and beverages account for almost half of the portfolio.

Dow Jones U.S. Consumer Services Sector Index comprises the stocks of food and drug retailers, media companies, general retailers, and travel and leisure companies. Stocks of general retailers constitute 50 percent of the index. The top five holdings are Walmart, Home Depot, Time Warner, Walt Disney, and Viacom.

Dow Jones U.S. Energy Sector Index consists of stocks of companies that construct or provide oil rigs, drilling equipment, or other energy-related equipment or services; and, the exploration production, marketing, refining, or transporting of natural gas, coal, and other consumable fuels. Stocks of oil and gas producers make up about 80 percent of the index.

Dow Jones U.S. Financial Sector Index comprises the stocks of banks, nonlife insurance companies, life insurance companies, real estate companies (including REITs), and general finance companies. Banks and general finance stocks account for about two-thirds of the portfolio.

Dow Jones U.S. Financial Services Sector Index includes stocks of banks, brokerage firms, mortgage lenders, and credit-card companies. The top five stocks in the index are Citigroup, Bank of America, JPMorgan Chase, Wells Fargo, and Wachovia.

Dow Jones U.S. Healthcare Sector Index includes the stocks of companies involved in providing healthcare services, healthcare supplies and equipment, and healthcare facilities; and that conduct research in pharmaceuticals and biotechnology. The top five companies in the index are Johnson & Johnson, Pfizer, Amgen, United Health group, and Abbott Labs.

Dow Jones U.S. Industrial Sector Index comprises stocks in defense, aerospace, heavy equipment, industrial construction, and shipping industries. General Electric alone represents 22 percent of the portfolio. The next four biggest stock holdings are Tyco, 3M, Boeing, and United Technology.

Dow Jones U.S. Basic Materials Sector Index has mining, metals, forest and paper products, and chemical stocks. Component companies are involved in the production of aluminum, commodity chemicals, specialty chemicals, forest products, nonferrous metals, glass, paper products, precious metals, and steel. Dow Chemical, DuPont, Alcoa, Newmont Mining, and Monsanto are the top five companies in the index

Dow Jones U.S. Real Estate Index includes companies that invest directly or indirectly in the development, management or owner-ship of shopping malls, apartment buildings and housing develop-ments; and, real estate investment trusts ("REITs") that invest in apartments, office and retail properties. The list of companies in the index is topped by Simon Property Group, Equity Office Proper-ties, Vornado Realty, Equity Residential, and Prologis.

Dow Jones Select Dividend Index comprises 100 stocks that have a positive five-year per-share dividend growth rate, a five-year divi-dend payout ratio of 60 percent or more, and an average daily trad-ing volume of at least 200,000 shares.

Dow Jones U.S. Technology Sector Index includes companies in-volved in computers and office equipment, software, communica-tions technology, semiconductors, diversified technology services and Internet services. Microsoft, Intel , IBM, Cisco, and Hewlett-Packard. are the top five companies in the index.

Dow Jones U.S. Telecommunications Sector Index measures the performance of the telecommunications sector of the United States equity market. It includes companies that provide communication services through fixed-line, cellular, high bandwidth, and fiber-op-tic cable networks. The index's top five stocks are Verizon, SBC Communications, BellSouth, Alltel, and AT&T.

Dow Jones U.S. Utilities Sector Index is made up of stocks of companies that produce or distribute water, natural gas, electricity, and multi-utilities; and, companies that operate as independent producers and distributors of power. At the head of the list are Ex-celon, Dominion Resources, Southern Company, Duke, and EXU.

Goldman Sachs Indexes

Goldman Sachs has five sector indexes. The sectors are natural resources, networking, semiconductors, software, and technology.

Goldman Sachs Natural Resources Index comprises mostly oil-related issues, with oil stocks comprising 60 percent and oil service stocks 14 percent. The index also contains stocks of other industries, including metals (13 percent) and paper (8 percent). The addition of nonoil-related stocks lowers the fund's correlation with other natural resource ETFs. The fund's largest holdings are British Petroleum and Exxon Mobil.

Goldman Sachs Networking Index. The top three sectors in the index comprise companies that produce networking equipment, wireless equipment, and semiconductors; together, they represent 75 percent of the index. The top five companies in the index are Qualcomm, Motorola, Corning, Lucent Technologies, and Nortel Networks.

Goldman Sachs Software Index constitutes the stocks 46 software companies whose shares are publicly traded. They produce commercial software, and all except Red Hat produce software for pay. The index includes companies making operating systems, database software, video games, and automation software. The list of companies in the index is headed by Symantec, Microsoft, Oracle, Electronic Arts, and Computer Associates.

Goldman Sachs Technical Industry Semiconductor Index is an equity benchmark for U.S. traded semiconductor stocks. Companies represented include producers of capital equipment and manufacturers of wafers and chips. The top five holdings are Motorola, Texas Instruments, Applied Materials, Intel, and STMicroelectronics. Sectors represented in the index are semiconductors (90 percent) and multimedia networking (10 percent).

Goldman Sachs Technology Index includes computer-related, electronics, networking, Internet services, and Internet software companies. The sector breakdown of the index is software 20 percent, hardware 60 percent, media 13 percent, telecommunications 7 percent. The top five stocks in the index are Microsoft, Intel, IBM, Cisco, and Hewlett-Packard.

Halter USX China Index

The Halter USX China Index comprises some 55 Chinese companies whose stock is publicly traded on the New York Stock Exchange, American Stock Exchange or NASDAQ. The index allows U.S. investors to participate in the broad Chinese economy in a transparent U.S. market and without currency exchange considerations. For a company to be included in the Halter USX China Index. it must have had an average market capitalization of more than $50 million for the preceding 40 days.

KLD Select Social Index

The KLD Select Social Index is benchmarked to 250 to 350 nontobacco companies found in the Russell 1000 and ranked according to their social and environmental impact. Criteria used in selecting stocks for the index are the environment, labor relations, community relations, diversity, product safety, human rights, and governance.

Lehman Indexes

There are five Lehman Brothers fixed-income indexes that serve as benchmarks for ETFs.

Lehman Aggregate Bond Index is a composite of three Lehman indexes: Government/Credit Bond Index, Mortgage-Backed Securities Index, and Asset-backed Securities Index. Bonds are 95 percent U.S. and 5 percent foreign. The top holdings are Fannie Mae (28 percent), U.S. Treasury Notes (20 percent), and Federal Home Loan Mortgage Corporation (12 percent).

Lehman 1–3 Year Treasury Bond Index includes all publicly issued U.S. Treasury securities that have remaining maturity of from one to three years, are nonconvertible, are denominated in U.S. dollars, are rated *investment grade* (Baa3 or better) by Moody's, are fixed-rate, and have $250 million or more of outstanding face value. Excluded are flower bonds, state and local government bonds, targeted investor notes, and strips.

Lehman 7–10 Year Treasury Bond Index includes all publicly issued U.S. Treasury securities that have remaining maturity of from 7 to 10 years, are nonconvertible, are denominated in U.S. dollars, are rated investment grade (Baa3 or better) by Moody's or BBB- by

> **investment grade**
> denotes bonds rated in the top four rating categories by Standard & Poor's (AAA, AA, A, BBB) or Moody's (Aaa, Aa, A, Baa). Issuers of investment-grade bonds are considered to be very able to meet the bonds' financial obligations.

S&P, are fixed-rate, and have $250 million or more of outstanding face value. Excluded are flower bonds, state and local government bonds, targeted investor notes, and strips.

Lehman 20+ Year Treasury Bond Index includes all publicly issued U.S. Treasury securities that have remaining maturity of greater than 20 years, are nonconvertible, are denominated in U.S. dollars, are rated investment grade (Baa3 or better) by Moody's, are fixed-rate, and have more than $150 million par outstanding. Excluded are flower bonds, state and local government bonds, targeted investor notes, and strips.

Consumer Price Index
an index of consumer prices and price inflation determined by formula by the U.S. Bureau of Labor Statistics.

Lehman U.S. Treasury Inflation Notes Index measures the performance of inflation-protected notes and bonds issued by the U S. Treasury, also known as "TIPS." The principal amount of TIPs is adjusted monthly for inflation as measured by the U.S. *Consumer Price Index,* and interest is paid on the adjusted amount.

Lux Nanotech Index

The Lux Nanotech Index comprises stocks of companies involved in developing, manufacturing, and funding nanotechnology applications, including nanomaterials, nano-enabled products, and nanotools.

Mergent Dividend Achievers 50 Index

The Mergent Dividend Achievers 50 Index contains the 50 highest dividend-yielding U.S. companies with at least 10 years of consecutive dividend increases.

Mergent High Growth Rate Dividend Achievers Index

Mergent High Growth Rate Dividend Achievers Index is designed to track the performance of the top 100 dividend achieving companies by their 10-year compound annualized dividend growth rates. Component stocks must be incorporated in the United States; traded on the NYSE, NASDAQ or AMEX; and, must have increased their annual regular dividend payments each year for the last 10 or more consecutive years.

Morgan Stanley Consumer Index

The Morgan Stanley Consumer Index (MSCI) is designed to measure the performance of stable, consumer-oriented, U.S. growth industries. Its 30 component stocks represent 20 industries, including beverages, food, pharmaceuticals, tobacco, and personal products.

The Index is equal-dollar-weighted (each of the securities is represented in approximate equal dollar value). Index adjustments are made annually, based on closing prices on the third Friday in December. The following stocks comprise the MSCI:

Abbott Laboratories	Albertson's
American Home Products	American International Group
Anheuser-Busch	Automatic Data Processing
Coca-Cola	Colgate-Palmolive
ConAgra	Crown Cork & Seal
Disney	Emerson Electric
General Mills	Gillette
Grainger (W.W.)	International Flavors & Fragrances
Johnson & Johnson	Kimberly-Clark
McDonald's	Medtronic
Merck & Company	Newell Rubbermaid
PepsiCo	Philip Morris
Proctor & Gamble	Schering-Plough
Safeway	Sysco
Wal-Mart Stores	Walgreen

Morningstar Stock Indexes

The Morningstar family of 16 indexes targets 97 percent coverage of the U.S. equity market. The goals of the indexes are: to achieve broad market coverage without sacrificing liquidity, maximize the negative correlations between growth and value stocks, and to classify each stock uniquely (i.e., each stock belongs to only one of the nine style categories), and to minimize turnover. Morningstar indexes are rebalanced quarterly and reconstituted annually.

Nine the 16 Morningstar Stock Indexes provide the bases for ETFs. They are all style indexes.

Morningstar Large Core Index measures the performance of large-cap stocks where neither growth nor value characteristics predominate. Industry weightings in the Index are: Information 13.97 percent, Service 44.33 percent, and Manufacturing 41.71 percent.

Morningstar Large Growth Index measures the performance of large-cap stocks that are expected to grow at a faster pace than the rest of the market as measured by forward earnings, historical earnings, book value, cash flow, and sales. Industry weightings in the Index are: Information 37.63 percent, Service 51.71 percent, and Manufacturing 10.66 percent.

Morningstar Large Value Index measures the performance of large-cap stocks with relatively low prices in light of their anticipated per-share earnings, book value, cash flow, sales, and dividends. Industry weightings in the Index are: Information 12.46 percent, Service 45.97 percent, and Manufacturing 41.57 percent

Morningstar Mid-Core Index measures the performance of mid-cap stocks where neither growth nor value characteristics predominate. Industry weightings in the Index are: Information 13.25 percent, Service 50.23 percent, and Manufacturing 36.52 percent

Morningstar Mid-Growth Index measures the performance of midcap stocks that are expected to grow at a faster pace than the rest of the market as measured by forward earnings, historical earnings, book value, cash flow, and sales. Industry weightings in the Index are: Information 29.03 percent, Service 52.48 percent, and Manufacturing 18.49 percent.

Morningstar Mid-Value Index measures the performance of mid-cap stocks with relatively low prices given their anticipated per-share earnings, book value, cash flow, sales, and dividends. Industry weightings in the Index are: Information 6.11 percent, Service 52.50 percent, and Manufacturing 41.39 percent

Morningstar Small Core Index measures the performance of small-cap stocks where neither growth nor value characteristics predominate. Industry weightings in the Index are: Information 13.02 percent, Service 54.34 percent, and Manufacturing 32.64 percent.

Morningstar Small Growth Index measures the performance of small-cap stocks that are expected to grow at a faster pace than the rest of the market as measured by forward earnings, historical earnings, book value, cash flow and sales. Industry weightings in the Index are: Information 30.32 percent, Service 51.83 percent, and Manufacturing 17.85 percent.

Morningstar Small Value Index measures the performance of small-cap stocks with relatively low prices given their anticipated per-share earnings, book value, cash flow, sales, and dividends. Industry weightings in the Index are: Information 8.46 percent, Service 52.45 percent, and Manufacturing 39.09 percent.

MSCI Global Equity Indexes The widely followed MSCI Global Equity Indexes provide U.S.-dollar benchmarks for foreign products and services. Of the 29 ETFs that track MSCI Global Equity Indexes, three are global indexes, five are foreign regional indexes, and 21 are foreign country indexes.

A foreign company's weight in an MSCI Global Equity Index is not determined by the company's total market value. The weighting of companies in the index is determined by the company shares that are "free"—that is, available for purchase in the market. This rule excludes shares held by governments and company insiders. The aim of MSCI is to include in its global equity indexes 85 percent of the free-floating securities in each industry group.

As a rule, ETFs based on MSCI Global Equity Indexes use *representative sampling* rather than full index replication.

The largest global ETF is iShares MSCI EAFE (Europe, Australia, Far East), an equity benchmark for international stock performance. It comprises more than 1,000 securities with a total market capitalization close to U.S. $6 trillion. Financials, consumer discretionary, and healthcare are the top sectors represented. Sub-indexes to iShares MSCIEAFE include MSCI EAFE Growth Index and MSCI EAFE Value Index.

representative sampling

using selected stocks to create a sample portfolio that behaves like the benchmark index. Representative sampling is used when securities are unavailable to replicate the index, when the underlying index does not comply with the rules governing index structure, or when duplicating the index is not practicable because of the large number of stocks the index contains.

The MSCI foreign regions consist of EMU (countries that are members of the European Monetary Union), Pacific ex-Japan, and Emerging Markets. Two other indexes—MSCI Europe and MSCI Pacific—represent diverse portfolios of stocks held in Vanguard ETFs.

MSCI foreign country indexes are the most numerous. They comprise the securities of enterprises in Australia, Austria, Belgium, Brazil, Canada, China, France, Germany, Hong Kong, Italy, Japan, Malaysia, Mexico, Netherlands, Singapore, South Africa, South Korea, Spain, Sweden, Switzerland, Taiwan, and the United Kingdom.

The most active ETF is a foreign country fund: the iShares MSCI Japan Index Fund, which trades more than 12 million shares a day.

Further information about MSCI may be found at their website, *www.msci.com.*

MSCI Europe Index comprises a total of 500 stocks in the indexes of 16 developed countries outside North and South America, representing about 85 percent of the total market capitalization in those countries. As of May 2005, the countries represented are Austria, Belgium, Denmark, Finland, France, Germany, Greece, Ireland, Italy, the Netherlands, Norway, Portugal, Spain, Sweden, Switzerland, and the United Kingdom.

MSCI Pacific Index is designed to measure equity market performance of developed countries in the Pacific region. As of May 2005, the Index consisted of the stocks of companies in Australia, Hong Kong, Japan, New Zealand, and Singapore.

MSCI U.S. Equity Indexes

MSCI introduced U.S. Equity Indexes in 2003. There are 18 indexes that form the basis for ETFs. The MSCI U.S. Investable Market 2500 Index, a broad-based measure that represents 98 percent of the U.S. equity market, does not itself form the basis for an ETF; but several of its subset indexes do. Components of the MSCI sector indexes follow the Global Industry Classification Standards. Indexes are rebalanced quarterly.

MSCI U.S. Broad Market Index represents about 99 percent of the capitalization of the U.S. equity market and includes some 3,900 companies. It comprises the aggregation of four smaller

MSCI indexes, including a large-cap 300, a mid–cap 450, a small-cap 1,750 and a micro–cap index.

MSCI U.S. Prime Market 750 Index represents the universe of large- and midcap companies in the U.S. equity market. The index represents about 85 percent of the capitalization of the U.S. equity market.

MSCI U.S. Prime Market Growth Index represents the growth companies in the MSCI U.S. Prime Market 750 Index.

MSCI U.S. Prime Market Value Index represents the value stocks in the MSCI U.S. Prime Market 750 Index.

MSCI U.S. Small-Cap 1750 Index represents the universe of small capitalization companies in the U.S. equity market. This index targets for inclusion 1,750 companies that represent about 11 percent of the capitalization of the U.S. equity market.

MSCI U.S. Small-Cap Growth Index represents the growth companies of the MSCI U.S. Small Cap 1750 Index.

MSCI U.S. Small Cap Value Index represents the value companies of the MSCI U.S. Small Cap 1750 Index.

MSCI U.S. Investable Market Consumer Discretionary Index represents the companies of the MSCI U.S. Investable Market 2500 Index that produce or distribute automotive goods, household durable goods, textiles, apparel, and leisure equipment. Also in this category are media production services and consumer retailers.

MSCI U.S. Investable Market Consumer Staples Index represents the companies in the MSCI U.S. Investable Market 2500 Index that are involved in the development and production of consumables, and whose businesses are therefore less sensitive to economic cycles than consumer discretionary businesses. Products include food, beverages, tobacco, nondurable household goods and personal products.,

MSCI U.S. Investable Market Energy Index represents companies of the MSCI U.S. Investable Market 2500 Index that are involved with the production and distribution of energy and energy-producing products. Included are stocks of oil and natural gas producers, oil equipment, oil services, and power distributors.

MSCI U.S. Investable Market Industrials Index represents defense, aerospace, heavy equipment, industrial construction, and shipping companies that are part of the MSCI U.S. Investable Market 2500 Index.

MSCI U.S. Investable Market Telecommunications Services Index represents a subset of telecommunication equipment and services stocks in MSCI U.S. Investable Market 2500 Index, including fixed and mobile telecommunications.

NASDAQ Composite Stock Index

The NASDAQ Composite Stock Index includes the more than 3000 common stocks listed on the NASDAQ stock market. The types of securities in the index include American Depository Receipts, common stocks, real estate investment trusts (REITs), and tracking stocks. Excluded are derivatives, preferred shares, mutual funds, exchange-traded funds, and debentures.

New York Stock Exchange 100 Index

The NYSE 100 Index is a large-cap benchmark embracing 45 percent of the total U.S. stock market capitalization. Stocks are those of well established, blue-chip companies that meet NYSE's listings standards; they are well diversified across all economic sectors. The NYSE 100 has the lowest annualized volatility of all major large-cap stock indexes. Of the other major stock indexes, the NYSE correlates most highly (.94) with the S&P 100.

New York Stock Exchange Composite Index

In 1966, the NYSE established the NYSE Composite Index to provide a comprehensive measure of market trends. The index comprises all common stocks listed on the NYSE. Within the Index are four subgroup indexes—industrial, transportation, utility, and finance.

The indexes measure changes in aggregate market value of NYSE common stocks, adjusted to eliminate the effects of capitalization changes, new listings, and de-listings.

PowerShares Stock Indexes

The following indexes underlie PowerShares ETFs. Those based on "intellidexes" are semimanaged—that is, stocks are selected for their potential for capital appreciation using a rules-based stock selection process that differs from traditional benchmark indexing. Stock selection criteria include fundamentals, market valuation, timeliness, and relative risk.

ETFs based on these intellidexes have the word "dynamic" in their names. Each intellidex is rebalanced quarterly.

The six dynamic intellidexes for growth and value stocks in small-cap, mid–cap, and large-cap denominations each hold the style of stocks that their names promise. The difference, as mentioned, is that the stocks do not comprise a benchmark index but are chosen for their appreciation potential.

Broad Dividend Achievers Index contains a diversified group of U.S. companies that have increased their annual dividends for 10 or more consecutive years. They are typically companies with strong cash reserves, solid balance sheets, and a proven record of consistent earnings growth.

Dynamic Biotech and Genome Intellidex comprises the stocks of 30 U.S. biotechnology and genome companies that are involved in the research, development, and marketing of biotechnology products and services, including human pharmaceuticals and veterinary drugs.

Dynamic Energy Exploration & Production Intellidex contains 30 large-cap energy stocks. The largest single sector is exploration and production of oil and gas, at 64 percent. The next two biggest sectors are integrated oil and gas (15 percent) and oil and gas marketing (14 percent). The index is well diversified. The largest single holding is Valero, at 6.3 percent.

Dynamic Food and Beverage Intellidex comprises the stocks of 30 U.S. companies engaged in the manufacture, sale, or distribution of food and beverages, agricultural products, or products related to the development of new food technologies.

Dynamic Leisure and Entertainment Intellidex comprises stocks of 30 U.S. companies that serve all aspects of leisure and entertainment. Products include books and magazine, broadcasting, motion pictures, musical instruments, leisure apparel, camping and sporting goods, toys, and amusement parks.

Dynamic Market Intellidex is the flagship. Established in 1993, the index comprises 2000 of the largest and most liquid U.S. stocks, so as to represent the broad U.S. economy.

Dynamic Media Intellidex contains the stocks of 30 U.S. companies engaged in developing, producing, or selling media-related products and services, including free or pay television, satellite radio, films, cellular communications, advertising, newspapers, theaters, movie programming, and video products.

Dynamic Networking Intellidex contains stocks in three main technologies: wireless LANs (local area networks), VoIP (voice over Internet Protocol), and security.

Dynamic Oil & Gas Services Intellidex comprises 30 large-, mid-, and small-cap companies involved in oil and gas drilling, equipment, and services. The top five companies in the portfolio are BJ Services, Halliburton, National Oilwell Varco, Diamond Offshore Drilling, and Transocean.

Dynamic OTC Intellidex comprises 100 stocks drawn from the 1,000 largest U.S. headquartered stocks listed on the NASDAQ Stock Exchange. Its holdings comprise 56 percent information technology stocks.

Dynamic Pharmaceuticals Intellidex comprises stocks of 30 U.S. companies involved in the research, development, sale, or distribution of drugs, including companies that facilitate the testing and regulatory approval of drugs.

Dynamic Semiconductor Intellidex contains the stocks of 30 semiconductor companies involved in all aspects of the electronics business, including advanced design and manufacturing technologies, lasers, electro-optics,

Dynamic Software Intellidex contains the stocks of 30 U.S. companies that produce systems-level software, applications software, time-sharing services, Internet software, and software for home entertainment.

PowerShares International Dividend Achiever Portfolio typically includes companies with strong cash reserves, solid balance sheets, and a proven record of consistent earnings growth. The Broad Dividend Achievers Index comprises all US companies listed on major U.S. stock exchanges that have increased their regular dividends for a minimum of 10 consecutive years.

Russell Stock Indexes

Russell produces a family of U.S. equity indexes. The indexes include only common stocks of companies incorporated in the United States and its territories. The Russell 1000 and 2000 indexes are subsets of the Russell 3000 Index. Russell indexes rebalance once a year to ensure full and precise coverage of their universes.

Russell 3000 Stock Index measures the performance of the 3,000 largest U.S. companies, based on total market capitalization. These companies represent approximately 98 percent of the investible U.S. equity market.

The Russell 3000 Index was created in 1984 by Frank Russell Company and was designed to offer investors access to the broad U.S. equity universe. The market capitalizations of the companies in the Index range from $31 million to $379 billion. The median market cap is $1.02 billion.

The largest five sectors in the Index by weight are financial services, consumer discretionary and services, information technology, health care, and utilities. The top 10 stock holdings comprise the following:

General Electric	Exxon Mobil
Microsoft	Citigroup
Procter & Gamble	Bank of America
Johnson & Johnson	Intel
Pfizer	American International Group

Russell 2000 Stock Index is a barometer of small stocks in the U.S. The index comprises the bottom two-thirds of the stocks in the Russell 3000 Index, which are about 10 percent of the Russell 3000's total market capitalization. At its most recent setting, the average market capitalization of the Russell 2000 Index was about $467 million.

Russell 1000 Stock Index measures the performance of the largest companies in the Russell 3000 Index. These 1000 companies represent about 90 percent of the total market capitalization of the Russell 3000 Index. Its average market capitalization today is about $7.6 billion.

Russell MicroCapX Index measures the micro–cap sector of the U.S. equity market. It comprises the 1,000 stocks in the Russell MicroCap Index that have the biggest historical trading volume. The larger Russell MicroCap Index embraces the stocks of about 2,000 companies with market capitalizations ranging from $50 million to $550 million, representing 3 percent of the market capitalization of listed U.S. securities.

Spade Defense Index

The Spade Defense Index is made up of the stocks of about 60 companies involved with defense, homeland security, and space. Representative business activities include construction of naval vessels, military aircraft, missiles, and munitions; and, battle-space awareness, network centric warfare, border security, biometric and screening systems, space systems, and satellite services.

Standard & Poor's Indexes

Standard & Poor's 500 Stock Index dates back to 1923, when Standard and Poor's first introduced a stock index covering 233 companies. In 1957, the index was expanded to include 500 companies.

The S&P 500 Index today represents more than $1 trillion in listed and over-the-counter stocks. It is a major international benchmark for U.S. stock market performance and the foundation for two ETFs. About three-fourths of the stocks are industrial companies. The remaining one-fourth comprises stocks of utilities, transportation companies, and financial institutions.

Standard & Poor's Composite 1500 Index combines three leading indexes—the S&P 500, the S&P MidCap 400, and the S&P SmallCap 600—to form an investable benchmark of the U.S. equity market. Covering approximately 90 percent of the U.S. market capitalization, the S&P Composite 1500 offers investors an index with the familiar characteristics of the S&P 500 but with broader market exposure.

Standard & Poor's O-strip Index constitutes those stocks of the S&P 500 that are also listed on the NASDAQ, currently 75 stocks. Dividends, constituent changes, and share count adjustments are treated in the same manner and implemented at the same time in both the S&P 500 Index and the S&P 500 O-Strip Index. The proportional weight of any stock in the S&P 500 O-Strip Index will be larger than that stock's proportional weight in the S&P 500 because the S&P 500 O-Strip Index is a subset of the S&P 500.

Standard & Poor's MidCap 400 Stock Index reflects the group performance of the stocks of 400 moderately sized U.S. companies. Predominant index sectors are technology, finance, utilities, and consumer cyclicals.

Membership in the S&P MidCap 400 is limited to stocks listed on the New York Stock Exchange, the American Stock Exchange, and NASDAQ. Foreign ADRs, mutual funds, limited partnerships, and real estate investments trusts are excluded. No stock can be a member of both the S&P MidCap 400 and the S&P 500.

Rydex Standard & Poor's Equal-Weight Index comprises the same 500 stocks that make up the S&P 500 Index. However, unlike the S&P 500 (which is capitalization-weighted) the Rydex S&P Equal Weight Index is weighted so that each stock constitutes an equal percentage of the total index. The Index is rebalanced quarterly to ensure that it maintains its equal-weight status.

Standard & Poor's BARRA Stock Indexes   In 1992, Standard & Poor's and Barra began a collaboration to produce growth and value subsets of S&P's equity indexes.

The S&P/Barra Growth and Value indexes are constructed by dividing the stocks in the index according to a single attribute: book-to-price ratio. The value index contains firms with higher book-to-price ratios; the growth index has firms with lower book-to-price ratios.

This distinction (book-to-price ratio) has several advantages. It is simple and easy to understand; it is mutually exclusive; and, as mentioned earlier, the book-to-price ratio captures one of the fundamental differences between companies generally classified as value companies or growth companies.

Additionally, book-to-price ratios tend to be more stable over time than alternative measures such as price-to-earnings ratios, historical earnings, growth rates, or return on equity. These qualities result in indexes with relatively low turnover.

Each company in the index is assigned to either the value or growth index so that the two style indexes "add up" to the full index.

There are 6 S&P BARRA Indexes that underlie ETFs. They include:

S&P 500/BARRA Growth Index

S&P 500/BARRA Value Index

S&P MidCap 400/BARRA Growth Index

S&P MidCap 400/BARRA Value Index

S&P Small Cap 600/BARRA Index

S&P Small Cap 66/BARRA Value Index

Standard & Poor's Foreign Stock Indexes

S&P Global 100 Stock Index is designed to track the performances of 100 of the world's largest multinational companies that do significant business outside the countries where they are based. Seventy of the 100 companies included in the index are listed on the New York Stock Exchange. Sectors represented are telecommunications, health care, technology and consumer cyclicals. On a geographic basis, the index has roughly a 60 percent weighting in the United States, with 39 U.S.-based companies included.

S&P Global Energy Sector Index comprises stocks of companies in the energy sector of the S&P Global 1200 Index. Component companies are those that S&P believes are important to global energy markets. They include oil equipment and services companies; oil exploration and production companies; and oil refineries, principally in the United States, Great Britain, and Canada.

S&P Global Financials Sector Index component companies ostensibly include major banks, financial companies, insurance companies, real estate companies, and securities brokers. However, it is skewed heavily toward stocks in the financial services sector, which represent 99 percent of the holdings. Foreign stocks account for about 60 percent. Geographically, companies in the United States, Great Britain, and Japan predominate.

S&P Global Healthcare Sector Index. Component companies of the S&P Global Healthcare Sector Index include health care providers, biotech companies, manufacturers of medical supplies, and pharmaceutical companies. The index is not diversified. Virtually the entire portfolio is concentrated in healthcare securities. About 65 percent of the companies are located in the United States.

S&P Global Information Technology Sector Index component companies are involved in the development and production of computer and telecommunications products and equipment. Hardware comprises 62 percent, software comprises 20 percent. About 70 percent of the companies in the index are located in the United States. The index is more diversified than some of the other S&P global sector indexes; the top 10 holdings represent 44 percent of the portfolio.

S&P Global Telecommunications Sector Index component companies include diversified communication carriers and wireless communication companies. About 1/3 of the companies are in the United States; the balance are foreign, mostly in Great Britain and Spain. The portfolio is devoted almost entirely to telecommunication services companies.

S&P Europe 350 Stock Index measures the performance of the stocks of leading companies in continental Europe. The market capitalization of constituent companies is adjusted to reflect only those stocks that are available to foreign investors. The fund holds 347 stocks, no bonds. The top 10 holdings represent 22 percent of the portfolio.

S&P Latin America 40 Index comprises selected equities trading on the exchanges of Mexico, Brazil, Argentina, and Chile. The index is dominated by Mexico and Brazil, and by its top five markets sectors: materials, telecommunication services, financials, energy, and consumer staples stocks account for about 90 percent of the portfolio.

S&P Tokyo Stock Price 150 Index comprises 150 highly liquid securities selected from each major sector of Japanese equities. The index represents 70 percent of the total market value of the Japanese equity market. The index is not well diversified. The top four sectors—financials, consumer discretionary, industrials, and information technology—account for about half of the portfolio.

Standard & Poor's (U.S.) Sector Indexes   Standard & Poor's has 9 Select Sector indexes. They include consumer discretionary, consumer staples, energy, financial, health care, industrial, materials, technology, and utilities.

Basic Industries Select Sector Index comprises the stocks of companies involved in producing chemicals, paper and forest products, containers, and construction materials. Metal mining companies are also in this category. The two predominant sectors represented are chemicals (55 percent) and mining (22 percent).

Consumer Discretionary Select Sector Index. Consumer discretionary stocks are those of companies that are the most sensitive to economic cycles. In this category are producers of automobiles, media, household durable goods, textiles, and leisure equipment. Services include hotels, restaurants, and consumer retailers. The top three sectors represented are media (31 percent), specialty retailers (20 percent), and restaurants and leisure (14 percent).

Consumer Staples Select Sector Index includes stocks of manufacturers and distributors of food, beverages and tobacco; and nondurable household goods, and personal products. Food and drug retailers are also in this category. Stocks of consumer staples companies are less sensitive to economic cycles than stocks of consumer discretionary companies.

Energy Select Sector Index comprises companies engaged in the construction or provision of energy related equipment and services, such as oil rigs and drilling equipment; and, the exploration, production, refining, and marketing of oil, natural gas, and other consumable fuels. Leaders in the group include Exxon Mobil, Chevron Texaco, and Conoco Phillips.

Financial Select Sector Index consists of the stocks of companies involved in banking, mortgage finance, consumer finance, asset management, insurance, financial investments, and real estate. About 70 percent of the index comprises the stocks of commercial banks, insurance companies, and diversified financial services.

Health Care Select Sector Index includes companies that make healthcare equipment and supplies and provide healthcare-related services; and, companies involved in the research, development of pharmaceuticals and biotechnology. The top two sectors represented are pharmaceuticals (53 percent) and healthcare products and services (20 percent).

Industrial Select Sector Index stocks are those of companies that make and distribute capital goods, such as construction equipment, industrial machinery, and aerospace and defense products; and companies that provide printing, employment, land and marine transportation, airlines, and environmental services.

Technology Select Sector Index comprises stocks of companies involved in information technology consulting, computers and peripherals, manufacturing of semiconductor equipment and products, and providing diversified land and wireless telecommunication services. The top three sectors are computers and peripherals (20 percent), software (20 percent), and semiconductors (18 percent).

Utilities Select Sector Index. Companies represented in this index primarily produce, generate, transmit, or distribute electricity or natural gas. Electric utility and multi-utility companies comprise more than 80 percent of the index.

WilderHill Clean Energy Index

This index normally invests at least 80 percent of its total assets in common stocks of companies engaged in advancing the causes of cleaner energy and conservation.

The Wilshire Indexes

Wilshire 4500 Completion Index   The Wilshire 4500 Completion Index comprises a broadly diversified group of stocks from small and medium-sized U.S. companies. The Index consists of all the common stocks regularly traded on the New York Stock Exchange, the American Stock Exchange, and the NASDAQ—except that the stocks in the S&P 500 Index have been removed.

Wilshire 5000 Stock Index   The Wilshire 5000 is considered the "total market index." Designed to track the value of the entire stock market, it presently comprises about 6,700 different stocks. Financial services, health care, computer hardware, industrial materials, and consumer services stocks account for more than 65 percent of the index.

Stocks in the Wilshire 5000 must meet three criteria: the firm's headquarters must be based in the United States, the stock must be actively traded on a U.S. exchange, and the stock must have widely available pricing information. This last requirement disqualifies most bulletin board and over-the-counter stocks.

The top 10 weighted stocks in the Wilshire 5000 include:

General Electric	Microsoft
Exxon Mobil	Pfizer
Citigroup	Wal-Mart
Intel	American International Group
Cisco Systems	IBM

Wilshire Real Estate Investment Trust (REIT) Index   The Dow Jones Wilshire REIT Index measures the performance of U.S. publicly traded real estate investment trusts. To be in the index, a company must be an equity owner and operator of commercial or residential real estate. Other REITs and companies that have more than 25 percent of their assets in direct mortgage investments are excluded. The eligible company must also have a minimum total market capitalization of at least $200 million at the time of its inclusion, and at least 75 percent of its total revenue must be derived from the ownership and operation of real estate assets.

Zacks MicroCap Index

Zacks MicroCap Index comprises between 300 and 500 microcap stocks that are selected, on the basis of technical analysis, for their promise to outperform benchmark microcap indexes.

A Gallery of Exchange-Traded Funds

The following are thumbnail descriptions of every domestic ETF traded as of this writing. The ETFs are arranged alphabetically by their trading symbols. The statistical information is provided courtesy of *etfconnect.com* and Thomson Financial.

The number of ETFs continues to grow, so there may be new ETFs not in this list. Some of the short-term performance data may change over time. Before you invest in any ETF, it is wise to read its complete prospectus.

ADRA BLDRS Asia 50 ADR Index Fund
Inception date: 11/8/2002
Asset size ($mil.): 45
Average daily volume: 41,400
Expense ratio (%): 0.30
Category: Non-U.S. equity
Investment objective: Emulate the performance of the Bank of New York Asia 50 ADR Index.

	Annualized Total Returns (% share price)	ETF Facts	
1 year	29.48	Marginable:	Yes
3 year	20.65	Options:	No
5 year	—	Short sales:	Yes
10 year	—	Minimum purchase:	1
Since inception:	19.78		

ADRD BLDRS Developed Markets 100 ADR Index Fund
Inception date: 11/8/2002
Asset size ($mil.): 42
Average daily volume: 14,700
Expense ratio (%): 0.30
Category: Non-U.S. equity
Investment objective: Emulate the performance of the subject index.

	Annualized Total Returns (% share price)	ETF Facts	
1 year	21.37	Marginable:	Yes
3 year	20.25	Options:	No
5 year	—	Short sales:	Yes
10 year	—	Minimum purchase:	1
Since inception:	19.58		

ADRE BLDRS Emerging Markets 50 ADR Index Fund
Inception date: 11/8/2002
Asset size ($mil.): 212
Average daily volume: 257,800
Expense ratio (%): 0.30
Category: Emerging market equity
Investment objective: Emulate the performance of the Bank of New York Emerging Markets 50 ADR Index.

	Annualized Total Returns (% share price)	ETF Facts	
1 year	34.47	Marginable:	Yes
3 year	29.22	Options:	No
5 year	—	Short sales:	Yes
10 year	—	Minimum purchase:	1
Since inception:	33.48		

ADRU BLDRS Europe 100 ADR Index Fund
Inception date: 11/8/2002
Asset size ($mil.): 28
Average daily volume: 10,600
Expense ratio (%): 0.30
Category: Non-U.S. equity
Investment objective: Emulate the performance of the Bank of New York Europe 100 ADR Index.

	Annualized Total Returns (% share price)	ETF Facts	
1 year	18.74	Marginable:	Yes
3 year	20.67	Options:	No
5 year	—	Short sales:	Yes
10 year	—	Minimum purchase:	1
Since inception:	19.67		

AGG iShares Lehman Aggregate Fund Index
    Inception date: 9/26/2003
    Asset size ($mil.): 2,347
    Average daily volume: 202,400
    Expense ratio (%): 0.20
    Category: General bond–Investment grade
    Investment objective: Emulate the performance of the total U.S. in-
    vestment-grade bond market, including Treasury bonds, corporate
    bonds, and municipal bonds.

	Annualized Total Returns (% share price)	Bond Facts	
1 year	0.86	Avg. maturity:	6.96 yrs
3 year	—	Avg. coupon:	5.19%
5 year	—	Avg. duration::	5.29 yrs
10 year	—		
Since inception:	2.36		

BBH Biotechnology HOLDERS
    Inception date: 11/23/1999
    Asset size ($mil.): 1,370
    Average daily volume: 556,800
    Expense ratio (%): —
    Category: Sector–Health/biotech
    Investment objective: Deliver the returns of a nondiversified group
    of health and biotechnology stocks.

	Annualized Total Returns (% share price)	ETF Facts	
1 year	−2.90	Marginable:	Yes
3 year	11.32	Options:	Yes
5 year	9.72	Short sales:	Yes
10 year	—	Minimum purchase:	100
Since inception:	9.50		

BDH Merrill Lynch Broadband HOLDRs
Inception date: 4/6/2000
Asset size ($mil.): 118
Average daily volume: 157,800
Expense ratio (%): —
Category Growth–Domestic
Investment objective: Holds a group of securities of U.S. companies affiliated with broadband communications.

	Annualized Total Returns (% share price)	ETF Facts	
1 year	–6.61	Marginable:	Yes
3 year	18.63	Options:	Yes
5 year	–4.40	Short sales:	Yes
10 year	—	Minimum purchase:	100
Since inception:	–24.64		

BHH Merrill Lynch B2B Internet HOLDRs
Inception date: 2/4/2000
Asset size ($mil.): 32
Average daily volume: 74,800
Expense ratio (%): —
Category: Growth–Domestic
Investment objective: Hold the common stock of a group of business-to-business (B2B) Internet product and service companies.

	Annualized Total Returns (% share price)	ETF Facts	
1 year	19.10	Marginable:	Yes
3 year	1.93	Options:	Yes
5 year	–10.42	Short sales:	Yes
10 year	—	Minimum purchase:	100
Since inception:	–40.92		

DBH Deutsche Bank Commodity Index Tracking Fund

No results found

DGT streetTracks Dow Jones Global Titans Index Fund
   Inception date: 9/29/2000
   Asset size ($mil.): 91
   Average daily volume: 7,100
   Expense ratio (%): 0.50
   Category: Global equity
   Investment objective: Emulate the performance of subject index.

Annualized Total Returns (% share price)		ETF Facts	
1 year	10.08	Marginable:	Yes
3 year	10.62	Options:	No
5 year	1.74	Short sales:	Yes
10 year	—	Minimum purchase:	1
Since inception:	−1.70		

DIA Diamond Trust Series 1
   Inception date: 1/20/1998
   Asset size ($mil.): 77,669
   Average daily volume: 7,216,800
   Expense ratio (%): 0.18
   Category: Growth–Domestic
   Investment objective: Emulate the performance of the Dow Jones
   Industrial Average.

Annualized Total Returns (% share price)		ETF Facts	
1 year	7.29	Marginable:	Yes
3 year	8.82	Options:	Yes
5 year	3.37	Short sales:	Yes
10 year	—	Minimum purchase:	1
Since inception:	6.11		

DSG streetTracks Dow Jones U.S. Small-Cap Growth Index Fund
Inception date: 9/29/2000
Asset size ($mil.): 53
Average daily volume: 7,000
Expense ratio (%): 0.25
Category: Growth–Domestic
Investment objective: Emulate the performance of the subject index.

	Annualized Total Returns (% share price)	ETF Facts	
1 year	3.58	Marginable:	Yes
3 year	13.80	Options:	No
5 year	3.06	Short sales:	Yes
10 year	—	Minimum purchase:	1
Since inception:	-2.90		

DSV streetTracks Dow Jones U.S. Small-Cap Value Index Fund
Inception date: 9/29/2000
Asset size ($mil.): 89
Average daily volume: 8,400
Expense ratio (%): 0.25
Category: Growth–Domestic
Investment objective: Emulate the performance of the subject index.

	Annualized Total Returns (% share price)	ETF Facts	
1 year	7.63	Marginable:	Yes
3 year	19.79	Options:	No
5 year	15.04	Short sales:	Yes
10 year	—	Minimum purchase:	1
Since inception:	18.35		

DVY iShares Dow Jones U.S. Select Dividend Index Fund
>Inception date: 11/3/2003
>Asset size ($mil.): 6,371
>Average daily volume: 460,000
>Expense ratio (%): 0.40
>Category: Equity income
>Investment objective: Emulate the performance of the subject ndex.

	Annualized Total Returns (% share price)	ETF Facts	
1 year	5.26	Marginable:	No
3 year	—	Options:	No
5 year	—	Short sales:	No
10 year	—	Minimum purchase:	1
Since inception:	14.09		

EEM iShares MSCI Emerging Markets Index Fund
>Inception date: 4/7/2003
>Asset size ($mil.): 4,720
>Average daily volume: 4,142,000
>Expense ratio (%): 0.75
>Category: Emerging market equity
>Investment objective: Emulate the performance of the subject index.

	Annualized Total Returns (% share price)	ETF Facts	
1 year	26.03	Marginable:	No
3 year	32.76	Options:	No
5 year	—	Short sales:	No
10 year	—	Minimum purchase:	1
Since inception:	39.71		

EFA iShares MSCI EAFE Index Fund
 Inception date: 8/14/2001
 Asset size ($mil.): 15,993
 Average daily volume: 3,571,600
 Expense ratio (%): 0.35
 Category: Non-U.S. equity
 Investment objective: Emulate the performance of the subject index.

	Annualized Total Returns (% share price)	ETF Facts	
1 year	24.45	Marginable:	Yes
3 year	23.45	Options:	No
5 year	—	Short sales:	Yes
10 year	—	Minimum purchase:	1
Since inception:	10.79		

EKH Merrill Lynch HOLDRs Europe 2001
 Inception date: 1/18/2001
 Asset size ($mil.): 19
 Average daily volume: 1,700
 Expense ratio (%): —
 Category: Non-U.S. equity
 Investment objective: Hold the securities of the 45 largest European companies that are listed for trading on the New York Stock Exchange, the American Stock Exchange, and NASDAQ.

	Annualized Total Returns (% share price)	ETF Facts	
1 year	11.65	Marginable:	Yes
3 year	15.74	Options:	Yes
5 year	2.16	Short sales:	Yes
10 year	—	Minimum purchase:	100
Since inception:	–3.93		

ELG streetTracks Dow Jones U.S. Large-Cap Growth Index Fund
     Inception date: 9/25/2000
     Asset size ($mil.): 81
     Average daily volume: 20,600
     Expense ratio (%): 0.20
     Category: Growth–Domestic
     Investment objective: Emulate the performance of the subject index.

	Annualized Total Returns (% share price)	ETF Facts	
1 year	−0.25	Marginable:	Yes
3 year	5.29	Options:	No
5 year	−3.12	Short sales:	Yes
10 year	—	Minimum purchase:	1
Since inception:	−10.94		

ELV streetTracks Dow Jones U.S. Large-Cap Value Index Fund
     Inception date: 9/29/2000
     Asset size ($mil.): 135
     Average daily volume: 4,800
     Expense ratio (%): 0.20
     Category: Equity income
     Investment objective: Emulate the performance of the subject index.

	Annualized Total Returns (% share price)	ETF Facts	
1 year	11.21	Marginable:	Yes
3 year	13.20	Options:	No
5 year	4.96	Short sales:	Yes
10 year	—	Minimum purchase:	1
Since inception:	4.19		

EPP iShares MSCI Pacific ex-Japan Index Fund
  Inception date: 10/25/2001
  Asset size ($mil.): 1,522
  Average daily volume: 134,300
  Expense ratio (%): 0.50
  Category: Non-U.S. equity
  Investment objective: Emulate the performance of the subject index.

	Annualized Total Returns (% share price)	ETF Facts	
1 year	15.74	Marginable:	Yes
3 year	25.35	Options:	No
5 year	—	Short sales:	Yes
10 year	—	Minimum purchase:	1
Since inception:	20.52		

EWA iShares MSCI Australia Index Fund
  Inception date: 3/12/1996
  Asset size ($mil.): 369
  Average daily volume: 350,600
  Expense ratio (%): 0.59
  Category: Non-U.S. equity
  Investment objective: Emulate the performance of the subject index.

	Annualized Total Returns (% share price)	ETF Facts	
1 year	20.56	Marginable:	Yes
3 year	28.38	Options:	No
5 year	21.20	Short sales:	Yes
10 year	10.88	Minimum purchase:	1
Since inception:	10.56		

EWC iShares MSCI Canada Index Fund
Inception date: 3/12/1996
Asset size ($mil.): 420
Average daily volume: 599,300
Expense ratio (%): 0.59
Category: Non-U.S. equity
Investment objective: Emulate the performance of the subject index.

	Annualized Total Returns (% share price)	ETF Facts	
1 year	24.64	Marginable:	Yes
3 year	28.19	Options:	No
5 year	16.93	Short sales:	Yes
10 year	13.70	Minimum purchase:	1
Since inception:	13.44		

EWD iShares MSCI Sweden Index Fund
Inception date: 3/12/1996
Asset size ($mil.): 61
Average daily volume: 96,700
Expense ratio (%): 0.59
Category: Non-U.S. equity
Investment objective: Emulate the performance of the subject index.

	Annualized Total Returns (% share price)	ETF Facts	
1 year	19.15	Marginable:	Yes
3 year	28.84	Options:	No
5 year	13.78	Short sales:	Yes
10 year	10.67	Minimum purchase:	1
Since inception:	11.06		

EWG iShares MSCI Germany Index Fund
    Inception date: 3/12/1996
    Asset size ($mil.): 315
    Average daily volume: 695,400
    Expense ratio (%): 0.59
    Category: Non-U.S. equity
    Investment objective: Emulate the performance of the subject index.

	Annualized Total Returns (% share price)	ETF Facts	
1 year	21.65	Marginable:	Yes
3 year	22.89	Options:	No
5 year	8.00	Short sales:	Yes
10 year	7.60	Minimum purchase:	1
Since inception:	7.75		

EWH iShares MSCI Hong Kong Index Fund
    Inception date: 3/12/1996
    Asset size ($mil.): 638
    Average daily volume: 931,400
    Expense ratio (%): 0.59
    Category: Non-U.S. equity
    Investment objective: Emulate the performance of the subject index.

	Annualized Total Returns (% share price)	ETF Facts	
1 year	7.09	Marginable:	Yes
3 year	21.59	Options:	No
5 year	9.34	Short sales:	Yes
10 year	3.47	Minimum purchase:	1
Since inception:	3.49		

EWI iShares MSCI Italy Index Fund
Inception date: 3/12/1996
Asset size ($mil.): 43
Average daily volume: 54,600
Expense ratio (%): 0.59
Category: Non-U.S. equity
Investment objective: Emulate the performance of the subject index.

	Annualized Total Returns (% share price)	ETF Facts	
1 year	17.37	Marginable:	Yes
3 year	2.50	Options:	No
5 year	12.50	Short sales:	Yes
10 year	12.41	Minimum purchase:	1
Since inception:	12.53		

EWJ iShares MSCI Japan Index Fund
Inception date: 3/12/1996
Asset size ($mil.): 6,297
Average daily volume: 23,284,100
Expense ratio (%): 0.59
Category: Non-U.S. equity
Investment objective: Emulate the performance of the subject index.

	Annualized Total Returns (% share price)	ETF Facts	
1 year	32.95	Marginable:	Yes
3 year	21.66	Options:	No
5 year	7.80	Short sales:	Yes
10 year	−0.61	Minimum purchase:	1
Since inception:	−0.38		

EWK iShares MSCI Belgium Index Fund

    Inception date: 3/12/1996

    Asset size ($mil.): 47

    Average daily volume: 51,000

    Expense ratio (%): 0.59

    Category: Non-U.S. equity

    Investment objective: Emulate the performance of the subject index.

	Annualized Total Returns (% share price)	ETF Facts	
1 year	22.32	Marginable:	Yes
3 year	30.57	Options:	No
5 year	17.24	Short sales:	Yes
10 year	9.81	Minimum purchase:	1
Since inception:	9.84		

EWL iShares MSCI Switzerland Index Fund

    Inception date: 3/12/1996

    Asset size ($mil.): 79

    Average daily volume: 123,300

    Expense ratio (%): 0.59

    Category: Non-U.S. equity

    Investment objective: Emulate the performance of the subject index.

	Annualized Total Returns (% share price)	ETF Facts	
1 year	26.99	Marginable:	Yes
3 year	22.71	Options:	No
5 year	11.50	Short sales:	Yes
10 year	8.12	Minimum purchase:	1
Since inception:	7.85		

EWM iShares MSCI Malaysia Index Fund
    Inception date: 3/12/1996
    Asset size ($mil.): 388
    Average daily volume: 67,400
    Expense ratio (%): 0.59
    Category: Non-U.S. equity
    Investment objective: Emulate the performance of the subject index.

	Annualized Total Returns (% share price)	ETF Facts	
1 year	5.52	Marginable:	Yes
3 year	11.41	Options:	No
5 year	12.18	Short sales:	Yes
10 year	–3.25	Minimum purchase:	1
Since inception:	–3.14		

EWN iShares MSCI Netherlands Index Fund
    Inception date: 3/12/1996
    Asset size ($mil.): 64
    Average daily volume: 67,400
    Expense ratio (%): 0.59
    Category: Non-U.S. equity
    Investment objective: Emulate the performance of the subject index.

	Annualized Total Returns (% share price)	ETF Facts	
1 year	24.48	Marginable:	Yes
3 year	20.87	Options:	No
5 year	5.69	Short sales:	Yes
10 year	6.26	Minimum purchase:	1
Since inception:	6.96		

EWO iShares MSCI Austria Index Fund
   Inception date: 3/12/1996
   Asset size ($mil.): 197
   Average daily volume: 162,100
   Expense ratio (%): 0.59
   Category: Non-U.S. equity
   Investment objective: Emulate the performance of the subject index.

	Annualized Total Returns (% share price)	ETF Facts	
1 year	26.17	Marginable:	Yes
3 year	42.38	Options:	No
5 year	31.96	Short sales:	Yes
10 year	12.73	Minimum purchase:	1
Since inception:	12.20		

EWP iShares MSCI Spain Index Fund
   Inception date: 3/12/1996
   Asset size ($mil.): 67
   Average daily volume: 54,300
   Expense ratio (%): 0.59
   Category: Non-U.S. equity
   Investment objective: Emulate the performance of the subject index.

	Annualized Total Returns (% share price)	ETF Facts	
1 year	24.80	Marginable:	Yes
3 year	26.09	Options:	No
5 year	17.11	Short sales:	Yes
10 year	14.81	Minimum purchase:	1
Since inception:	15.09		

EWQ iShares MSCI France Index Fund
    Inception date: 3/12/1996
    Asset size ($mil.): 81
    Average daily volume: 138,700
    Expense ratio (%): 0.59
    Category: Non-U.S. equity
    Investment objective: Emulate the performance of the subject index.

	Annualized Total Returns (% share price)	ETF Facts	
1 year	21.19	Marginable:	Yes
3 year	23.09	Options:	No
5 year	9.69	Short sales:	Yes
10 year	10.61	Minimum purchase:	1
Since inception:	11.09		

EWS iShares MSCI Singapore Index Fund
    Inception date: 3/12/1996
    Asset size ($mil.): 341
    Average daily volume: 617,000
    Expense ratio (%): 0.59
    Category: Non-U.S. equity
    Investment objective: Emulate the performance of the subject index.

	Annualized Total Returns (% share price)	ETF Facts	
1 year	12.63	Marginable:	Yes
3 year	22.45	Options:	No
5 year	13.67	Short sales:	Yes
10 year	−0.22	Minimum purchase:	1
Since inception:	−1.08		

EWT iShares MSCI Taiwan Index
  Inception date: 6/20/2000
  Asset size ($mil.): 753
  Average daily volume: 2,768,100
  Expense ratio (%): 0.74
  Category: Non-U.S. equity
  Investment objective: Emulate the performance of the subject index.

	Annualized Total Returns (% share price)	ETF Facts	
1 year	1.26	Marginable:	Yes
3 year	6.98	Options:	No
5 year	7.29	Short sales:	Yes
10 year	—	Minimum purchase:	1
Since inception:	−6.32		

EWU iShares MSCI United Kingdom Index Fund
  Inception date: 3/12/1996
  Asset size ($mil.): 465
  Average daily volume: 280,600
  Expense ratio (%): 0.59
  Category: Non-U.S. equity
  Investment objective: Emulate the performance of the subject index.

	Annualized Total Returns (% share price)	ETF Facts	
1 year	23.05	Marginable:	Yes
3 year	21.67	Options:	No
5 year	9.71	Short sales:	Yes
10 year	9.15	Minimum purchase:	1
Since inception:	9.47		

EWW iShares MSCI Mexico Index Fund
Inception date: 3/12/1996
Asset size ($mil.): 256
Average daily volume: 972,900
Expense ratio (%): 0.59
Category: Non-U.S. equity
Investment objective: Emulate the performance of the subject index.

	Annualized Total Returns (% share price)	ETF Facts	
1 year	37.14	Marginable:	Yes
3 year	39.80	Options:	No
5 year	22.29	Short sales:	Yes
10 year	16.64	Minimum purchase:	1
Since inception:	16.67		

EWY iShares MSCI South Korea Index Fund
Inception date: 5/9/2000
Asset size ($mil.): 698
Average daily volume: 995,600
Expense ratio (%): 0.74
Category: Non-U.S. equity
Investment objective: Emulate the performance of the subject index.

	Annualized Total Returns (% share price)	ETF Facts	
1 year	26.19	Marginable:	Yes
3 year	28.47	Options:	No
5 year	28.76	Short sales:	Yes
10 year	—	Minimum purchase:	1
Since inception:	14.27		

EWZ iShares MSCI Brazil Index
   Inception date: 7/10/2000
   Asset size ($mil.): 552
   Average daily volume: 2,984,100
   Expense ratio (%): 0.74
   Category: Non-U.S. equity
   Investment objective: Emulate the performance of the subject index.

	Annualized Total Returns (% share price)	ETF Facts	
1 year	58.29	Marginable:	Yes
3 year	56.23	Options:	No
5 year	28.59	Short sales:	Yes
10 year	—	Minimum purchase:	1
Since inception:	14.48		

EZA iShares MSCI South Africa Index Fund
   Inception date: 2/7/2003
   Asset size ($mil.): 154
   Average daily volume: 93,600
   Expense ratio (%): 0.74
   Category: Non-U.S. equity
   Investment objective: Emulate the performance of the subject index.

	Annualized Total Returns (% share price)	ETF Facts	
1 year	28.96	Marginable:	Yes
3 year	33.53	Options:	No
5 year	—	Short sales:	Yes
10 year	—	Minimum purchase:	1
Since inception:	33.73		

EZU iShares MSCI EMU Index
Inception date: 7/25/2000
Asset size ($mil.): 547
Average daily volume: 98,100
Expense ratio (%): 0.59
Category: Non-U.S. equity
Investment objective: Emulate the performance of the subject index, which tracks the aggregate performance of publicly traded securities in European Monetary Union markets.

	Annualized Total Returns (% share price)	ETF Facts	
1 year	21.85	Marginable:	Yes
3 year	23.26	Options:	No
5 year	9.79	Short sales:	Yes
10 year	—	Minimum purchase:	1
Since inception:	2.85		

FEU streetTracks Dow Jones STOXX 50 Index Fund
Inception date: 10/21/2002
Asset size ($mil.): 31
Average daily volume: 7,700
Expense ratio (%): 0.29
Category: Non-U.S. equity
Investment objective: Emulate the performance of the subject index.

	Annualized Total Returns (% share price)	ETF Facts	
1 year	19.09	Marginable:	No
3 year	19.63	Options:	No
5 year	—	Short sales:	No
10 year	—	Minimum purchase:	1
Since inception:	18.25		

FEZ streetTracks Dow Jones Euro STOXX 50 Index
    Inception date: 10/21/2002
    Asset size ($mil.): 180
    Average daily volume: 309,900
    Expense ratio (%): 0.29
    Category: Non-U.S. equity
    Investment objective: Emulate the performance of the subject index.

	Annualized Total Returns (% share price)	ETF Facts	
1 year	19.90	Marginable:	No
3 year	21.79	Options:	No
5 year	—	Short sales:	No
10 year	—	Minimum purchase:	1
Since inception:	21.42		

FXE Rydex Euro Currency Trust
    Inception date: 12/2/2005
    Asset size ($mil.): 103
    Average daily volume: —
    Expense ratio (%): 0.40
    Investment objective: Track the price of the euro expressed in U.S. dollars.

	Annualized Total Returns (% share price)	ETF Facts	
1 year	—	Marginable:	Yes
3 year	—	Options:	No
5 year	—	Short sales:	Yes
10 year	—	Minimum purchase:	100
Since inception:	8.04		

FXI IShares FTSE/Xinhua China 25 Index Fund
  Inception date: 10/5/2004
  Asset size ($mil.): 1,000
  Average daily volume: 442,100
  Expense ratio (%): 0.74
  Category: Non-U.S. equity
  Investment objective: Emulate the performance of the subject index.

	Annualized Total Returns (% share price)	ETF Facts	
1 year	29.94	Marginable:	No
3 year	—	Options:	No
5 year	—	Short sales:	No
10 year	—	Minimum purchase:	1
Since inception:	24.97		

GLD streetTracks Gold Shares
  Inception date: 11/18/2004
  Asset size ($mil.): 3,115
  Average daily volume: 4,821,500
  Expense ratio (%): 0.40
  Category: Sector–Precious metals
  Investment objective: track the price gold bullion.

	Annualized Total Returns (% share price)	ETF Facts	
1 year	47.50	Marginable:	Yes
3 year	—	Options:	Yes
5 year	—	Short sales:	Yes
10 year	—	Minimum purchase:	1
Since inception:	23.58		

HHH Merrill Lynch Internet HOLDRs
Inception date: 9/24/1999
Asset size ($mil.): 251
Average daily volume: 357,600
Expense ratio (%): —
Category: Growth–Domestic
Investment objective: Hold stocks of major companies who produce software, produce hardware, act as Internet service providers, and sell via the Internet.

	Annualized Total Returns (% share price)	ETF Facts	
1 year	−24.75	Marginable:	Yes
3 year	4.82	Options:	Yes
5 year	3.09	Short sales:	Yes
10 year	—	Minimum purchase:	1
Since inception:	−11.45		

IAH Merrill Lynch Internet Architecture HOLDRs
Inception date: 2/25/2000
Asset size ($mil.): 83
Average daily volume: 31,900
Expense ratio (%): —
Category: Growth–Domestic
Investment objective: Hold stocks of major U.S. companies involved in designing or supporting the infrastructure of the Internet.

	Annualized Total Returns (% share price)	ETF Facts	
1 year	−7.24	Marginable:	Yes
3 year	1.41	Options:	Yes
5 year	−3.67	Short sales:	Yes
10 year	—	Minimum purchase:	100
Since inception:	−14.38		

IAU iShares COMEX Gold Trust
Inception date: 1/28/2005
Asset size ($mil.): 174
Average daily volume: 160,700
Expense ratio (%): 0.40
Category: Sector—Precious metals
Investment objective: Tracks the COMEX spot month settlement price for gold futures.

	Annualized Total Returns (% share price)	ETF Facts	
1 year	47.49	Marginable:	No
3 year	—	Options:	No
5 year	—	Short sales:	No
10 year	—	Minimum purchase:	1
Since inception:	29.98		

IBB iShares NASDAQ Biotechnology Index Fund
Inception date: 2/5/2001
Asset size ($mil.): 1,079
Average daily volume: 1,268,600
Expense ratio (%): 0.50
Category: Sector–Health/biotech
Investment objective: Emulate the performance of the subject index.

	Annualized Total Returns (% share price)	ETF Facts	
1 year	−5.93	Marginable:	Yes
3 year	−0.76	Options:	No
5 year	−3.85	Short sales:	Yes
10 year	—	Minimum purchase:	1
Since inception:	−5.95		

ICF iShares Cohen & Steers Realty Majors Index Fund
    Inception date: 1/29/2001
    Asset size ($mil.): 1,298
    Average daily volume: 270,000
    Expense ratio (%): 0.35
    Category: Sector–Real estate
    Investment objective: Emulate the performance of the subject index.

	Annualized Total Returns (% share price)	ETF Facts	
1 year	17.49	Marginable:	Yes
3 year	27.74	Options:	No
5 year	22.02	Short sales:	Yes
10 year	—	Minimum purchase:	1
Since inception:	21.14		

IDU iShares Dow Jones U.S. Utilities Sector Index Fund
    Inception date: 6/12/2000
    Asset size ($mil.): 646
    Average daily volume: 82,300
    Expense ratio (%): 0.48
    Category: Sector–Utilities
    Investment objective: Emulate the performance of the subject index.

	Annualized Total Returns (% share price)	ETF Facts	
1 year	7.83	Marginable:	Yes
3 year	20.87	Options:	No
5 year	5.48	Short sales:	Yes
10 year	—	Minimum purchase:	1
Since inception:	6.13		

IEF iShares Lehman 7-10 Year Treasury Bond Fund
Inception date: 7/22/2002
Asset size ($mil.): 1,120
Average daily volume: 176,100
Expense ratio (%): 0.15
Category: Government bond
Investment objective: Emulate the performance of the subject index.

	Annualized Total Returns (% share price)	Bond Facts
1 year	−0.06	U.S Treasuries with 7 to 10 years to maturity, nonconvertible, priced in U.S. dollars, more than $150 million par outstanding, rated Baa3 or better by Moodys.
3 year	3.10	
5 year	—	
10 year	—	
Since inception:	3.71	

IEV iShares S&P Europe 350 Index Fund
Inception date: 7/25/2000
Asset size ($mil.): 1,182
Average daily volume: 147,300
Expense ratio (%): 0.60
Category: Non-U.S. equity
Investment objective: Emulate the performance of the subject index.

	Annualized Total Returns (% share price)	ETF Facts	
1 year	23.84	Marginable:	Yes
3 year	22.77	Options:	No
5 year	10.08	Short sales:	Yes
10 year	—	Minimum purchase:	1
Since inception:	4.40		

IGE iShares Goldman Sachs Natural Resources Index Fund
Inception date: 10/22/2001
Asset size ($mil.): 801
Average daily volume: 114,600
Expense ratio (%): 0.48
Category: Sector- energy
Investment objective: Emulate the performance of the subject index.

	Annualized Total Returns (% share price)	ETF Facts	
1 year	27.21	Marginable:	Yes
3 year	34.40	Options:	No
5 year	—	Short sales:	Yes
10 year	—	Minimum purchase:	1
Since inception:	19.02		

IGM iShares Goldman Sachs Technology Index Fund
Inception date: 3/13/2001
Asset size ($mil.): 295
Average daily volume 61,600
Expense ratio (%): 0.48
Category: Sector–Technology
Investment objective: Emulate the performance of the subject index.

	Annualized Total Returns (% share price)	ETF Facts	
1 year	-7.00	Marginable:	Yes
3 year	3.77	Options:	No
5 year	-4.79	Short sales:	Yes
10 year	—	Minimum purchase:	1
Since inception:	-4.98		

IGN iShares Goldman Sachs Networking Index Fund
     Inception date: 7/10/2001
     Asset size ($mil.): 148
     Average daily volume: 168,400
     Expense ratio (%): 0.48
     Category: Sector–Technology
     Investment objective: Emulate the performance of the Goldman
     Sachs Network Index.

	Annualized Total Returns (% share price)	ETF Facts	
1 year	−12.47	Marginable:	Yes
3 year	8.39	Options:	No
5 year	−7.29	Short sales:	Yes
10 year	—	Minimum purchase:	1
Since inception:	−6.28		

IGV iShares Goldman Sachs Software Index Fund
     Inception date: 7/10/2001
     Asset size ($mil.): 230
     Average daily volume: 100,300
     Expense ratio (%): 0.48
     Category: Sector–Technology
     Investment objective: Emulate the performance of the subject index.

	Annualized Total Returns (% share price)	ETF Facts	
1 year	−6.60	Marginable:	Yes
3 year	6.27	Options:	No
5 year	−5.14	Short sales:	Yes
10 year	—	Minimum purchase:	1
Since inception:	−5.07		

IGW iShares Goldman Sachs Semiconductor Index Fund
　　Inception date: 7/10/2001
　　Asset size ($mil.): 544
　　Average daily volume: 219,700
　　Expense ratio (%): 0.48
　　Category: Sector–Technology
　　Investment objective: Emulate the performance of the subject index.

	Annualized Total Returns (% share price)	ETF Facts	
1 year	−5.64	Marginable:	Yes
3 year	4.76	Options:	No
5 year	−5.56	Short sales:	Yes
10 year	—	Minimum purchase:	1
Since inception:	−3.29		

IIH Merrill Lynch Internet Infrastructure HOLDRs
　　Inception date: 2/25/2000
　　Asset size ($mil.): 37
　　Average daily volume: 137,800
　　Expense ratio (%): —
　　Category: Sector–Technology
　　Investment objective: Hold the stocks of companies that provide software and technology services, enhance Internet content and functionality, and improve network performance and web site service, and analysis for Internet companies.

	Annualized Total Returns (% share price)	ETF Facts	
1 year	16.28	Marginable:	Yes
3 year	9.37	Options:	Yes
5 year	−12.20	Short sales:	Yes
10 year	—	Minimum purchase:	100
Since inception:	−37.31		

IJH iShares S&P Midcap 400 Index Fund
    Inception date: 5/22/2000
    Asset size ($mil.): 18
    Average daily volume: 330,600
    Expense ratio (%): 0.20
    Category: Growth–Domestic
    Investment objective: Emulate the performance of the subject index.

	Annualized Total Returns (% share price)	ETF Facts	
1 year	3.70	Marginable:	Yes
3 year	15.41	Options:	No
5 year	8.87	Short sales:	Yes
10 year	—	Minimum purchase:	1
Since inception:	8.98		

IJJ iShares S&P Midcap 400 Value Index Fund
    Inception date: 7/24/2000
    Asset size ($mil.): 1,852
    Average daily volume: 330,600
    Expense ratio (%): 0.20
    Category: Growth–Domestic
    Investment objective: Emulate the performance of the subject index.

	Annualized Total Returns (% share price)	ETF Facts	
1 year	3.70	Marginable:	Yes
3 year	15.41	Options:	No
5 year	8.87	Short sales:	Yes
10 year	—	Minimum purchase:	1
Since inception:	8.98		

IJK iShares S&P Midcap 400 Growth index Fund
    Inception date: 7/24/2000
    Asset size ($mil.): 1,112
    Average daily volume: 172,600
    Expense ratio (%): 0.25
    Category: Growth–Domestic
    Investment objective: Emulate the performance of the subject index.

	Annualized Total Returns (% share price)	ETF Facts	
1 year	2.11	Marginable:	Yes
3 year	12.01	Options:	No
5 year	5.88	Short sales:	Yes
10 year	—	Minimum purchase:	1
Since inception:	1.83		

IJR iShares S&P Small-Cap 600 Index Fund
    Inception date: 5/22/2000
    Asset size ($mil.): 3,245
    Average daily volume: 1,712,400
    Expense ratio (%): 0.20
    Category: Growth–Domestic
    Investment objective: Emulate the performance of the subject index.

	Annualized Total Returns (% share price)	ETF Facts	
1 year	3.17	Marginable:	Yes
3 year	16.87	Options:	No
5 year	10.45	Short sales:	Yes
10 year	—	Minimum purchase:	1
Since inception:	11.25		

IJS iShares S&P Small-Cap 600 Value Index Fund
  Inception date: 7/24/2000
  Asset size ($mil.): 1,572
  Average daily volume: 203,000
  Expense ratio (%): 0.25
  Category: Growth–Domestic
  Investment objective: Emulate the performance of the subject index.

	Annualized Total Returns (% share price)	ETF Facts	
1 year	4.31	Marginable:	Yes
3 year	17.60	Options:	No
5 year	10.91	Short sales:	Yes
10 year	—	Minimum purchase:	1
Since inception:	13.12		

IJT iShares S&P Small-Cap 600 Growth index Fund
  Inception date: 7/24/2000
  Asset size ($mil.): 990
  Average daily volume: 95,700
  Expense ratio (%): 0.25
  Category: Growth–Domestic
  Investment objective: Emulate the performance of the subject index.

	Annualized Total Returns (% share price)	ETF Facts	
1 year	2.25	Marginable:	Yes
3 year	15.79	Options:	No
5 year	9.74	Short sales:	Yes
10 year	—	Minimum purchase:	1
Since inception:	6.46		

ILF iShares S&P Latin America 40 Index Fund
  Inception date: 10/25/2001
  Asset size ($mil.): 336
  Average daily volume: 232,600
  Expense ratio (%): 0.50
  Category: Non-U.S. equity
  Investment objective: Emulate the performance of the subject index.

	Annualized Total Returns (% share price)	ETF Facts	
1 year	44.01	Marginable:	Yes
3 year	46.78	Options:	No
5 year	—	Short sales:	Yes
10 year	—	Minimum purchase:	1
Since inception:	31.03		

IOO iShares S&P Global 100 Index Fund
  Inception date: 12/5/2000
  Asset size ($mil.): 343
  Average daily volume: 41,600
  Expense ratio (%): 0.40
  Category: Global equity
  Investment objective: Emulate the performance of the subject index.

	Annualized Total Returns (% share price)	ETF Facts	
1 year	11.22	Marginable:	Yes
3 year	12.73	Options:	No
5 year	3.33	Short sales:	Yes
10 year	—	Minimum purchase:	1
Since inception:	−0.01		

ISI iShares S&P 1500 Index Fund
   Inception date: 1/20/2004
   Asset size ($mil.): 131
   Average daily volume: 26,200
   Expense ratio (%): 0.20
   Category: Equity income
   Investment objective: Emulate the performance of the subject index.

	Annualized Total Returns (% share price)	ETF Facts	
1 year	5.12	Marginable:	No
3 year	—	Options:	No
5 year	—	Short sales:	No
10 year	—	Minimum purchase:	1
Since inception:	6.97		

ITF iShares S&P/TOPIX 150 Index Fund
   Inception date: 10/23/2001
   Asset size ($mil.): 126
   Average daily volume: 33,200
   Expense ratio (%): 0.50
   Category: Non-U.S. equity
   Investment objective: Emulate the performance of the S&P/Tokyo Stock Price 150 Index.

	Annualized Total Returns (% share price)	ETF Facts	
1 year	35.55	Marginable:	Yes
3 year	21.36	Options:	No
5 year	—	Short sales:	Yes
10 year	—	Minimum purchase:	1
Since inception:	10.02		

IVE iShares S&P 500 Value Index
Inception date: 5/22/2000
Asset size ($mil.): 2,704
Average daily volume: 264,500
Expense ratio (%): 0.18
Category: Equity income
Investment objective: Emulate the performance of the subject index.

	Annualized Total Returns (% share price)	ETF Facts	
1 year	9.96	Marginable:	Yes
3 year	14.56	Options:	No
5 year	4.63	Short sales:	Yes
10 year	—	Minimum purchase:	1
Since inception:	4.13		

IVV iShares S&P 500 Index Fund
Inception date: 5/15/2000
Asset size ($mil.): 1,329
Average daily volume: 1,125,200
Expense ratio (%): 0.09
Category: Growth–Domestic
Investment objective: Emulate the performance of the subject index.

	Annualized Total Returns (% share price)	ETF Facts	
1 year	5.22	Marginable:	Yes
3 year	10.72	Options:	No
5 year	2.78	Short sales:	Yes
10 year	—	Minimum purchase:	1
Since inception:	−0.52		

IVW iShares S&P 500 Growth Index Fund
    Inception date: 5/22/2000
    Asset size ($mil.): 2,341
    Average daily volume: 310,200
    Expense ratio (%): 0.18
    Category: Growth–Domestic
    Investment objective: Emulate the performance of the subject index.

	Annualized Total Returns (% share price)	ETF Facts	
1 year	.42	Marginable:	Yes
3 year	6.70	Options:	Yes
5 year	.49	Short sales:	Yes
10 year	—	Minimum purchase:	1
Since inception:	−4.29		

IWB iShares Russell 1000 Index Fund
    Inception date: 5/15/2000
    Asset size ($mil.): 1,984
    Average daily volume: 260,500
    Expense ratio (%): 0.15
    Category: Growth–Domestic
    Investment objective: Emulate the performance of the subject index.

	Annualized Total Returns (% share price)	ETF Facts	
1 year	4.95	Marginable:	Yes
3 year	11.19	Options:	Yes
5 year	3.29	Short sales:	Yes
10 year	—	Minimum purchase:	1
Since inception:	−0.17		

IWC iShares Russell Microcap Index Fund
>   Inception date: 8/12/2005
>   Asset size ($mil.): 51
>   Average daily volume: —
>   Expense ratio (%): 0.60
>   Category: Growth–Domestic
>   Investment objective: Emulate the performance of the Russell MicroCapX Index.

	Annualized Total Returns (% share price)	ETF Facts	
1 year	—	Marginable:	No
3 year	—	Options:	No
5 year	—	Short sales:	No
10 year	—	Minimum purchase:	1
Since inception:	4.35		

IWD iShares Russell 1000 Value Index Fund
>   Inception date: 5/22/2000
>   Asset size ($mil.): 4,791
>   Average daily volume: 805,600
>   Expense ratio (%): 0.20
>   Category: Equity income
>   Investment objective: Emulate the performance from subject index.

	Annualized Total Returns (% share price)	ETF Facts	
1 year	11.30	Marginable:	Yes
3 year	15.84	Options:	No
5 year	7.21	Short sales:	Yes
10 year	—	Minimum purchase:	1
Since inception:	6.84		

IWF iShares Russell 1000 Growth Index Fund
    Inception date: 5/22/2000
    Asset size ($mil.): 3,129
    Average daily volume: 955,900
    Expense ratio (%): 0.20
    Category: Growth–Domestic
    Investment objective: Emulate the performance of the subject index.

	Annualized Total Returns (% share price)	ETF Facts	
1 year	−1.09	Marginable:	Yes
3 year	6.56	Options:	No
5 year	−0.80	Short sales:	Yes
10 year	—	Minimum purchase:	1
Since inception:	−6.65		

IWM iShares Russell 2000 Index Fund
    Inception date: 5/22/2000
    Asset size ($mil.): 7,281
    Average daily volume: 38,803,000
    Expense ratio (%): 0.20
    Category: Growth–Domestic
    Investment objective: Emulate the performance of the subject index.

	Annualized Total Returns (% share price)	ETF Facts	
1 year	3.73	Marginable:	Yes
3 year	15.01	Options:	Yes
5 year	8.89	Short sales:	Yes
10 year	—	Minimum purchase:	1
Since inception:	7.74		

IWN iShares Russell 2000 Value Stock Index
    Inception date: 7/24/2000
    Asset size ($mil.): 2,711
    Average daily volume: 1,129,800
    Expense ratio (%): 0.25
    Category: Growth–Domestic
    Investment objective: Emulate the performance of the subject index.

	Annualized Total Returns (% share price)	ETF Facts	
1 year	6.54	Marginable:	Yes
3 year	18.47	Options:	Yes
5 year	13.07	Short sales:	Yes
10 year	—	Minimum purchase:	1
Since inception:	14.89		

IWO iShares Russell 2000 Growth Index Fund
    Inception date: 7/24/2000
    Asset size ($mil.): 2,105
    Average daily volume: 1,383,600
    Expense ratio (%): 0.25
    Category: Growth–Domestic
    Investment objective: Emulate the performance of the subject index.

	Annualized Total Returns (% share price)	ETF Facts	
1 year	1.21	Marginable:	Yes
3 year	11.32	Options:	Yes
5 year	4.14	Short sales:	Yes
10 year	—	Minimum purchase:	1
Since inception:	–2.11		

IWP iShares Russell Midcap Growth index Fund
    Inception date: 7/17/2001
    Asset size ($mil.): 842
    Average daily volume: 139,000
    Expense ratio (%): 0.25
    Category: Growth–Domestic
    Investment objective: Emulate the performance of the subject index.

	Annualized Total Returns (% share price)	ETF Facts	
1 year	2.83	Marginable:	Yes
3 year	13.88	Options:	No
5 year	5.18	Short sales:	Yes
10 year	—	Minimum purchase:	1
Since inception:	5.18		

IWR iShares Russell Midcap Index Fund
    Inception date: 7/17/2001
    Asset size ($mil.): 1,202
    Average daily volume: 152,600
    Expense ratio (%): 0.20
    Category: Growth–Domestic
    Investment objective: Emulate the performance of the subject index.

	Annualized Total Returns (% share price)	ETF Facts	
1 year	5.17	Marginable:	Yes
3 year	17.48	Options:	No
5 year	10.01	Short sales:	Yes
10 year	—	Minimum purchase:	1
Since inception:	9.88		

IWS iShares Russell Midcap Value Index Fund
Inception date: 7/17/2001
Asset size ($mil.): 1,148
Average daily volume: 148,600
Expense ratio (%): 0.25
Category: Growth–Domestic
Investment objective: Emulate the performance of the subject index.

	Annualized Total Returns (% share price)	ETF Facts	
1 year	8.24	Marginable:	Yes
3 year	20.08	Options:	No
5 year	12.87	Short sales:	Yes
10 year	—	Minimum purchase:	1
Since inception:	12.77		

IWV iShares Russell 3000 Index Fund
Inception date: 5/22/2000
Asset size ($mil.): 1,957
Average daily volume: 172,200
Expense ratio (%): 0.20
Category: Equity income
Investment objective: Emulate the performance of the subject index.

	Annualized Total Returns (% share price)	ETF Facts	
1 year	5.09	Marginable:	Yes
3 year	11.51	Options:	No
5 year	3.60	Short sales:	Yes
10 year	—	Minimum purchase:	1
Since inception:	.91		

IWW iShares Russell 3000 Value Index Fund
    Inception date: 7/24/2000
    Asset size ($mil.): 364
    Average daily volume: 35,700
    Expense ratio (%): 0.25
    Category: Equity income
    Investment objective: Emulate the performance of the subject index.

	Annualized Total Returns (% share price)	ETF Facts	
1 year	10.91	Marginable:	Yes
3 year	15.94	Options:	No
5 year	7.51	Short sales:	Yes
10 year	—	Minimum purchase:	1
Since inception:	7.80		

IWZ iShares Russell 3000 Growth Index Fund
    Inception date: 7/24/2000
    Asset size ($mil.): 182
    Average daily volume: 38,000
    Expense ratio (%): 0.25
    Category: Equity income
    Investment objective: Emulate the performance of the subject index.

	Annualized Total Returns (% share price)	ETF Facts	
1 year	−0.93	Marginable:	Yes
3 year	6.76	Options:	No
5 year	−0.48	Short sales:	Yes
10 year	—	Minimum purchase:	1
Since inception:	−7.87		

IXC iShares S&P Global Energy Index Fund
Inception date: 11/12/2001
Asset size ($mil.): 323
Average daily volume: 70,300
Expense ratio (%): 0.48
Category: Sector–Energy
Investment objective: Emulate the performance of the subject index.

	Annualized Total Returns (% share price)	ETF Facts	
1 year	22.44	Marginable:	Yes
3 year	33.31	Options:	No
5 year	—	Short sales:	Yes
10 year	—	Minimum purchase:	1
Since inception:	20.19		

IXG iShares S&P Global Financial Index Fund
Inception date: 11/12/2001
Asset size ($mil.): 83
Average daily volume: 17,800
Expense ratio (%): 0.48
Category: Sector–Financial services
Investment objective: Emulate the performance of the S&P Global
Financials Sector Index.

	Annualized Total Returns (% share price)	ETF Facts	
1 year	22.06	Marginable:	Yes
3 year	18.23	Options:	No
5 year	—	Short sales:	Yes
10 year	—	Minimum purchase:	1
Since inception:	11.71		

IXJ iShares S&P Global Healthcare Sector index Fund
    Inception date: 11/13/2001
    Asset size ($mil.): 229
    Average daily volume: 61,800
    Expense ratio (%): 0.48
    Category: Sector–Health/biotech
    Investment objective: Emulate the performance of the subject index.

Annualized Total Returns (% share price)		ETF Facts	
1 year	8.55	Marginable:	Yes
3 year	8.76	Options:	No
5 year	—	Short sales:	Yes
10 year	—	Minimum purchase:	1
Since inception:	3.06		

IXN iShares S&P Global Technology Sector Index Fund
    Inception date: 11/12/2001
    Asset size ($mil.): 56
    Average daily volume: 17,100
    Expense ratio (%): 0.48
    Category: Global equity
    Investment objective: Emulate the performance of the subject index.

Annualized Total Returns (% share price)		ETF Facts	
1 year	−3.32	Marginable:	Yes
3 year	5.35	Options:	No
5 year	—	Short sales:	Yes
10 year	—	Minimum purchase:	1
Since inception:	−1.40		

IXP iShares S&P Global Telecommunications Sector index Fund
    Inception date: 11/12/2001
    Asset size ($mil.): 60
    Average daily volume: 14,600
    Expense ratio (%): 0.48
    Category: Global equity
    Investment objective: Emulate the performance of the subject index.

	Annualized Total Returns (% share price)	ETF Facts	
1 year	7.20	Marginable:	Yes
3 year	12.89	Options:	No
5 year	—	Short sales:	Yes
10 year	—	Minimum purchase:	1
Since inception:	2.87		

IYC iShares Dow Jones U.S. Consumer Services Sector Index Fund
    Inception date: 6/12/2000
    Asset size ($mil.): 251
    Average daily volume: 45,000
    Expense ratio (%): 0.48
    Category: Equity income
    Investment objective: Emulate the performance of the subject index.

	Annualized Total Returns (% share price)	ETF Facts	
1 year	−5.65	Marginable:	Yes
3 year	5.55		No
5 year	−0.49	Short sales:	Yes
10 year	—	Minimum purchase:	1
Since inception:	−0.16		

IYE iShares Dow Jones U.S. Energy Sector Index Fund
Inception date: 6/12/2000
Asset size ($mil.): 639
Average daily volume: 149,400
Expense ratio (%): 0.48
Category: Sector–Energy
Investment objective: Emulate the performance of the subject index.

Annualized Total Returns (% share price)		ETF Facts	
1 year	23.35	Marginable:	Yes
3 year	35.82	Options:	No
5 year	16.29	Short sales:	Yes
10 year	—	Minimum purchase:	1
Since inception:	13.23		

IYF iShares Dow Jones U.S. Financial Sector Index Fund
Inception date: 5/22/2000
Asset size ($mil.): 300
Average daily volume: 37,500
Expense ratio (%): 0.48
Category: Sector–Financial services
Investment objective: Emulate the performance of the subject index.

Annualized Total Returns (% share price)		ETF Facts	
1 year	11.69	Marginable:	Yes
3 year	12.13	Options:	No
5 year	6.60	Short sales:	Yes
10 year	—	Minimum purchase:	1
Since inception:	8.59		

IYG iShares Dow Jones U.S. Financial Services Index Fund
Inception date: 6/12/2000
Asset size ($mil.): 142
Average daily volume: 18,500
Expense ratio (%): 0.48
Category: Sector–Financial services
Investment objective: Emulate the performance of the subject index.

	Annualized Total Returns (% share price)	ETF Facts	
1 year	13.77	Marginable:	Yes
3 year	11.51	Options:	No
5 year	6.64	Short sales:	Yes
10 year	—	Minimum purchase:	1
Since inception:	7.82		

IYH iShares Dow Jones U.S. Healthcare Sector Index Fund
Inception date: 6/12/2000
Asset size ($mil.): 1,169
Average daily volume: 148,400
Expense ratio (%): 0.48
Category: Sector–Health/biotech
Investment objective: Emulate the performance of the subject index.

	Annualized Total Returns (% share price)	ETF Facts	
1 year	1.27	Marginable:	Yes
3 year	5.83	Options:	No
5 year	0.92	Short sales:	Yes
10 year	—	Minimum purchase:	1
Since inception:	1.64		

IYJ iShares Dow Jones U.S. Industrial Sector Index Fund
    Inception date: 6/12/2000
    Asset size ($mil.): 237
    Average daily volume: 33,700
    Expense ratio (%): 0.48
    Category: Equity income
    Investment objective: Emulate the performance of the subject index.

	Annualized Total Returns (% share price)	ETF Facts	
1 year	5.76	Marginable:	Yes
3 year	12.76	Options:	No
5 year	3.76	Short sales:	Yes
10 year	—	Minimum purchase:	1
Since inception:	1.05		

IYK iShares Dow Jones U.S. Consumer Goods Sector Index Fund
    Inception date: 6/12/2000
    Asset size ($mil.): 421
    Average daily volume: 69,900
    Expense ratio (%): 0.48
    Category: Equity income
    Investment objective: Emulate the performance of the subject index.

	Annualized Total Returns (% share price)	ETF Facts	
1 year	1.84	Marginable:	Yes
3 year	9.80	Options:	No
5 year	7.01	Short sales:	Yes
10 year	—	Minimum purchase:	1
Since inception:	6.32		

IYM iShares Dow Jones U.S. Basic Materials Sector Index Fund
    Inception date: 6/12/2000
    Asset size ($mil.): 413
    Average daily volume: 103,800
    Expense ratio (%): 0.48
    Category: Equity income
    Investment objective: Emulate the performance of the subject index.

	Annualized Total Returns (% share price)	ETF Facts	
1 year	10.09	Marginable:	Yes
3 year	13.70	Options:	No
5 year	8.20	Short sales:	Yes
10 year	—	Minimum purchase:	1
Since inception:	8.56		

IYR iShares Dow Jones U.S. Real Estate Index Fund
    Inception date: 6/12/2000
    Asset size ($mil.): 737
    Average daily volume: 2,266,700
    Expense ratio (%): 0.48
    Category: Growth & income
    Investment objective: Emulate the performance of the subject index.

	Annualized Total Returns (% share price)	ETF Facts	
1 year	13.24	Marginable:	Yes
3 year	23.78	Options:	No
5 year	18.92	Short sales:	Yes
10 year	—	Minimum purchase:	1
Since inception:	19.30		

IYT iShares Dow Jones Transportation Average Index Fund
Inception date: 10/10/2003
Asset size ($mil.): 99
Average daily volume: 415,500
Expense ratio (%): 0.48
Category: Equity income
Investment objective: Emulate the performance of the subject index.

	Annualized Total Returns (% share price)	ETF Facts	
1 year	15.89	Marginable:	No
3 year	—	Options:	No
5 year	—	Short sales:	No
10 year	—	Minimum purchase:	1
Since inception:	18.08		

IYW iShares Dow Jones Technology Index Fund
Inception date: 5/15/2000
Asset size ($mil.): 395
Average daily volume: 72,400
Expense ratio (%): 0.48
Category: Sector–Technology
Investment objective: Emulate the performance of the subject index.

	Annualized Total Returns (% share price)	ETF Facts	
1 year	−5.93	Marginable:	Yes
3 year	4.43	Options:	No
5 year	−3.98	Short sales:	Yes
10 year	—	Minimum purchase:	1
Since inception:	−13.84		

IYY iShares Dow Jones U.S. Total Market Index Fund
    Inception date: 6/12/2000
    Asset size ($mil.): 415
    Average daily volume: 36,400
    Expense ratio (%): 0.20
    Category: Growth–Domestic
    Investment objective: Emulate the performance of the subject index.

	Annualized Total Returns (% share price)	ETF Facts	
1 year	5.15	Marginable:	Yes
3 year	11.56	Options:	No
5 year	3.50	Short sales:	Yes
10 year	—	Minimum purchase:	1
Since inception:	0.03		

IYZ iShares Dow Jones U.S. Telecommunications Sector Index Fund
    Inception date: 5/22/2000
    Asset size ($mil.): 313
    Average daily volume: 275,100
    Expense ratio (%): 0.48
    Category: Equity income
    Investment objective: Emulate the performance of the subject index.

	Annualized Total Returns (% share price)	ETF Facts	
1 year	12.02	Marginable:	Yes
3 year	12.94	Options:	No
5 year	−4.86	Short sales:	Yes
10 year	—	Minimum purchase:	1
Since inception:	−9.85		

JKD iShares Morningstar Large Core Index Fund
    Inception date: 7/2/2004
    Asset size ($mil.): 80
    Average daily volume: 7,700
    Expense ratio (%): 0.20
    Category: Growth–Domestic
    Investment objective: Emulate the performance of the subject index.

	Annualized Total Returns (% share price)	ETF Facts	
1 year	4.92	Marginable:	No
3 year	—	Options:	No
5 year	—	Short sales:	No
10 year	—	Minimum purchase:	1
Since inception:	8.11		

JKE iShares Morningstar Large Growth Index Fund
    Inception date: 7/2/2004
    Asset size ($mil.): 104
    Average daily volume: 22,900
    Expense ratio (%): 0.25
    Category: Growth–Domestic
    Investment objective: Emulate the performance of the subject index.

	Annualized Total Returns (% share price)	ETF Facts	
1 year	−4.83	Marginable:	No
3 year	—	Options:	No
5 year	—	Short sales:	No
10 year	—	Minimum purchase:	1
Since inception:	−0.76		

JKF iShares Morningstar Large Value Index Fund
Inception date: 7/2/2004
Asset size ($mil.): 87
Average daily volume: 20,900
Expense ratio (%): 0.25
Category: Equity income
Investment objective: Emulate the performance of the subject index.

	Annualized Total Returns (% share price)	ETF Facts	
1 year	15.64	Marginable:	No
3 year	—	Options:	No
5 year	—	Short sales:	No
10 year	—	Minimum purchase:	1
Since inception:	15.92		

JKG iShares Morningstar Mid-Core Index Fund
Inception date: 7/2/2004
Asset size ($mil.): 85
Average daily volume: 7,400
Expense ratio (%): 0.25
Category: Growth–Domestic
Investment objective: Emulate the performance of the subject index.

	Annualized Total Returns (% share price)	ETF Facts	
1 year	2.49	Marginable:	No
3 year	—	Options:	No
5 year	—	Short sales:	No
10 year	—	Minimum purchase:	1
Since inception:	11.59		

JKH iShares Morningstar Mid-Growth Index Fund
Inception date: 7/2/2004
Asset size ($mil.): 58
Average daily volume: 24,000
Expense ratio (%): 0.30
Category: Growth–Domestic
Investment objective: Emulate the performance of the subject index.

	Annualized Total Returns (% share price)	ETF Facts	
1 year	5.12	Marginable:	No
3 year	—	Options:	No
5 year	—	Short sales:	No
10 year	—	Minimum purchase:	1
Since inception:	14.33		

JKI iShares Morningstar Mid-Value Index Fund
Inception date: 7/2/2004
Asset size ($mil.): 71
Average daily volume: 6,600
Expense ratio (%): 0.30
Category: Growth–Domestic
Investment objective: Emulate the performance of the Russell Mid-cap Value Index.

	Annualized Total Returns (% share price)	ETF Facts	
1 year	5.96	Marginable:	No
3 year	—	Options:	No
5 year	—	Short sales:	No
10 year	—	Minimum purchase:	1
Since inception:	16.31		

JKJ iShares Morningstar Small Core Index Fund
    Inception date: 7/2/2004
    Asset size ($mil.): 48
    Average daily volume: 15,100
    Expense ratio (%): 0.25
    Category: Growth–Domestic
    Investment objective: Emulate the performance of the subject index.

	Annualized Total Returns (% share price)	ETF Facts	
1 year	7.47	Marginable:	No
3 year	—	Options:	No
5 year	—	Short sales:	No
10 year	—	Minimum purchase:	1
Since inception:	14.16		

JKK iShares Morningstar Small Growth Index Fund
    Inception date: 7/7/2004
    Asset size ($mil.): 32
    Average daily volume: 14,300
    Expense ratio (%): 0.30
    Category: Growth–Domestic
    Investment objective: Emulate the performance of the subject index.

	Annualized Total Returns (% share price)	ETF Facts	
1 year	–0.03	Marginable:	No
3 year	—	Options:	No
5 year	—	Short sales:	No
10 year	—	Minimum purchase:	1
Since inception:	7.45		

JKL iShares Morningstar Small Value Index Fund
Inception date: 7/6/2004
Asset size ($mil.): 58
Average daily volume: 11,100
Expense ratio (%): 0.30
Category: Growth–Domestic
Investment objective: Emulate the performance of the subject index.

	Annualized Total Returns (% share price)	ETF Facts	
1 year	3.61	Marginable:	No
3 year	—	Options:	No
5 year	—	Short sales:	No
10 year	—	Minimum purchase:	1
Since inception:	13.17		

KLD iShares KLD Select Social Index
Inception date: 1/24/2005
Asset size ($mil.): 113
Average daily volume: 15,300
Expense ratio (%): 0.50
Category: Growth–Domestic
Investment objective: Emulate the performance of the subject index.

	Annualized Total Returns (% share price)	ETF Facts	
1 year	3.14	Marginable:	No
3 year	—	Options:	No
5 year	—	Short sales:	No
10 year	—	Minimum purchase:	1
Since inception:	5.83		

LQD iShares Goldman Sachs $ InvesTop Corporate Bond Fund Index
Inception date: 7/22/2002
Asset size ($mil.): 2,540
Average daily volume: 132,100
Expense ratio (%): 0.15
Category: Corporate–Investment grade
Investment objective: Emulates the index, which captures the return of the U.S. investment grade corporate bond market.

	Annualized Total Returns (% share price)	Bond Facts	
1 year	−0.92	Avg. maturity:	9.93 yrs
3 year	3.99	Avg. coupon::	5.11%
5 year	—	Avg. duration:	6.57 yrs
10 year	—		
Since inception:	5.30		

MDY MidCap SPDR Trust Series 1
Inception date: 5/4/1995
Asset size ($mil.): 7,313
Average daily volume: 2,602,900
Expense ratio (%): 0.25
Category: Growth–Domestic
Investment objective: Emulate the performance of the S&P Midcap 400 Stock Index.

	Annualized Total Returns (% share price)	ETF Facts	
1 year	3.89	Marginable:	Yes
3 year	15.36	Options:	Yes
5 year	8.72	Short sales:	Yes
10 year	13.86	Minimum purchase:	1
Since inception:	14.14		

MKH Merrill Lynch Market 2000 + HOLDRs
    Inception date: 8/30/2000
    Asset size ($mil.): 54
    Average daily volume: 2,200
    Expense ratio (%): —
    Category: Growth–Domestic
    Investment objective: Hold the common stocks 51 specified companies that are among the largest companies traded on the New York Stock Exchange, American Stock Exchange, and NASDAQ.

Annualized Total Returns (% share price)		ETF Facts	
1 year	2.46	Marginable:	Yes
3 year	6.39	Options:	Yes
5 year	–2.03	Short sales:	Yes
10 year	—	Minimum purchase:	100
Since inception:	–7.44		

MTK streetTracks Morgan Stanley Technology Index Fund
    Inception date: 9/29/2000
    Asset size ($mil.): 31
    Average daily volume: 58,700
    Expense ratio (%): 0.50
    Category: Growth–Domestic
    Investment objective: Emulate the performance of the subject index.

Annualized Total Returns (% share price)		ETF Facts	
1 year	–6.82	Marginable:	Yes
3 year	6.22	Options:	No
5 year	–3.30	Short sales:	Yes
10 year	—	Minimum purchase:	1
Since inception:	–11.50		

NY iShares NYSE 100 Index Fund
    Inception date: 3/29/2004
    Asset size ($mil.): 32
    Average daily volume: 25,400
    Expense ratio (%): 0.20
    Category: Equity income
    Investment objective: Emulate the performance of the subject index.

	Annualized Total Returns (% share price)	ETF Facts	
1 year	8.07	Marginable:	No
3 year	—	Options:	No
5 year	—	Short sales:	No
10 year	—	Minimum purchase:	1
Since inception:	6.68		

NYC iShares NYSE Composite Index Fund
    Inception date: 3/30/2004
    Asset size ($mil.): 14
    Average daily volume: 8.000
    Expense ratio (%): 0.25
    Category: Equity income
    Investment objective: Emulate the performance of the subject index.

	Annualized Total Returns (% share price)	ETF Facts	
1 year	11.35	Marginable:	No
3 year	—	Options:	No
5 year	—	Short sales:	No
10 year	—	Minimum purchase:	1
Since inception:	11.72		

OEF iShares S&P 100 Index Fund
  Inception date: 10/23/2000
  Asset size ($mil.): 795
  Average daily volume: 332,300
  Expense ratio (%): 0.20
  Category: Growth–Domestic
  Investment objective: Emulate the performance of the subject index.

	Annualized Total Returns (% share price)	ETF Facts	
1 year	4.86	Marginable:	Yes
3 year	7.61	Options:	No
5 year	.38	Short sales:	Yes
10 year	—	Minimum purchase:	1
Since inception:	−2.19		

OIH Merrill Lynch Market Oil Service HOLDRs
  Inception date: 2/6/2001
  Asset size ($mil.): 933
  Average daily volume: 9,500,300
  Expense ratio (%): —
  Category: Sector–Energy
  Investment objective: Deliver the returns of a group of stocks of major oil service companies.

	Annualized Total Returns (% share price)	ETF Facts	
1 year	29.58	Marginable:	Yes
3 year	38.47	Options:	Yes
5 year	18.47	Short sales:	Yes
10 year	—	Minimum purchase:	100
Since inception:	8.47		

ONEQ Fidelity NASDAQ Composite Index Tracking Stock
  Inception date: 9/25/2003
  Asset size ($mil.): 131
  Average daily volume: 48,200
  Expense ratio (%): 0.30
  Category: Growth–Domestic
  Investment objective: Emulate the performance of the NASDAQ Composite Index.

	Annualized Total Returns (% share price)	ETF Facts	
1 year	−3.76	Marginable:	No
3 year	—	Options:	No
5 year	—	Short sales:	No
10 year	—	Minimum purchase:	1
Since inception:	6.77		

OOO streetTracks SPDR O-Strip Index Fund
  Inception date: 9/15/2004
  Asset size ($mil.): 70
  Average daily volume: 19,300
  Expense ratio (%): 0.35
  Category: Growth–Domestic
  Investment objective: Emulate the performance of the S&P 500 O-Strip Index.

	Annualized Total Returns (% share price)	ETF Facts	
1 year	−11.72	Marginable:	No
3 year	—	Options:	No
5 year	—	Short sales:	No
10 year	—	Minimum purchase:	1
Since inception:	0.02		

PBE PowerShares Dynamic Biotech & Genome Portfolio
Inception date: 6/23/2005
Asset size ($mil.): 122
Average daily volume: 159,300
Expense ratio (%): 0.60
Category: Sector–Health/biotech
Investment objective: Emulate the performance of the PowerShares Dynamic Biotech & Genome Intellidex.

Annualized Total Returns (% share price)		ETF Facts	
1 year	–4.98	Marginable:	No
3 year	—	Options:	No
5 year	—	Short sales:	No
10 year	—	Minimum purchase:	1
Since inception:	7.00		

PBJ PowerShares Dynamic Food and Beverage Portfolio
Inception date: 6/23/2005
Asset size ($mil.): 23
Average daily volume: 13,800
Expense ratio (%): 0.60
Category: Equity income
Investment objective: Emulate the performance of the PowerShares Dynamic Food and Beverage Intellidex.

Annualized Total Returns (% share price)		ETF Facts	
1 year	–0.19	Marginable:	No
3 year	—	Options:	No
5 year	—	Short sales:	No
10 year	—	Minimum purchase:	1
Since inception:	1.62		

PBS PowerShares Dynamic Media Portfolio
  Inception date: 6/23/2005
  Asset size ($mil.): 24
  Average daily volume: 11,200
  Expense ratio (%): 0.63
  Category: Equity income
  Investment objective: Emulate the performance of the PowerShares
  Dynamic Media Intellidex.

	Annualized Total Returns (% share price)	ETF Facts	
1 year	−9.08	Marginable:	No
3 year	—	Options:	No
5 year	—	Short sales:	No
10 year	—	Minimum purchase:	1
Since inception:	−8.75		

PBW PowerShares Wilder Clean Energy Index Fund
  Inception date: 3/3/2005
  Asset size ($mil.): 169
  Average daily volume: 354,700
  Expense ratio (%): 0.60
  Category: Sector–Energy
  Investment objective: Emulate the performance of the subject index.

	Annualized Total Returns (% share price)	ETF Facts	
1 year	10.85	Marginable:	Yes
3 year	—	Options:	Yes
5 year	—	Short sales:	Yes
10 year	—	Minimum purchase:	1
Since inception:	9.27		

PEJ PowerShares Dynamic Leisure and Entertainment Portfolio
Inception date: 6/23/2005
Asset size ($mil.): 24
Average daily volume: 10,900
Expense ratio (%): 0.60
Category: Equity income
Investment objective: Emulate the performance of the PowerShares Dynamic and Leisure Intellidex.

	Annualized Total Returns (% share price)	ETF Facts	
1 year	−1.90	Marginable:	No
3 year	—	Options:	No
5 year	—	Short sales:	No
10 year	—	Minimum purchase:	1
Since inception:	−0.96		

PEY PowerShares High Yield Equity Dividend Achievers Fund
Inception date: 12/9/2004
Asset size ($mil.): 314
Average daily volume: 144,200
Expense ratio (%): 0.50
Category: Equity income
Investment objective: Emulate the performance of the Mergent Dividend Achievers 50 Index.

	Annualized Total Returns (% share price)	ETF Facts	
1 year	1.86	Marginable:	Yes
3 year	—	Options:	Yes
5 year	—	Short sales:	Yes
10 year	—	Minimum purchase:	1
Since inception:	5.77		

PFM PowerShares Dividend Achievers Portfolio
　　Inception date: 9/15/2005
　　Asset size ($mil.): 26
　　Average daily volume: —
　　Expense ratio (%): 0.50
　　Category: Equity income
　　Investment objective: Emulate the performance of the Broad Dividend Achievers Index.

Annualized Total Returns (% share price)		ETF Facts	
1 year	—	Marginable:	Yes
3 year	—	Options:	Yes
5 year	—	Short sales:	Yes
10 year	—	Minimum purchase:	1
Since inception:	7.27		

PGJ PowerShares Golden Dragon Halter USX China Portfolio
　　Inception date: 12/9/2004
　　Asset size ($mil.): 66
　　Average daily volume: 119,200
　　Expense ratio (%): 0.60
　　Category: Non-U.S. equity
　　Investment objective: Emulate the performance of the Halter USX China Index.

Annualized Total Returns (% share price)		ETF Facts	
1 year	10.37	Marginable:	Yes
3 year	—	Options:	Yes
5 year	—	Short sales:	Yes
10 year	—	Minimum purchase:	1
Since inception:	5.19		

PHJ PowerShares High Growth Dividend Achiever Portfolio Fund
Inception date: 9/15/2005
Asset size ($mil.): 27
Average daily volume: —
Expense ratio (%): 0.50
Category: Equity income
Investment objective: Emulate the performance of the Mergent High Growth Rate Dividend Achiever Index.

	Annualized Total Returns (% share price)	ETF Facts	
1 year	—	Marginable:	Yes
3 year	—	Options:	Yes
5 year	—	Short sales:	Yes
10 year	—	Minimum purchase:	1
Since inception:	6.96		

PIC PowerShares Dynamic Insurance Portfolio Fund
Inception date: 10/26/2005
Asset size ($mil.): 8
Average daily volume: —
Expense ratio (%): 0.60
Category: Equity income
Investment objective: Emulate the performance of the PowerShares Dynamic Insurance Intellidex.

	Annualized Total Returns (% share price)	ETF Facts	
1 year	—	Marginable:	Yes
3 year	—	Options:	Yes
5 year	—	Short sales:	Yes
10 year	—	Minimum purchase:	1
Since inception:	9.59		

PID PowerShares International Dividend Achiever Portfolio Fund
Inception date: 9/15/2005
Asset size ($mil.): 56
Average daily volume: —
Expense ratio (%): 0.50
Category: Equity income
Investment objective: Emulate the performance of the Broad Dividend Achievers Index.

	Annualized Total Returns (% share price)	ETF Facts	
1 year	—	Marginable:	Yes
3 year	—	Options:	Yes
5 year	—	Short sales:	Yes
10 year	—	Minimum purchase:	1
Since inception:	13.01		

PJP PowerShares Dynamic Pharmaceuticals Portfolio Fund
Inception date: 6/23/2005
Asset size ($mil.): 31
Average daily volume: 52,700
Expense ratio (%): 0.60
Category: Sector–Health/biotech
Investment objective: Emulate the performance of the PowerShares Dynamic Pharmaceuticals Intellidex.

	Annualized Total Returns (% share price)	ETF Facts	
1 year	6.28	Marginable:	No
3 year	—	Options:	No
5 year	—	Short sales:	No
10 year	—	Minimum purchase:	1
Since inception:	10.45		

PKB PowerShares Dynamic Building & Construction Portfolio Fund
Inception date: 10/26/2005
Asset size ($mil.): 5
Average daily volume: —
Expense ratio (%): 0.60
Category: Equity income
Investment objective: Emulate the performance of the PowerShares
Building & Construction Intellidex.

Annualized Total Returns (% share price)		ETF Facts	
1 year	—	Marginable:	Yes
3 year	—	Options:	Yes
5 year	—	Short sales:	Yes
10 year	—	Minimum purchase:	1
Since inception:	−5.69		

PMR PowerShares Dynamic Retail Portfolio Fund
Inception date: 10/26/2005
Asset size ($mil.): 31
Average daily volume: —
Expense ratio (%): 0.60
Category: Equity income
Investment objective: Emulate the performance of the PowerShares
Dynamic Retail Intellidex.

Annualized Total Returns (% share price)		ETF Facts	
1 year	—	Marginable:	Yes
3 year	—	Options:	Yes
5 year	—	Short sales:	Yes
10 year	—	Minimum purchase:	1
Since inception:	8.98		

PPA PowerShares Aerospace & Defense Fund
Inception date: 10/26/2005
Asset size ($mil.): 4
Average daily volume: —
Expense ratio (%): 0.60
Category: Equity income
Investment objective: Emulate the performance of the SPADE Defense Index.

	Annualized Total Returns (% share price)	ETF Facts	
1 year	—	Marginable:	Yes
3 year	—	Options:	Yes
5 year	—	Short sales:	Yes
10 year	—	Minimum purchase:	1
Since inception:	10.60		

PPH Merrill Lynch Pharmaceutical HOLDRs
Inception date: 2/1/2000
Asset size ($mil.): 1,037
Average daily volume: 760,500
Expense ratio (%): —
Category: Sector–Health/biotech
Investment objective: Deliver the returns of a group of stocks of leading pharmaceutical companies.

	Annualized Total Returns (% share price)	ETF Facts	
1 year	6.19	Marginable:	Yes
3 year	1.27	Options:	Yes
5 year	-3.84	Short sales:	Yes
10 year	—	Minimum purchase:	1
Since inception:	-1.18		

PSI PowerShares Dynamic Semiconductor Portfolio Fund
   Inception date: 6/23/2005
   Asset size ($mil.): 60
   Average daily volume: 96,600
   Expense ratio (%): 0.60
   Category: Equity income
   Investment objective: Emulate the performance of the PowerShares
   Dynamic Semiconductors Intellidex.

	Annualized Total Returns (% share price)	ETF Facts	
1 year	0.44	Marginable:	No
3 year	—	Options:	No
5 year	—	Short sales:	No
10 year	—	Minimum purchase:	1
Since inception:	6.95		

PSJ PowerShares Dynamic Software Portfolio Fund
   Inception date: 6/3/2005
   Asset size ($mil.): 32
   Average daily volume: 26,600
   Expense ratio (%): 0.60
   Category: Growth–Domestic
   Investment objective: Emulate the performance of the PowerShares
   Dynamic Software Intellidex.

	Annualized Total Returns (% share price)	ETF Facts	
1 year	3.74	Marginable:	No
3 year	—	Options:	No
5 year	—	Short sales:	No
10 year	—	Minimum purchase:	1
Since inception:	8.91		

PUI PowerShares Dynamic Utilities Portfolio Fund
> Inception date: 10/26/2005
> Asset size ($mil.): 5
> Average daily volume: —
> Expense ratio (%): 0.60
> Category: Sector–Utilities
> Investment objective: Emulate the performance of the PowerShares Dynamic Utilities Intellidex.

	Annualized Total Returns (% share price)	ETF Facts	
1 year	—	Marginable:	Yes
3 year	—	Options:	Yes
5 year	—	Short sales:	Yes
10 year	—	Minimum purchase:	1
Since inception:	16.92		

PWB PowerShares Dynamic Large-Cap Growth Index Portfolio Fund
> Inception date: 3/3/2005
> Asset size ($mil.): 44
> Average daily volume: 71,100
> Expense ratio (%): 0.60
> Category: Growth–Domestic
> Investment objective: Emulate the performance of the PowerShares Dynamic Large-Cap Growth Intellidex.

	Annualized Total Returns (% share price)	ETF Facts	
1 year	-3.06	Marginable:	Yes
3 year	—	Options:	Yes
5 year	—	Short sales:	Yes
10 year	—	Minimum purchase:	1
Since inception:	1.07		

PWC PowerShares Dynamic Market Portfolio Fund
    Inception date: 4/29/2003
    Asset size ($mil.): 284
    Average daily volume: 102,300
    Expense ratio (%): 0.60
    Category: Growth–Domestic
    Investment objective: Emulate the performance of the PowerShares
    Dynamic Market Intellidex.

	Annualized Total Returns (% share price)	ETF Facts	
1 year	4.97	Marginable:	Yes
3 year	16.20	Options:	No
5 year	—	Short sales:	Yes
10 year	—	Minimum purchase:	1
Since inception:	18.78		

PWJ PowerShares Dynamic Midcap Growth Fund
    Inception date: 3/3/2005
    Asset size ($mil.): 26
    Average daily volume: 56,600
    Expense ratio (%): 0.60
    Category: Growth–Domestic
    Investment objective: Emulate the performance of the Dynamic
    Midcap Growth Intellidex.

	Annualized Total Returns (% share price)	ETF Facts	
1 year	8.61	Marginable:	Yes
3 year	—	Options:	Yes
5 year	—	Short sales:	Yes
10 year	—	Minimum purchase:	1
Since inception:	11.34		

PWO PowerShares Dynamic OTC Portfolio Fund
　　Inception date: 4/29/2003
　　Asset size ($mil.): 133
　　Average daily volume: 33,600
　　Expense ratio (%): 0.60
　　Category: Growth–Domestic
　　Investment objective: Emulate the performance of the PowerShares
　　Dynamic OTC Intellidex.

	Annualized Total Returns (% share price)	ETF Facts	
1 year	-1.56	Marginable:	Yes
3 year	13.25	Options:	No
5 year	—	Short sales:	Yes
10 year	—	Minimum purchase:	1
Since inception:	16.73		

PWP PowerShares Dynamic Midcap Value Fund
　　Inception date: 3/3/2005
　　Asset size ($mil.): 19
　　Average daily volume: 23.900
　　Expense ratio (%): 0.60
　　Category: Growth–Domestic
　　Investment objective: Emulate the performance of the Dynamic
　　Midcap Value Intellidex.

	Annualized Total Returns (% share price)	ETF Facts	
1 year	5.19	Marginable:	Yes
3 year	—	Options:	Yes
5 year	—	Short sales:	Yes
10 year	—	Minimum purchase:	1
Since inception:	9.55		

PWT PowerShares Dynamic Small-Cap Growth Fund
Inception date: 3/3/2005
Asset size ($mil.): 19
Average daily volume: 63,800
Expense ratio (%): 0.60
Category: Growth–Domestic
Investment objective: Emulate the performance of the Dynamic Small-Cap Growth Intellidex.

	Annualized Total Returns (% share price)	ETF Facts	
1 year	−3.30	Marginable:	Yes
3 year	—	Options:	Yes
5 year	—	Short sales:	Yes
10 year	—	Minimum purchase:	1
Since inception:	3.20		

PWV PowerShares Dynamic Large-Cap Value Fund
Inception date: 3/3/2005
Asset size ($mil.): 30
Average daily volume: 42,100
Expense ratio (%): 0.60
Category: Equity income
Investment objective: Emulate the performance of the PowerShares Dynamic Large-Cap Value Intellidex.

	Annualized Total Returns (% share price)	ETF Facts	
1 year	14.69	Marginable:	Yes
3 year	—	Options:	Yes
5 year	—	Short sales:	Yes
10 year	—	Minimum purchase:	1
Since inception:	15.76		

PWY PowerShares Dynamic Small-Cap Value Fund
>   Inception date: 3/3/2005
>   Asset size ($mil.): 29
>   Average daily volume: 28,100
>   Expense ratio (%): 0.60
>   Category: Growth–Domestic
>   Investment objective: Emulate the performance of the PowerShares
>   Dynamic Small-Cap Value Intellidex

Annualized Total Returns (% share price)		ETF Facts	
1 year	1.54	Marginable:	Yes
3 year	—	Options:	Yes
5 year	—	Short sales:	Yes
10 year	—	Minimum purchase:	1
Since inception:	5.97		

PXE PowerShares Dynamic Energy Exploration and Production Portfolio Fund
>   Inception date: 10/26/2005
>   Asset size ($mil.): 41
>   Average daily volume: —
>   Expense ratio (%): 0.60
>   Category: Sector–Energy
>   Investment objective: Emulate the performance of the subject index.

Annualized Total Returns (% share price)		ETF Facts	
1 year	—	Marginable:	Yes
3 year	—	Options:	Yes
5 year	—	Short sales:	Yes
10 year	—	Minimum purchase:	1
Since inception:	23.42		

PXJ PowerShares Dynamic Oil & Gas Exploration Services Portfolio Fund

Inception date: 10/26/2005
Asset size ($mil.): 33
Average daily volume: —
Expense ratio (%): 0.60
Category: Sector–Energy
Investment objective: Emulate the performance of the subject index.

Annualized Total Returns (% share price)		ETF Facts	
1 year	—	Marginable:	Yes
3 year	—	Options:	Yes
5 year	—	Short sales:	Yes
10 year	—	Minimum purchase:	1
Since inception:	25.26		

PXN PowerShares Lux Nanotech Portfolio Fund

Inception date: 10/26/2005
Asset size ($mil.): 30
Average daily volume: —
Expense ratio (%): 0,60
Category: Growth–Domestic
Investment objective: Emulate the performance of the Lux Nanotech Index

Annualized Total Returns (% share price)		ETF Facts	
1 year	—	Marginable:	Yes
3 year	—	Options:	Yes
5 year	—	Short sales:	Yes
10 year	—	Minimum purchase:	1
Since inception:	8.74		

PXQ PowerShares Dynamic Networking Portfolio
   Inception date: 6/23/2005
   Asset size ($mil.): 24
   Average daily volume: 23,000
   Expense ratio (%): 0.60
   Category: Growth–Domestic
   Investment objective: Emulate the performance of the PowerShares Dynamic Networking Intellidex.

	Annualized Total Returns (% share price)	ETF Facts	
1 year	−12.30	Marginable:	No
3 year	—	Options:	No
5 year	—	Short sales:	No
10 year	—	Minimum purchase:	1
Since inception:	−7.18		

PZI PowerShares Zacks Microcap Portfolio Fund
   Inception date: 8/18/2005
   Asset size ($mil.): 84
   Average daily volume: —
   Expense ratio (%): 0.60
   Category: Growth–Domestic
   Investment objective: Emulate the performance of the subject index.

	Annualized Total Returns (% share price)	ETF Facts	
1 year	—	Marginable:	Yes
3 year	—	Options:	No
5 year	—	Short sales:	Yes
10 year	—	Minimum purchase:	1
Since inception:	6.82		

QQQQ NASDAQ 100 Trust Series 1
Inception date: 3/5/1999
Asset size ($mil.): 20,649
Average daily volume: 97,608,200
Expense ratio (%): 0.20
Category: Growth–Domestic
Investment objective: Emulate the performance of the NASDAQ 100 Index.

	Annualized Total Returns (% share price)	ETF Facts	
1 year	−5.89	Marginable:	Yes
3 year	5.79	Options:	Yes
5 year	−2.05	Short sales:	Yes
10 year	—	Minimum purchase:	1
Since inception:	−4.09		

RKH Merrill Lynch Regional Bank HOLDRs
Inception date: 6/26/2000
Asset size ($mil.): 200
Average daily volume: 765,800
Expense ratio (%): —
Category: Sector–Financial services
Investment objective: Holds stocks of regional banks in the United States.

	Annualized Total Returns (% share price)	ETF Facts	
1 year	14.30	Marginable:	Yes
3 year	12.20	Options:	Yes
5 year	7.19	Short sales:	Yes
10 year	—	Minimum purchase:	100
Since inception:	10.37		

RSP Rydex S&P Equal-Weight Trust Index Fund
Inception date: 4/24/2003
Asset size ($mil.): 708
Average daily volume: 419,300
Expense ratio (%): 0.40
Category: Equity income
Investment objective: Emulate the performance of the subject index.

	Annualized Total Returns (% share price)	ETF Facts	
1 year	4.57	Marginable:	No
3 year	14.85	Options:	No
5 year	—	Short sales:	No
10 year	—	Minimum purchase:	1
Since inception:	18.01		

RTH Merrill Lynch Retail HOLDRs
Inception date: 5/2/2001
Asset size ($mil.): 440
Average daily volume: 3,413,100
Expense ratio (%): —
Category: Growth–Domestic
Investment objective: Holds the stocks of companies that sell clothing, drugs, books, homeowner products, and other goods directly to customers via retail outlets or via the Internet.

	Annualized Total Returns (% share price)	ETF Facts	
1 year	−9.78	Marginable:	Yes
3 year	5.05	Options:	Yes
5 year	0.40	Short sales:	Yes
10 year	—	Minimum purchase:	100
Since inception:	0.15		

RWR streetTracks Wilshire REIT Index Fund
    Inception date: 4/27/2001
    Asset size ($mil.): 659
    Average daily volume: 76,400
    Expense ratio (%): 0.25
    Category: Growth–Income
    Investment objective: Emulate the performance of the subject index.

	Annualized Total Returns (% share price)	ETF Facts	
1 year	17.06	Marginable:	Yes
3 year	26.54	Options:	No
5 year	20.64	Short sales:	Yes
10 year	—	Minimum purchase:	1
Since inception:	21.15		

SHY iShares Lehman 1- to 3-Year Treasury Bond Index Fund
    Inception date: 7/22/2002
    Asset size ($mil.): 4,221
    Average daily volume: 531,900
    Expense ratio (%): 0.15
    Category: Government bond
    Investment objective: Emulate the performance of the subject index.

	Annualized Total Returns (% share price)	Bond Facts	
1 year	2.72	Avg. maturity:	1.77 yrs
3 year	1.67	Avg. coupon:	3.33%
5 year	—	Avg. duration:	1.67 yrs
10 year	—		
Since inception:	2.03		

SLV iShares Silver Trust
   Inception date: 4/30/2006
   Asset size ($mil.): —
   Average daily volume: —
   Expense ratio (%): 0.50
   Investment objective: Track the price of actual silver held by the trust

	Annualized Total Returns (% share price)	ETF Facts	
1 year	—	Marginable:	No
3 year	—	Options:	No
5 year	—	Short sales:	No
10 year	—	Minimum purchase:	1
Since inception:	−17.35		

SMH HOLDRs Semiconductor
   Inception date: 5/6/2000
   Asset size ($mil.): 2,422
   Average daily volume: 17,788,100
   Expense ratio (%): —
   Category: Growth–Domestic
   Investment objective: Deliver the returns of a portfolio of semiconductor stocks.

	Annualized Total Returns (% share price)	ETF Facts	
1 year	−15.16	Marginable:	Yes
3 year	−0.73	Options:	Yes
5 year	−7.36	Short sales:	Yes
10 year	—	Minimum purchase:	100
Since inception:	−13.72		

SPY SPDR Trust Series 1
Inception date: 2/18/1993
Asset size: ($mil.): 54,364
Average daily volume: 68,508,300
Expense ratio (%): 0.10
Category: Growth–Domestic
Investment objective: Emulate the performance of the S&P 500 Stock Index.

	Annualized Total Returns (% share price)	ETF Facts	
1 year	5.18	Marginable:	Yes
3 year	10.70	Options:	No
5 year	2.76	Short sales:	Yes
10 year	8.71	Minimum purchase:	1
Since inception:	10.08		

SWH Merrill Lynch Software HOLDRs
Inception date: 9/27/2000
Asset size ($mil.): 202
Average daily volume: 212,200
Expense ratio (%): —
Category: Growth–Domestic
Investment objective: Holds stocks of U.S. producers of computer software, services, and associated products.

	Annualized Total Returns (% share price)	ETF Facts	
1 year	–3.11	Marginable:	Yes
3 year	5.54	Options:	Yes
5 year	–4.16	Short sales:	Yes
10 year	—	Minimum purchase:	100
Since inception:	–14.13		

TBH Telecom Brasil SA TE HOLDR
 Inception date: 7/28/1998
 Asset size ($mil.): 763
 Average daily volume: 78,700
 Expense ratio (%): —
 Category: Non-U.S. equity
 Investment objective: Earn the aggregate returns of a portfolio of Brazilian telecommunication stocks,.

	Annualized Total Returns (% share price)	ETF Facts	
1 year	3.03	Marginable:	Yes
3 year	9.66	Options:	Yes
5 year	−1.98	Short sales:	Yes
10 year	—	Minimum purchase:	1
Since inception:	−7.30		

TIP iShares Lehman TIPS Bond Fund
 Inception date: 12/4/2003
 Asset size ($mil.): 2,810
 Average daily volume: 185,300
 Expense ratio (%): 0.20
 Category: Government bond
 Investment objective: Emulates the return of the Lehman Brothers U.S. Treasury Inflation Notes Index, which measures the performance of inflation-protected Treasury bonds.

	Annualized Total Returns (% share price)	Bond Facts	
1 year	2.13	Avg. maturity:	10.74 yrs
3 year	—	Avg. coupon:	2.58%
5 year	—	Avg. duration:	5.26 yrs
10 year	—		
Since inception:	4.07		

TLT iShares Lehman 20+ Year Treasury Bond Fund index
Inception date: 7/22/2002
Asset size ($mil.): 719
Average daily volume: 1,007,600
Expense ratio (%): 0.15
Category: Government bond
Investment objective: Emulate the performance of the subject index.

	Annualized Total Returns (% share price)	Bond Facts
1 year	−3.42	U.S. Treasuries with remaining life of more 20 years, nonconvertible, grade Baa3 or better, more than $150 million outstanding.
3 year	6.08	
5 year	—	
10 year	—	
Since inception:	5.84	

TMW streetTracks Total Market Index Fund
Inception date: 10/11/2000
Asset size ($mil.): 107
Average daily volume: 3,900
Expense ratio (%): 0.20
Category: Growth–Domestic
Investment objective: Emulate the performance of the Dow Jones Wilshire 5000 Composite Index.

	Annualized Total Returns (% share price)	ETF Facts	
1 year	4.68	Marginable:	Yes
3 year	10.58	Options:	Yes
5 year	2.74	Short sales:	Yes
10 year	—	Minimum purchase:	1
Since inception:	1.06		

TTH Merrill Lynch Telecom HOLDRs
   Inception date: 2/2/2000
   Asset size ($mil.): 202
   Average daily volume: 328,400
   Expense ratio (%): —
   Category: Growth–Domestic
   Investment objective: Holds the stocks of major U.S. telephone and communications companies.

	Annualized Total Returns (% share price)	ETF Facts	
1 year	13.91	Marginable:	Yes
3 year	10.87	Options:	Yes
5 year	–6.91	Short sales:	Yes
10 year	—	Minimum purchase:	1
Since inception:	–12.28		

USO The United States Oil Fund
   Inception date: 4/10/06
   Asset size ($mil.): —
   Average daily volume: —
   Expense ratio (%): 0.50
   Category: <SUPPLY MISSING CATEGORY>
   Investment objective: Track the price of West Texas Intermediate light sweet crude oil. The ETF invests in near-term energy futures contracts, cash-settled options on crude oil futures contracts, and short-term U.S. Treasury securities.

	Annualized Total Returns (% share price)	ETF Facts	
1 year	—	Marginable:	Yes
3 year	—	Options:	No
5 year	—	Short sales:	Yes
10 year	—	Minimum purchase:	1
Since inception:	2.21		

UTH Merrill Lynch Utilities HOLDRs
    Inception date: 6/26/2000
    Asset size ($mil.): 405
    Average daily volume: 372,400
    Expense ratio (%): —
    Category: Sector–Utilities
    Investment objective: Holds the common stocks of major electric and gas utility companies in the United States.

	Annualized Total Returns (% share price)	ETF Facts	
1 year	10.27	Marginable:	Yes
3 year	24.44	Options:	Yes
5 year	6.75	Short sales:	Yes
10 year	—	Minimum purchase:	100
Since inception:	8.05		

VAW Vanguard Materials VIPERs
    Inception date: 1/26/2004
    Asset size ($mil.): 50
    Average daily volume: 13,400
    Expense ratio (%): 0.26
    Category: Equity income
    Investment objective: Emulate the performance of the MSCI U.S. Investable Market Materials Index

	Annualized Total Returns (% share price)	ETF Facts	
1 year	8.88	Marginable:	No
3 year	—	Options:	No
5 year	—	Short sales:	No
10 year	—	Minimum purchase:	1
Since inception:	10.85		

VB Vanguard Small-Cap VIPERs
Inception date: 1/6/2004
Asset size ($mil.): 182
Average daily volume: 38,600
Expense ratio (%): 0.10
Category: Growth–Domestic
Investment objective: Emulate the performance of the MSCI U.S. Small-Cap 1750 Index

	Annualized Total Returns (% share price)	ETF Facts	
1 year	3.59	Marginable:	No
3 year	—	Options:	No
5 year	—	Short sales:	No
10 year	—	Minimum purchase:	1
Since inception:	9.11		

VBK Vanguard Small-Cap Growth VIPERs
Inception date: 1/26/2004
Asset size ($mil.): 93
Average daily volume: 34,800
Expense ratio (%): 0.12
Category: Growth–Domestic
Investment objective: Emulate the performance of the MSCI U.S. Small-Cap Growth Index.

	Annualized Total Returns (% share price)	ETF Facts	
1 year	1.98	Marginable:	No
3 year	—	Options:	No
5 year	—	Short sales:	No
10 year	—	Minimum purchase:	1
Since inception:	6.12		

VBR Vanguard Small-Cap Value VIPERs
Inception date: 1/26/2004
Asset size ($mil.): 90
Average daily volume: 23,800
Expense ratio (%): 0.12
Category: Growth–Domestic
Investment objective: Emulate the performance of the MSCI U.S. Small-Cap Value Index.

	Annualized Total Returns (% share price)	ETF Facts	
1 year	5.52	Marginable:	No
3 year	—	Options:	No
5 year	—	Short sales:	No
10 year	—	Minimum purchase:	1
Since inception:	12.10		

VCR Vanguard Consumer Discretionary VIPERs
Inception date: 1/26/2004
Asset size ($mil.): 32
Average daily volume: 10,400
Expense ratio (%): 0.26
Category: Equity income
Investment objective: Emulate the performance of the MSCI U.S. Investable Consumer Discretionary Index.

	Annualized Total Returns (% share price)	ETF Facts	
1 year	-7.91	Marginable:	No
3 year	—	Options:	No
5 year	—	Short sales:	No
10 year	—	Minimum purchase:	1
Since inception:	1.29		

VDC Vanguard Consumer Staples VIPERs
Inception date: 1/26/2004
Asset size ($mil.): 73
Average daily volume: 14,600
Expense ratio (%): 0.26
Category: Equity income
Investment objective: Emulate the performance of the MSCI U.S. Investable Market Consumer Staples Index.

	Annualized Total Returns (% share price)	ETF Facts	
1 year	6.19	Marginable:	No
3 year	—	Options:	No
5 year	—	Short sales:	No
10 year	—	Minimum purchase:	1
Since inception:	6.05		

VDE Vanguard Energy VIPERs
Inception date: 9/23/2004
Asset size ($mil.): 182
Average daily volume: 49,400
Expense ratio (%): 0.26
Category: Sector–Energy
Investment objective: Emulate the performance of the MSCI U.S. Investable Market Energy Index

	Annualized Total Returns (% share price)	ETF Facts	
1 year	24.92	Marginable:	No
3 year	—	Options:	No
5 year	—	Short sales:	No
10 year	—	Minimum purchase:	1
Since inception:	34.24		

VFH Vanguard Financials VIPERs
   Inception date: 1/6/2004
   Asset size ($mil.): 53
   Average daily volume: 13,800
   Expense ratio (%): 0.26
   Category: Sector–Financial services
   Investment objective: Emulate the performance of the MSCI Investable Market Financials Index

Annualized Total Returns (% share price)		ETF Facts	
1 year	11.80	Marginable:	No
3 year	—	Options:	No
5 year	—	Short sales:	No
10 year	—	Minimum purchase:	1
Since inception:	8.37		

VGT Vanguard Information Technology VIPERs
   Inception date: 1/26/2004
   Asset size ($mil.): 51
   Average daily volume: 23,700
   Expense ratio (%): 0.26
   Category: Growth–Domestic
   Investment objective: Emulate the performance of the MSCI U.S. Investable Market Information Technology Index.

Annualized Total Returns (% share price)		ETF Facts	
1 year	−5.59	Marginable:	No
3 year	—	Options:	No
5 year	—	Short sales:	No
10 year	—	Minimum purchase:	1
Since inception:	−5.25		

VHT Vanguard Health Care VIPERs
　　Inception date: 1/26/2004
　　Asset size ($mil.): 205
　　Average daily volume: 34,300
　　Expense ratio (%): 0.26
　　Category: Sector–Health
　　Investment objective: Emulate the performance of the MSCI U.S.
　　Investable Market Health Care Index.

	Annualized Total Returns (% share price)	ETF Facts	
1 year	1.77	Marginable:	No
3 year	—	Options:	No
5 year	—	Short sales:	No
10 year	—	Minimum purchase:	1
Since inception:	3.42		

VIS Vanguard Industrials VIPERs
　　Inception date: 9/23/2004
　　Asset size ($mil.): 16
　　Average daily volume: 12,700
　　Expense ratio (%): 0.26
　　Category: Equity income
　　Investment objective: Emulate the performance of the MSCI U.S.
　　Investable Market Industrials Index.

	Annualized Total Returns (% share price)	ETF Facts	
1 year	7.81	Marginable:	No
3 year	—	Options:	No
5 year	—	Short sales:	No
10 year		Minimum purchase:	1
Since inception:	11.29		

VNQ Vanguard REIT Vipers
    Inception date: 9/23/2004
    Asset size ($mil.): 348
    Average daily volume: 89,100
    Expense ratio (%): 0.12
    Category: Growth and income
    Investment objective: Tracks the MSCI REIT Index.

	Annualized Total Returns (% share price)	ETF Facts	
1 year	15.51	Marginable:	No
3 year	—	Options:	No
5 year	—	Short sales:	No
10 year	—	Minimum purchase:	1
Since inception:	25.40		

VO Vanguard Midcap VIPERS
    Inception date: 1/26/2004
    Asset size ($mil.): 651
    Average daily volume: 75,000
    Expense ratio (%): 0.13
    Category: Growth–Domestic
    Investment objective: Emulate the performance of the MSCI U.S. Midcap 450 Index

	Annualized Total Returns (% share price)	ETF Facts	
1 year	6.25	Marginable:	No
3 year	—	Options:	No
5 year	—	Short sales:	No
10 year	—	Minimum purchase:	1
Since inception:	12.46		

VOX Vanguard Telecommunications Services VIPERs
>   Inception date: 9/23/2004
>   Asset size ($mil.): 16
>   Average daily volume: 13,800
>   Expense ratio (%): 0.26
>   Category: Equity income
>   Investment objective: Emulate the performance of the MSCI U.S.
>   Investable Market Telecommunications Services Index

	Annualized Total Returns (% share price)	ETF Facts	
1 year	15.28	Marginable:	No
3 year	—	Options:	No
5 year	—	Short sales:	No
10 year	—	Minimum purchase:	1
Since inception:	16.67		

VPU Vanguard Utilities VIPERs
>   Inception date: 1/26/2004
>   Asset size ($mil.): 95
>   Average daily volume: 13,800
>   Expense ratio (%): 0.26
>   Category: Sector–Utilities
>   Investment objective: Emulate the performance of the MSCI U.S.
>   Investable Market Utilities Index.

	Annualized Total Returns (% share price)	ETF Facts	
1 year	8.54	Marginable:	No
3 year	—	Options:	No
5 year	—	Short sales:	No
10 year	—	Minimum purchase:	1
Since inception:	18.69		

VTI Vanguard Total Stock Market VIPERs
Inception date: 5/24/2001
Asset size ($mil.): 4,565
Average daily volume: 194,000
Expense ratio (%): 0.07
Category: Growth–Income
Investment objective: Emulate the performance of the Wilshire 5000 Stock Index.

	Annualized Total Returns (% share price)	ETF Facts	
1 year	5.07	Marginable:	Yes
3 year	11.93	Options:	No
5 year	4.24	Short sales:	Yes
10 year	—	Minimum purchase:	1
Since inception:	2.57		

VTV Vanguard Value VIPERS
Inception date: 1/26/2004
Asset size ($mil.): 517
Average daily volume: 51,300
Expense ratio (%): 0.11
Category: Equity income
Investment objective: Emulate the performance of the MSCI U.S. Prime Market Value index.

	Annualized Total Returns (% share price)	ETF Facts	
1 year	12.03	Marginable:	No
3 year	—	Options:	No
5 year	—	Short sales:	No
10 year	—	Minimum purchase:	1
Since inception:	11.19		

VUG Vanguard Growth VIPERs
    Inception date: 1/26/2004
    Asset size ($mil.): 163
    Average daily volume: 59,800
    Expense ratio (%): 0.11
    Category: Growth–Domestic
    Investment objective: Emulate the performance of the MSCI U.S. Prime Market Growth Index.

	Annualized Total Returns (% share price)	ETF Facts	
1 year	−0.75	Marginable:	No
3 year	—	Options:	No
5 year	—	Short sales:	No
10 year	—	Minimum purchase:	1
Since inception:	1.96		

VV Vanguard Large-Cap VIPERs
    Inception date: 1/27/2004
    Asset size ($mil.): 121
    Average daily volume: 41,600
    Expense ratio (%): 0.07
    Category: Growth–Domestic
    Investment objective: Emulate the performance of the MSCI Prime Market 750 Index.

	Annualized Total Returns (% share price)	ETF Facts	
1 year	5.77	Marginable:	No
3 year	—	Options:	No
5 year	—	Short sales:	No
10 year	—	Minimum purchase:	1
Since inception:	7.03		

VXF Vanguard Extended Market VIPERs
  Inception date: 12/27/2001
  Asset size ($mil.): 315
  Average daily volume: 28,800
  Expense ratio (%): 0.08
  Category: Growth–Domestic
  Investment objective: Track the Wilshire 4500 Stock Index/S&P Extended Stock Market Index

	Annualized Total Returns (% share price)	ETF Facts	
1 year	4.71	Marginable:	Yes
3 year	16.32	Options:	Yes
5 year	—	Short sales:	Yes
10 year	—	Minimum purchase:	1
Since inception:	10.90		

WMH Merrill Lynch Wireless HOLDRs
  Inception date: 11/1/2000
  Asset size ($mil.): 74
  Average daily volume: 10,700
  Expense ratio (%): —
  Category: Growth–Domestic
  Investment objective: Hold stocks of international companies involved in the production of wireless communications equipment and the establishment and maintenance of wireless networks.

	Annualized Total Returns (% share price)	ETF Facts	
1 year	−2.03	Marginable:	Yes
3 year	15.33	Options:	Yes
5 year	−1.27	Short sales:	Yes
10 year	—	Minimum purchase:	100
Since inception:	−7.62		

XLE Select Sector SPDR–Energy
Inception date: 12/22/1998
Asset size ($mil.): 2,057
Average daily volume: 21,873,100
Expense ratio (%): 0.24
Category: Sector–Energy
Investment objective: Emulate the performance of the subject index.

	Annualized Total Returns (% share price)	ETF Facts	
1 year	24.61	Marginable:	Yes
3 year	38.16	Options:	Yes
5 year	16.27	Short sales:	Yes
10 year	—	Minimum purchase:	1
Since inception:	14.81		

XLF Select Sector SDPR–Financial Index Fund
Inception date: 12/22/1998
Asset size ($mil.): 1,483
Average daily volume: 8,954,600
Expense ratio (%): 0.25
Category: Sector–Financial services
Investment objective: Emulate the performance of the subject index.

	Annualized Total Returns (% share price)	ETF Facts	
1 year	13.12	Marginable:	Yes
3 year	11.35	Options:	Yes
5 year	5.46	Short sales:	Yes
10 year	—	Minimum purchase:	1
Since inception:	6.57		

XLG Rydex Russell Top 50 Index Fund
    Inception date: 5/10/2005
    Asset size ($mil.): 137
    Average daily volume: 19,400
    Expense ratio (%): 0.20
    Category: Equity income
    Investment objective: Emulate the performance of the Russell Top
    50 Index

	Annualized Total Returns (% share price)	ETF Facts	
1 year	4.95	Marginable:	No
3 year	—	Options:	No
5 year	—	Short sales:	No
10 year	—	Minimum purchase:	1
Since inception:	6.76		

XLI Select Sector SPDR Fund–Industrial Index
    Inception date: 12/22/1998
    Asset size ($mil.): 771
    Average daily volume: 1,196,300
    Expense ratio (%): 0.24
    Category: Growth–Domestic
    Investment objective: Emulate the performance of the subject index.

	Annualized Total Returns (% share price)	ETF Facts	
1 year	6.27	Marginable:	Yes
3 year	12.97	Options:	Yes
5 year	3.48	Short sales:	Yes
10 year	—	Minimum purchase:	1
Since inception:	5.62		

XLK Select Sector SPDR Fund–Technology
   Inception date: 12/22/1998
   Asset size ($mil.): 1,040
   Average daily volume: 1,567,500
   Expense ratio (%): 0.25
   Category: Growth–Domestic
   Investment objective: Emulate the performance of the subject index.

	Annualized Total Returns (% share price)	ETF Facts	
1 year	−5.29	Marginable:	Yes
3 year	5.20	Options:	Yes
5 year	−4.76	Short sales:	Yes
10 year	—	Minimum purchase:	1
Since inception:	−5.69		

XLP Select Sector SPDR Fund–Consumer Staples Index
   Inception date: 12/22/1998
   Asset size ($mil.): 762
   Average daily volume: 1,282,800
   Expense ratio (%): 0.25
   Category: Growth–Domestic
   Investment objective: Emulate the performance of the subject index.

	Annualized Total Returns (% share price)	ETF Facts	
1 year	6.82	Marginable:	Yes
3 year	8.77	Options:	Yes
5 year	1.38	Short sales:	Yes
10 year	—	Minimum purchase:	1
Since inception:	0.55		

XLU Select Sector SPDR Fund–Utilities
  Inception date: 12/22/1998
  Asset size ($mil.): 1,830
  Average daily volume: 2,871,800
  Expense ratio (%): 0.25
  Category: Sector–Utilities
  Investment objective: Emulate the performance of the subject index.

	Annualized Total Returns (% share price)	ETF Facts	
1 year	8.28	Marginable:	Yes
3 year	21.87	Options:	Yes
5 year	5.38	Short sales:	Yes
10 year	—	Minimum purchase:	1
Since inception:	5.15		

XLV Select Sector SPDR Fund–Health Care
  Inception date: 12/22/1998
  Asset size ($mil.): 1,287
  Average daily volume: 1,168,600
  Expense ratio (%): 0.24
  Category: Sector–Health/biotech
  Investment objective: Emulate the performance of the Health Care Select Sector Index.

	Annualized Total Returns (% share price)	ETF Facts	
1 year	1.84	Marginable:	Yes
3 year	4.65	Options:	Yes
5 year	3.02	Short sales:	Yes
10 year	—	Minimum purchase:	1
Since inception:	4.12		

XLY Select Sector SPDR Fund–Consumer Discretionary
   Inception date: 12/22/1998
   Asset size ($mil.): 364
   Average daily volume: 1,024,300
   Expense ratio (%): 0.25
   Category: Growth–Domestic
   Investment objective: Emulate the performance of the subject index.

	Annualized Total Returns (% share price)	ETF Facts	
1 year	−5.94	Marginable:	Yes
3 year	6.20	Options:	Yes
5 year	3.07	Short sales:	Yes
10 year	—	Minimum purchase:	1
Since inception:	3.97		

Finding More Information

Periodicals

The Journal of Indexes, published every two months, features articles discussing the philosophy, current status, and future prospects for ETFs. Authors are leading names in the field. Also included are historical performance data on the indexes themselves; overviews of Dow Jones economic sectors; a table of the largest U.S. ETFs arranged in order of total net assets; an overview of comparative (Morningstar) ETF asset-class performance over the past 1,3, 5, and 10 years; and selected major indexes sorted by year-over-year total returns. *The Journal of Indexes* is published by Charter Financial Publishing Network, P.O. Box 7550, Shrewsbury, NJ 07702. You can find out more about the journal and current issues at *www.indexuniverse.com/joi*.

    Exchange-Traded Funds Report (*ETFR*) contains news items. Its most important content, however, is its Databank section, which presents comprehensive current information on the size, prices, and performance of all U.S., European, and international exchange-traded funds. *ETFR* is published every month by Index Publications LLC. For further information, visit its website at *www.indexuniverse.com/etfr* or call 732-450-8866, extension 207.

Online

The Internet is a rich source of historical and current information about exchange-traded funds. The following websites provide specifications, trading help, and performance data for ETFs traded on U.S. exchanges.

adr.com is an excellent source for researching ADRs, Search results show an ADR's type, country of origin, and industry. Links are provided for charts, financials, and earnings estimates.

morningstar.com provides a virtual online prospectus for each ETF. Included are the ETF's short- and long-term performance, asset class, total assets, expense ratio, stock holdings by industry and sector, proprietary five-star rating system (by subscription), tax analysis, standard deviation, Sharpe ratio, valuation and growth rates, a table of fees and expenses, beta, and asset allocation and sector weightings.

etfconnect.com is a comprehensive source for up-to-date fundamental and price information. Several pages are presented for each ETF, describing the ETF in detail. Included are the date the ETF began trading; its 1-, 3-, 5-, and 10-year performance numbers; its asset size; average daily trading volume; top 10 stock holdings; country and industry diversification; expense ratio; and a description of the index it tracks. The site also allows you to search for ETFs by asset class, region (U.S., global, or international), sponsor, yield, asset size, or annual return.

indexuniverse.com presents current performance charts and news and feature articles on ETFs as well as article archives dating back to September 2003. The site also provides a unique set of tools: A click on "data" opens up a search engine that allows you to search a complete ETF data base by symbol, total net assets, asset class, expense ratio, price-to-book ratio, NAV, Sharpe ratio, beta, or standard deviation. There is also a tool for sorting underlying indexes using some of the same criteria. Access is free.

prudenttrader.com focuses on technical analysis. Included in its weekly letter is an overview of the current technical situation and outlook for ETFs, an analysis of one particular industry or sector, a list of ETFs that prudenttrader.com considers promising on the basis of their relative strength or other technical criteria, a minicourse on how a certain technical tool works, and tables that allow you to compare the performance of ETFs within industry groups. Access is free upon registration, although the site's editor keeps promising that free won't last forever.

agileinvesting.com is an investment advisory service that uses exchange-traded funds to construct low-cost, diversified investment portfolios. Its services to subscribers include model portfolios, weekly commentary and strategy updates, and a detailed monthly review of asset class performance and valuation levels. A free 60-day trial subscription is available.

etfzone.com presents model portfolios, fundamental analysis, discussions of tax issues, a public bulletin board, a glossary, a fund screener to help you find the ETF that suits your investment goals, and the answers to frequently asked questions about ETFs.

smartmoney.com covers all aspects of the stock market, but the website has a special section that shows each ETF's expense ratio, beta, net assets, turnover, price/book ratio, standard deviation, volume, the day's price range, 1-, 3-, and 5-year annualized returns, and a pie chart showing a breakdown of the ETF's holdings. A free membership is required to explore the site.

yahoo.com is the gateway to more than 100 websites that bear on the subject of ETFs, including periodicals, advisory services, charting services, and other information sources. Yahoo's own *finance.yahoo.com/etf* enables a reader to rank ETFs by size, performance, volume, or family. It also presents a glossary; a screener; and, a series of articles written by the yahoo staff about the nature and use of ETFs.

midnighttrader.com is a news and information service. It specializes in premarket and after hours trading, allowing traders to react to news and events that occur outside of normal trading hours. The website provides market news and streaming quotes, full access to open bid and asked orders on ECN order books, and links to online brokers.

indexfunds.com is maintained by Index Funds, Inc. the publisher of *Index Funds; the 12-step Program for Active Investors*. The site offers a wealth of information, including data on historical ETF performance, online-readable articles on index investing, a questionnaire you can use to asses your own risk tolerance, a button to speak to a live advisor, and an online calculator that can be used to determine the performance of a sample portfolio that you design.

Sponsor Websites

Each ETF sponsor has a website that provides detailed descriptions of its ETFs. Included may be downloadable prospectuses, price histories, customized "watch lists," a description of each ETF's underlying index; and analysis of ETF asset classes, performance history, and tax efficiency.

The sponsor websites include:

www.holdrs.com
www.ishares.com
www.streetracks.com
www.vanguard.com
www.statestreet.com
www.barclaysglobal.com
www.powershares.com
www.morningstar.com

Exchange Websites

The exchanges where ETFs are traded are good sources of background information and current price data on ETFs, ETF options, and ETF futures.

AMEX—*amex.com*—was the birthplace of the exchange-traded fund and is today the exchange home of most U.S. ETFs and ETF options. Its website provides menus and links to current prices, an ETF screener, a glossary, historical data, market news, and education. Downloadable "Tear Sheets" contain comprehensive snapshots of each ETF, including its specifications, a one-year chart showing price and trading volume, year-over-year and month-over-month comparative performance, and a table showing distributions made since the ETF was launched.

The Chicago Mercantile Exchange—*cme.com*—trades futures contracts on three ETFs: SPDR Trust Series 1, iShares Russell 2000 Index Fund, and the NASDAQ 100 Index Tracking Stock. The exchange website presents contract specifications and performance data, plus links to pages for simulated trading, a broker locator, online and classroom courses, and downloadable brochures describing exchange products and services.

NASDAQ—*nasdaq.com*—is the home exchange of nine ETFs. These include NASDAQ 100 Tracking Stock (QQQQ), Fidelity NASDAQ Composite Index Tracking Stock (ONEQ), iShares NASDAQ Biotechnology Index Fund (IBB), First Trust NASDAQ 100 Equal Weighted Index Fund (QQEW), First Trust NASDAQ 100 Technology Index Fund (QTEC), and the four Bank of New York BLDRs. Also presented are price and trading volume indicators for premarket and after-hours trading, a "heat map" that shows which ETFs are on the move, an ETF screener, and a tutorial on ETFs.

The Chicago Board Options Exchange—*cboe.com*—trades put and call options on about 45 ETFs. Its website provides streaming real-time quotes, market statistics, volume reports, a volatility optimizer, online tutorials, and online educational courses in option trading strategies.

The New York Stock Exchange—*nyse.com*—provides an overview of each ETF at its website. Included are its market performance, historical data, and fact sheets. Also presented are regulations governing the trading of ETFs and a searchable archive of statistics. The New York Stock Exchange is currently the home exchange of about 20 U.S. ETFs that track domestic and foreign stock indexes.

Glossary

active management an investing style predicated on the use of good judgment and market knowledge to select securities with the potential for the greatest risk-adjusted returns.

ADRs the acronym for American Depositary Receipts, which are certificates representing ownership of shares of stock in a foreign company. Most ADRs are issued by U.S. banks. They are freely traded on U.S. stock exchanges.

adviser an individual or organization employed by a fund to give advice on the fund's investment and management practices.

arbitrage the purchase of one asset and the sale of another (usually related) asset when the price relationship between them has become distorted. The relatively high priced asset is sold and the relatively low priced asset is bought. Arbitrage profits accrue when market forces cause the price relationship between the two assets to return to normal.

asset class a description of the kind of stocks in an ETF, based on their location, nature, and size (e.g., large-cap U.S. value stocks). There are some 24 ETF asset classes.

at the money a call or put option is at the money when its market price and striking price are the same.

Authorized Participant (AP) a large institutional investor, specialist, or market-maker who has signed a participant agreement with a particular ETF sponsor.

basis the difference between the cash and futures price of an ETF, expressed as futures minus cash.

beta an index of the volatility of a security's price, compared to the volatility of the S&P 500 Index. Securities with betas higher than 1 are more volatile than the S&P 500 Index. Securities with betas of less than 1 are less volatile than the S&P 500 Index.

broker-dealer a securities firm that sells stocks, bond, funds, or other investments to the public.

call option the right to buy the underlying security at a specified price on or before a specified date.

capital leverage the effective ownership of an asset while possessing less than 100 percent of its equity. Leverage creates both opportunity and risk. In 50 percent margin trades, for example, a $1.00 price change in the asset will cause a $2.00 change in the

275

investor's equity. In single-stock futures, where the minimum margin is 20 percent, a $1.00 change in asset value can result in a $5.00 change in investor equity.

creation fee   the fee paid by the Authorized Participant for delivering shares of the underlying stocks and accepting one or more creation units of ETFs. The fee is expressed in dollars and is nominal, usually less than 1 percent.

creation unit   the minimum number of ETF shares that can be created by the fund sponsor and Associated Person in one transaction. The transaction is "in kind" and not for cash. Each ETF has its own creation unit size, ranging from 25,000 to 500,000 ETF shares, with 50,000 shares being the most common size. Creation of large numbers of ETF shares are made in multiples of the creation unit.

day order   an order to buy or sell that expires at the end of the trading day.

Depositary Trust Company (DTC)   a corporation owned collectively by broker-dealers and banks. The trust holds securities for shareholders and clients (including index shares in trust for ETFs) and arranges for the shares' electronic delivery, transfer, and settlement. DTC is part of the U.S. Depositary Trust and Clearing Corporation.

DIAMONDS   shares in Diamond Trust Series 1, an ETF that tracks the Dow Jones Industrial Average. Organized as a unit investment trust.

discount   The amount that an ETF's market price is below its net asset value, expressed as a percentage.

diversification   Lowering overall portfolio risk by investing in a variety of different asset types or classes that are not all likely to move in the same direction.

ECN   an acronym for "electronics communications network." ECNs are electronic trading systems for matching buy and sell orders received from the ECNs' subscribers, typically institutional investors, broker-dealers, and market-makers. ECNs connect buyers and sellers directly, bypassing third parties. An individual investor who wishes to trade via an ECN must have an account with a subscriber. Only limit orders are accepted.

ETF value   the value of ETF shares depends on two factors: the value of the stocks in the trust, and the market price set by bids and offers on the exchange.

expense ratio   the recurring charges against fund assets for investment management, custody, and administration, expressed as a percentage of the fund's net assets. Expense ratios do not includes nonroutine costs such as brokerage commissions or legal fees paid in a lawsuit against the fund.

fundamental analysis   the study of a company's business and financial situation in an attempt to predict the course of the company's stock price in coming weeks or months.

futures contract   A fungible agreement to buy or sell a specific quantity of a certain commodity (including financial instruments) at an agreed price at a certain time in the future.

gap   on a bar chart, the white space left when the trading ranges of two consecutive trading days do not overlap.

grantor trust   a trust certificate that represents literal ownership of a basket of stocks, including voting rights and the receipt of dividends. The certificate trades like a stock but is not issued by a company nor registered with the SEC. Merrill Lynch HOLDRs and Ryder Euro Currency Trust are grantor trusts.

growth stock a stock with above-average prospects for capital gains. Growth stocks typically have high price/earnings ratios and pay few or no dividends.

hedge a two-position strategy whereby the loss (including opportunity loss) in one asset is largely offset by the gain in a different but economically related asset.

HOLDR an unmanaged portfolio of 20 or more sector or industry stocks that are bought and sold as a unit, like an ETF.

in the money a call option is in the money when its market price is above the option's striking price; a put option in the money when its market price is below the option's striking price.

index fund a fund designed to emulate the market performance of securities that comprise a specific stock index, like the S&P 500 or the Dow Jones Industrial Average.

index tracking a measure of the correlation between the returns of a stock portfolio and the returns of the index to which to portfolio is benchmarked.

institutional investor banks, insurance companies, hedge funds, and other large fiduciaries that buy and sell securities for their own accounts.

intrinsic value the amount by which an option is in the money. In a call, intrinsic value equals the call's market price minus its striking price. In a put, intrinsic value equals the put's striking price minus its market price.

investment advisor in an actively managed mutual fund, a person or company who is paid to provide specific advice for selecting securities and timing market entry and exit. Some investment advisors may also manage portfolios of securities.

large-cap stock the stock of a company with an equity market capitalization of $2 billion or more.

leverage *see capital leverage.*

limit order a contingent order to buy or sell; it specifies the minimum selling price or maximum buying price that the person originating the order will accept.

margin a cash deposit made by the stock buyer to secure a margin loan.

market order an order to buy or sell a security immediately, at the best price available.

market timing an attempt to predict the movement of security prices, thereby enabling the purchase of shares just before their prices go up or the sale of shares just before their prices go down.

market-maker an exchange member who enhances market liquidity by providing continuous public bids and offers for its designated ETFs. There may be more than one market-maker in a heavily traded ETF. Market-makers are required by law to give a public customer the best available bid or asked price.

micro–cap stock the stock of a company with a market capitalization of "micro" proportions, generally less than $100 million.

mid–cap stock   the stock of a company with a market capitalization of between $500 million and $2 billion.

NASD   the abbreviation of the National Association of Securities Dealers. NASD is a private, nonprofit organization created by the Securities Exchange Act of 1934. NASD is responsible for standardizing investment practices and setting ethical criteria for the finance industry. Nearly every brokerage firm doing business in the United States is required by law to be a member of NASD.

NASDAQ   the acronym for National Association of Securities Dealers Automated Quotations, an electronic automated quote system. The system was established by NASD in 1968 and today reports price quotes, trading volume, and other market information for more than 5,000 over-the-counter stocks. NASDAQ later grew into the NASDAQ Stock Market, an electronic stock exchange where computer networks match orders from buyers and sellers. There are six ETFs traded on NASDAQ: NASDAQ 100 Index Tracking Stock Fund, iShares NASDAQ Biotechnology Index Fund, and the four BLDR (Baskets of Listed Depositary Receipt) funds based on the Bank of New York ADR indexes.

net asset value (NAV)   an ETF's net asset value comprises the fund's total assets (securities and cash), minus the fund's liabilities, divided by the number of fund shares outstanding.

opportunity loss   the return that could be earned if the money commited to an investment were employed elsewhere.

over-the-counter   an NASD-regulated market for stocks that are not traded on traditional brick-and-mortar stock exchanges. Also included are some listed securities that are traded off the exchange, and government and corporate bonds.

passive management   a money management strategy that seeks to match the return and risk characteristics of a market index by mirroring its composition. Passive managers do not actively buy and sell securities in a search for those with the greatest returns. They make as few portfolio decisions as possible, in order to minimize transaction costs and the accrual of capital gains. Semiactive management has another shade of meaning. PowerShares Dynamic ETFs, for example, are benchmarked to indexes ("Intellidexes") that comprise stocks selected quarterly for their performance potential.

portfolio manager   the person or firm who is responsible to administer the portfolio of ETF index stocks held in trust.

premium   the amount by which an ETF's market price is above its net asset value, expressed as a percentage of the net asset value. The word "premium" also refers to the amount of money paid by the option buyer to the option seller in an option transaction.

price/earnings ratio (P/E ratio)   a component of a company's fundamental analysis. To calculate the P/E ratio, you divide the company's current stock price by the company's earnings per share (EPS). An increase in the stock price or a decline in company's earnings will cause the company's P/E to increase. A P/E ratio that is calculated using EPS data from the last four quarters is known as the trailing P/E. A P/E ratio calculated using estimated earnings over the next four quarters is known as the leading or projected P/E.

price-to-book ratio (P/B)   is a company's assets minus its liabilities. It is what would be left over for shareholders if the company were sold and its debt retired. The price-to-book ratio equals the stock share price divided by the per-share book value.

put option   the right to sell a specific asset at a specified price on or before a specified date.

Qubes (QQQQ)   A heavily traded ETF that tracks the NASDAQ 100 Index. Structured as a unit investment trust.

redemption   exchanging ETF shares for the shares of their underlying stocks held in trust. Redemption is made in redemption units.

redemption fee   the fee paid by the Authorized Participant for redeeming one or more redemption units of ETFs and receiving shares of the underlying stocks. The fee is nominal; is expressed in dollars; and is paid per transaction, regardless of the number redemption units involved.

risk   the quantifiable likelihood of loss or less-than-expected returns.

secondary market   the traditional exchanges, over-the-counter markets, and electronic exchanges where securities previously issued are bought and sold by investors.

sector ETF   an ETF whose underlying index contains stocks in only one market sector such as iShares Dow Jones U.S. Telecommunications Sector Index Fund. Prices of sector ETFs are typically more volatile than the prices of broad-based ETFs.

short seller   a short seller borrows stock and sells it in the expectation that its price will go down. He buys it back later and returns it to the lender.

small-cap stock   the stock of a company whose market value is less than $250 million. Includes microcap stocks, which comprise companies with market values of $100 million or less.

SPDR   the acronym for S&P Depositary Receipt, the first ETF, introduced in 1993 and designed to track the S&P 500 Stock Index. Pronounced "spider," the acronym is also part of the name of several other ETFs, including SPDR O-Strip, SPDR MidCap, and several sector SPDRs.

specialist   responsible for maintaining fair and orderly markets in the stocks to which he (or she) is assigned. He does so by posting his best bid and asked prices, maintaining a record of orders that are away from the market, and by buying for or selling from his own inventory when there are not sufficient public buyers or sellers to maintain price equilibrium.

standard deviation   a gauge of volatility, standard deviation is a measure of dispersal in a group of numbers. It describes how tightly a set of values is clustered around the average of those same values. Stable investments like money market funds have standard deviations near zero. More volatile holdings may have standard deviations of 20 or more.

stop order   an order specifying a price that is away from the current price, to be executed when the stop price is reached. Buy stop orders are placed above the current price, sell stop orders are placed below the current price.

support level   a price level where declines tend to pause or stop. A strong support level can turn prices around and form the foundation for a subsequent rally. Most easily seen on a price chart.

systemic risk   risk that affects an entire system or market. Systemic risk cannot be reduced by diversification.

tax efficiency   the tax efficiency of an ETF is a function of the fund's capital gains that are passed through to the ETF holder. An ETF that is managed with tax efficiency as a goal will distribute few or no taxable capital gains to its holders.

technical analysis   the forecasting of stock prices based solely on the interpretation of price movement and trading volume. Supply, demand, and company business conditions are not components of technical analysis.

time value   a measure of how much investors will pay solely for the amount of time that the option has left to live; an option's market price minus its intrinsic value. The price of an out-of-the-money option comprises all time value, which will decrease at an increasing rate as the option approaches expiration and be zero on the day the option expires.

turnover   the number of purchases and sales of stocks for the portfolio. More precisely, (Purchases + Sales) divided by (Beginning value + Ending value). If a portfolio has an average annual turnover of 30 percent using this formula, it would mean that 30 percent of the stocks in the portfolio were replaced with new stocks during the year.

unit investment trust   an investment company that holds a fixed group of securities in trust until the trust is dissolved.

value stocks   a stock with a high-dividend yield, a low price-to-earnings ratio, a low price-to-book ratio, and that is currently priced below similar companies in the same business.

volatility   A measure of the fluctuations in the market price of a security. The greater the distance between a stock's average daily high and low prices, the greater is its volatility—and the greater is the short-term price risk in owning the stock.

Bibliography

Amott, Robert D., and Robert Jeffreys, "Is Your Alpha Big Enough to Cover Your Taxes," *The Journal of Portfolio Management* 19 (Spring 1993): 15–25.

Brinson, Gary, "Determinants of Portfolio Performance," *Financial Analysts Journal,* 42 (July/August 1986): 39–44.

Ellis, Charles D., "The Loser's Game," *Financial Analysts Journal,* 31 (July/August 1975): 19–26.

Fontanills, George A. *Trade Options Online* (New York: John Wiley & Sons, 1999).

Friedfertig, Marc, and George West, *Electronic Day Traders' Secrets* (New York: McGraw-Hill, 1999).

Gastineau, Gary L., *Someone Will Make Money in Mutual Funds—Why Not You?* (Hoboken, NJ: John Wiley & Sons, 2005).

Gastineau, Gary L., *The Exchange Traded Funds Manual* (Hoboken, NJ: John Wiley & Sons, 2002).

Gleick, James, *Chaos: Making a New Science* (New York: Penguin Books, 1987).

Greenblatt, Joel, *The Little Book That Beats the Market* (Hoboken, NJ: John Wiley & Sons, 2006).

Hebner, Mark T., *Index Funds: The 12-step Program for Active Investors* (Irvine, CA: IFA, 2005).

Levine, Michael, *Broken Windows, Broken Business*, Warner Business Books, New York, 2005.

Lofton, Todd, *Getting Started in Futures,* 5th ed. (Hoboken, NJ: John Wiley & Sons, 2005).

Malkiel, Burton, *A Random Walk Down Wall Street* (New York: Norton, 1990).

McClatchy, Will, and Jim Wiandt, *Exchange Traded Funds* (Hoboken, NJ: John Wiley & Sons, 2002).

Richards, Jr., Archie, *All About Exchange-Traded Funds* (New York: McGraw-Hill, 2003).

Schwager, Jack D., *Technical Analysis* (New York: John Wiley & Sons, 1996).

Schwager, Jack D., *A Complete Guide to the Futures Markets* (New York: John Wiley & Sons, 1984).

Singal, Vijay, *Beyond the Random Walk* (New York: Oxford University Press, 2004).

Thomsett, Michael C., *Getting Started in Options,* 6th ed. (Hoboken, NJ: John Wiley & Sons, 2006).

Burger, Edward B., and Michael Starbird, *Coincidences, Chaos, and All That Math Jazz* (New York: Norton, 2005).

Index